Procession of the Night Theatre

Procession
of the
NIGHT THEATRE

An Exposition on the Lunar Stations

J. M. Hamade

Revelore Press
Olympia, WA
2024

Procession of the Night Theatre:
An Exposition on the Lunar Stations

Copyright © 2024 J. M. Hamade.

All rights reserved. No part of this publication may be reproduced or transmitted in any form or by any means, electronic or mechanical, including photocopy, without permission in writing from the publisher. Reviewers may quote brief passages, as may scholars writing astrological journal articles.

Book and cover design by Joseph Uccello.
Illustrations and back cover art by J. M. Hamade.

PUBLISHER'S CATALOGING-IN-PUBLICATION
(PROVIDED BY CASSIDY CATALOGUING SERVICES, INC.)

Names:	Hamade, J. M., author, illustrator.
Title:	Procession of the night theatre : an exposition on the lunar stations / J. M. Hamade.
Description:	Olympia, WA: Revelore Press, [2024]	Includes bibliographical references.
Identifiers:	ISBN: 9781947544581 (paperback)	9781947544529 (hardback)
Subjects:	LCSH: Moon—Miscellanea.	Moon—Phases.	Moon—Poetry.	Zodiac.	Zodiac—Poetry.	Houses (Astrology)	Houses (Astrology)—Poetry.	LCGFT: Poetry.
Classification:	LCC: BF1723 .H36 2024	DDC: 133.532—dc23

ISBN: 9781947544581

Printed worldwide through Ingram.

Revelore Press
1910 4th AVE E PMB 141
Olympia WA 98506
United States
www.revelore.press

Contents

Introduction 9

I: Procession of the Night Theatre

THE THIRD NIGHT	19
THE FOURTH NIGHT	21
THE FIFTH NIGHT	23
THE SIXTH NIGHT	26
THE SEVENTH NIGHT	29
THE EIGHTH NIGHT	31
THE NINTH NIGHT	34
THE TENTH NIGHT	37
THE ELEVENTH NIGHT	39
THE TWELFTH NIGHT	41
THE THIRTEENTH NIGHT	44
THE FOURTEENTH NIGHT	46
THE FIFTEENTH NIGHT	48
THE SIXTEENTH NIGHT	50
THE SEVENTEENTH NIGHT	53
THE EIGHTEENTH NIGHT	56
THE NINETEENTH NIGHT	59
THE TWENTIETH NIGHT	62
THE TWENTY FIRST NIGHT	64
THE TWENTY SECOND NIGHT	66
THE TWENTY THIRD NIGHT	67
THE TWENTY FOURTH NIGHT	69
THE TWENTY FIFTH NIGHT	70
THE TWENTY SIXTH NIGHT	74
THE TWENTY SEVENTH NIGHT	76

THE TWENTY EIGHTH NIGHT..................... 78
THE FIRST NIGHT.. 81
THE SECOND NIGHT 83

II: An Exposition on the Lunar Stations

A Brief History of the Lunar Stations 87
A Note on Coordinates... 94
The 28 Lunar Stations..97

Scatter Stars and See What Grows/Ignite.....................97
Volcano/Bountiful 108
Head of a Doe/A Hunt at Twilight............................. 118
The Retaliating Body/An Instinct to End.................. 130
Born Again/Die Again... 141
A Blister, A Thought/Eye of Potential 151
Snake Pit/The Overcoming Eyes 161
Double-Chambered Heart/A Star Enthroned........... 170
Treasure of the Pyramid I/Marriage
    from One Side 180
Treasure of the Pyramid II/Marriage
    from Another Side.. 188
Whistling Hand/Time-of-Day.................................... 196
A Faceted Gem/The Measure of Heaven................... 205
The Long Breath/A Feather, Windswept,
    Metal-Sharpened.. 214
The Replicating Branch/Rain-Light........................... 224
Wreath of Flowers/A Hare Upon
    the Moon's Face.. 233
The Soaring Heart/Red-Ghost
    in the Machine.. 242
Origin/Red-Root of the Cosmos 251
Jamal (Divine Beauty)/The Water Sieve 261
Jalal (Divine Majesty)/Silence...................................... 269

A Thread to Heaven/Darkness at the Pole	279
Subtle Listening/A Walk Through Eternity	286
Reverberating Sound/Beauty Conquers All	295
Stirring of the Old Gods/Pharmacopeia	304
Water-Ash/Burning	313
Ash-Water/Drowning	322
Water Ways (Veins)/Mouth of the Whale	331
Two Horns/Lightning from Heaven	340
Kingdom of the Interior/The Relentless Weight of Existence	349

III: Waning

Waning	359
Bibliography	362

Introduction

IT is no accident that we deem the Moon ever fit for travel. Observable in constant motion she graces the sky with spans of distance unseen amidst the nighttime retinue. And, if we were to gaze upward on a clear night and witness her great presence, we would be remiss so as not to utter praises for her starry gown; a novel and ever more radiant one each night. Like the crab who is of her ilk, these gowns may also be her homes. A liquid, alabaster body seeking shape between the setting and rising of the Sun. Her migration persists, simultaneously resting amid the movement of a steady pace. In this way we can begin to conceive of the lunar stations, or mansions as they are sometimes called, as places along the Moon's nightly path.

Procession of the Night Theatre, at its ethos, is a tracking of these same movements through collected images and accretions of all kinds. They are gathered among these so-called places, stations, mansions, and all-around locales, designated by starlight and darkness in contrast. Just as we often conceive of the Sun's starry path—that of the solar 12 sign zodiac we often take for granted—the Moon also walks upon her road; though it is altogether different in quality and all the more mysterious in character.

Envisioning the pathway of the Sun, we may observe the obvious yet often forgotten fact that the stars and planets are not visible during daytime hours. It is this apparent reality that bears on the history of astrology as it has developed through our forms of perception. In other words, though the 12 familiar zodiac signs (Aries through Pisces) have their origins in asterisms, the astrology of the Sun has moved far beyond them. This is not to equate beyond with superiority. More likely the case, it would seem that these origins and their invisible backdrops of starlight have become increasingly less relevant in our modern technological age.

The trend has moved towards the diurnal dimension indefinitely. Though there is no lack of stellar characteristics (as we often forget the Sun remains a star!), it does exclude the many Others who reign free among the boundlessness of night. Technically speaking, we find a greater emphasis on the cardinal points of crossing, the seasons, and the stations of the Sun more broadly. Our interpretations of these once purely stellar origins are viewed through a washed-out solar lens. In this way, Sun-centered astrology lends itself to heightened 'rational' principles, as diurnal phenomenon is of a clearer and more predictable nature.

This is less the case in observing the Moon's pathway. Her light is of a gentler quality. Consequently, she lends herself to a kind of collective luminosity. The other stars and planets become visible under her terrestrial reign. Putting aside the ever-intrusive reality of light pollution (the diurnal colonization of the nocturnal dimension...) for the time being, it is the night in which the true origins of astrology persist. Similarly, our deeper imaginations flourish here, less obstructed by the day-time-rational-regimes of order and capitalist regularity.

This is not to posit the night or the Moon's light as representative of the irrational or chaotic. To do so, it would seem, is far too easy a binary. Rather, nocturnal regularity takes on the quality of dream and visionary experience. It is not that we cease breathing or having to sleep, or even that our dreams do not partake of diurnal consciousness in some capacity. It is that her rhythms are more akin to music, the tactility of a painter's brush strokes, or the utterings of a poet, than the strict definitions of scientific analysis might allow for.

It is in this spirit, or better yet *soul*, in which procession proceeds. Unlike the evermore rarified dimensions of spirit, it is the soul which roots deeper into the landscape. It is the soul which must be grown and tended amidst the hardest of circumstances. The byways of the Moon are closer to the Earth in character. Though her starry retinue persists, and her celestial credibility is never in question, her images are distinctly those of our immersion into matter and the creative ways that we navigate this question.

Our guiding image is of a Moon as traveler. This is where the term *station* becomes preferable, as there are 28 places of experience over 28 nights that the Moon finds herself along the journey. Though we more commonly hear of these 28 places referred to as the lunar mansions, lodgings, and domiciles, stations imply a continual movement and shape-shifting necessary for the process. Every stop is an unfurling of accouterment, color, adornment, and costume. Novel characters and personalities emerge in each new place. New becomings time and again, sometimes as skins, sometimes as times. It is only through star-dotted, oneiric vast-black, that we may become witness to the never-ending theatrics of imagination. This is the lunar zodiac.

The decor, the flavor, and the all-around feeling of each of the 28 stations depend upon a host of factors from individual perception, magic, and charm, to various cultural iterations and particular astronomies. *Station*, as an intentional word choice, is the recognition that these processes are constantly evolving. Just as the Moon in her ophidian-light sheds and re-dons new skins every month, so too do her reflections and artistries change shapes amidst the shadow play of time. The Moon as 'the nearest planet' ensures this reality, as these forms mirror that which we see before us night after night.

In this way, *Procession of the Night Theatre* speaks to the plurality of established forms that the stations have manifested through. They are born of cultures that have taken the tracking of the Moon to be of utmost import. In addition to this, the contents of this book have been garnered through the author's own aesthetic, magical, and astrological observations. As every chapter is aligned to a station, these cultural forms and observations are something of a furnish for their 28 unique stages, each one modifying the surroundings and the personalities of the characters who walk upon it. For example, the first station, *Al Sharatayn,* is passionate and charismatic. The prophet Elijah is a like character for this particular affair, howling and calling forth fire from the heavens to supplant the old gods. When the Moon moves through this place she experiences these qualities, beginning to act, dance, and sing in harmony with her surroundings. Unlike the Sun, who by nature will not reveal his company, we may witness with our naked eyes the Moon in her performance among the ever changing nightly-cast.

28 Nights

Many of our most well-known stories once traveled from distant lands on foot, horseback, and through dream. Due to the dangers of nighttime travel it was common for these groups of travelers or caravans to seek out resting places for the evening. The *caravanserai,* as many of these stops came to be known, were marked by replenishment, conversation and consequent imbibing, and sometimes, the occasional convivial-convergence with a fellow journeyer. Importantly, for our starry tale at hand, stories might be exchanged to pass the time. Perhaps told over the warmth of a fire, or, better yet, under a moonlit sky.

There is a resonance between these places and the lunar stations, in particular with the Arabic tradition of the *manzils* or mansions. Every night the Moon was thought to rest at each of these stations. It was the nearby stars that furnished the encounter. Her speedy passage through the sky assured her association with these same caravan travelers as well as their business dealings, conversations, and tale-tellings. One might gather much experience through these movements in the manner of the Moon. Of course, these locales all had their unique qualities. Depending on the culture and the night one happened to be present, these veritable stages would shift and change. New travelers were always passing through. Other times, it would be that same familiar from before, almost as if they never left. Other times there might be music and entertainment. The sounds, songs, and smells one might encounter through these stops were always on the move.

Many of the stories told would end up in collections such as the *1001 Nights*. Not unlike the movements of travelers who committed them to heart, these tales were structured over a series of consecutive nights, wherein each story might be carried over, adapted, and altered into never ending patterns of Sun sets and risings. Characters and stages were constantly shifting, yet a through-line of precessional nights remained the same. In this way, the reader of the Nights is not unlike the Moon; observing, listening, and taking in the scene. Each story becomes a stage all its own, capable of existence in a self-persistent world. Yet the story must continue. Each night we dream and emerge again in daylight. As such, this is the thread that binds them. That of travel and experience. That of rising and setting. That of contrast between night and day.

Just as Shahrazad must leave cliffhangers for the sake of survival, so must the nights persist for the sake of locomotion. Underneath the multitude of stories lies a perennial narration; one of movement in itself. So does any one story reveal the truth for all.

Night/Day

Following in the soul of night-side vision, a true sidereal picture show, *Procession of the Night Theatre* moves through 28 Nights as if a traveler in dream. It is through the medium of story that our 28 stations may be known at their roots; that is, in the realm of image-imagination. These byways emphasize intuition, poetry, spirit-contact, and oneiric sense above all else. At times, these methods are also capable of bypassing our more rigid inclinations and biases. Much like the 1001 Nights, each story, or, each station, may stand on its own. In this way, linear reading is not required nor encouraged per say. Move through as you wish.

As it is not our intention to abandon diurnal vision, this book has been separated into two parts. *Procession* moves through the stations as if a dream. Lucidity aside, the vast majority of our dreams are experienced as a cinema of images in which we are immersed. Us experiencers, donning reflective garments as such, both succumb to and radiate out phantasmagoria of astral airs with our immersion into the realm of sleep. Poetic-narrative language reflects these crooked dream-logics. The second part of this book, *An Exposition on the Lunar*

Stations, seeks to classify and categorize through means all too familiar in astrological research. Part II functions as a comprehensive guide through the many facets of the stations. Each one is broken down into its primary correspondances: *Manzils* (Arabic-Islamic), *Nakshatras* (Vedic-Indian), *Xiu* (Chinese), geomantic relationships, the Prayer to Mene list from *The Greek Magical Papyri,* and associations with the archaic Proto-Sinaitic alphabet and its Egyptian hieroglyphic origins. In addition to the gathering of published information, the author has provided keywords, a summary of the station, as well as brief delineations for each of the seven traditional planets and their placements in said region. If not footnoted, the authors and sources of this information are listed in the bibliography at the end of this book. The astronomical information in these same sections was garnered through the 'Stellarium Mobile Plus' application.

It must be stated from the outset that the vast majority of each station's correspondences emerge primarily from their signifying stars. If we return to the metaphor of a domicile, the stars figure as their primary occupants. This is not entirely unlike the familiar domicile schema in Western and Vedic astrology which has certain planets ruling certain signs. For example, the Moon is thought to rule Cancer, Mars over Aries and Scorpio, Jupiter over Sagittarius and Pisces, etc. Though the modern schema for nakshatras often mirrors this, we have chosen to maintain stellar sovereignty over that of their wandering siblings. In other words, the lunar stations do not have planetary rulers, only likenesses. If there were to be a planetary ruler, it would surely be the Moon, as her translation of starlight is integral to the task at hand.

The majority of works on the lunar stations have little in the way of natal interpretation. This is not ahistorical, as the lunar zodiac has largely been used for the purposes of electional, mundane, and magical astrologies. Nevertheless, pulling from this wealth of information one may still surmise how the Moon could function in the birth chart. In addition to this, each interpretation is informed by direct study of planetary behavior along the lunar zodiac. Though perhaps not as apparent as solar-zodiacal interpretations, this form of analysis is at least as rewarding as the study of decan, term, and other forms of 'minor' dignity.

Besides the critical placement of the Moon, the remaining six planets and their interpretation will vary depending on the circumstance. It is often the custom in Vedic astrology to focus on the Moon, followed by the Ascendant, the Sun, and sometimes the Atmakaraka (planet at the highest degree in the Vedic natal chart; thought to have great karmic significance). If one is looking for a schema of priority, indeed the Moon, the Ascendent, and the Sun would seem to be the most important. Though there is no direct interpretation of the Ascendent in each station, one may read the section for the Moon and Sun to ascertain that information. Similarly, it may be beneficial to observe the station of the 1st House lord, 9th and 10th lords, as well as angles and lots. In this respect, one's regular interpretative principles such as aspects, house placements and the like need not be abandoned. Once more the importance of the Moon must not be overstated as it is her zodiac. Unlike the other six planetary interpretations, all seven of them may be applied to the Moon in some fashion. In other words, if one is reading the interpretation of Mars, it still has some relevance to the placement of the Moon in that same station. The reverse is not necessarily true.

For fluidity of writing's sake, the planet's conventional genders found in Western astrological language have been used. Naturally, as there must always be an exception, the planet Mercury was given gender-queer pronouns. In all reality, every planet, star, or otherwise-being cannot be limited by our simple gender conventions. Though we have chosen to refer to the planets using gendered pronouns, it is important to recognize this as a convention of language and nothing more.

Planetary gendering follows similar notions of separating day and night perspectives as we have done here. Though the colonization of night by the diurnal dimension is a palpable reality, experiences born from the lunar zodiac rarely reify hard boundaries. Rather, it is that of infinite luminosities; or, the true origins of light itself. It is the plurality of darkness which is at stake. There are never simply two perspectives, two books, two ways of seeing, or even only day and night. As our two luminaries are sometimes thought of as the eyes of the cosmos, it is with both in unison that we must work for optimal vision. Though the left eye of the Moon has become weakened in our day-time striving culture, we must never sacrifice one for the other lest we lose our stride along the way.

* * *

It is the hope of this book that the lunar stations may be our guides toward holistic ways of seeing. That we may find the many Others on our journey. That we may recognize the brilliance and the multitudes of Them.

1001 is a large number, and ever growing. 'The Nights,' as it were, continue to fall as well as grace us with their never ending masquerades. The journey of the Moon, as well as the many stars along the way, are gateways to the rhythmic breath behind the dance. Each night, a hand extends to us so that we may join the swaying voyage. Each night a call to hum along in starlit chorus. This book is an answer to that call as well as a response. Tagging alongside the celestial retinue in tandem.

I
Procession of the Night Theatre

¶The Third Night

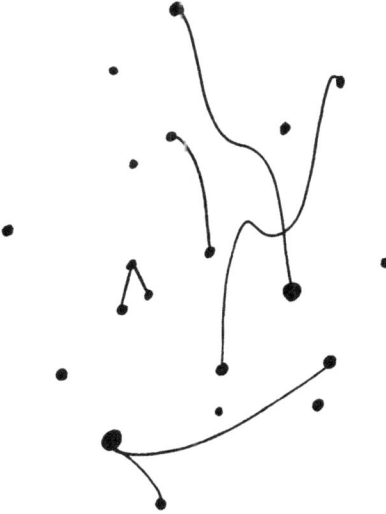

WHY DO THINGS NOT HAPPEN WHEN WE WANT them to? Perhaps we had already decided, in some twisted age before creation, when all the minds were one, that this would be *the moment* and nothing but? That I would force myself into the grand carousel of time, lest I forget why?

I arose startled by the sound of crackling fire. There were stars above me, and the sky had never seemed brighter or more awake. It might have been the stars and not the fire that stirred me from my slumber. Yet these are not terribly different at the end of the day.

Whether this was the first night of my journey or the last I could not recall. There had been so many like it… yet none quite like *this* one. This night would be branded upon my memory as the one which set a fire in my heart.

This is the night that I would notice the vault of heaven in all of its grandeur.

I couldn't recall the past with any clear sense of vision. Though it exerted weight behind and underneath me; as a feeling, as an urge. This sensation was enough to bring me back to a sense of time when there was no fire. When the way was not lit. To the times when lamps were extinguished. I could feel the cool ripple of air on my skin, as long-dead familiars blew out candles in earnest. If one were to walk across this scene as if a darkened landscape, an earthen fire would resemble a star. The kind of darkness where land and sky blend together into a single unapproachable vastness. When a lamp is lit here it cannot go unnoticed.

Such is the Moon in this place. Resplendent, the Queen of Heaven. If I followed that light with conviction I may begin to get somewhere. The stars that evening were approachable. Like I could sing to them and they would hear me. Perhaps even hum a tune back to me. They appeared reliable, but only so much as my humanity extended outward. Beautiful and vibrant as they were, if I followed them through the vast-black, I knew I could never return to the place from whence I came. The Moon was one thing. But to follow the stars meant death in certain terms. Unless you were at sea, of course. But I was not, and I knew these things.

A history of wandering in endless night took quite the toll on me and my people. Here was a decision if ever there was one. Standing between infinity in both directions I could see two ways. Behind me and underneath me a darkness forever. In front of me and above me the eternal lights. I hadn't yet learned that each way led to the other. My mind was still keen, sharp. I could forge pathways when I wanted. I could rally the crowd when I wanted. A real leader of the people type. It wasn't important at that moment that I didn't have the full picture. It was only critical that I make a choice.

¶The Fourth Night

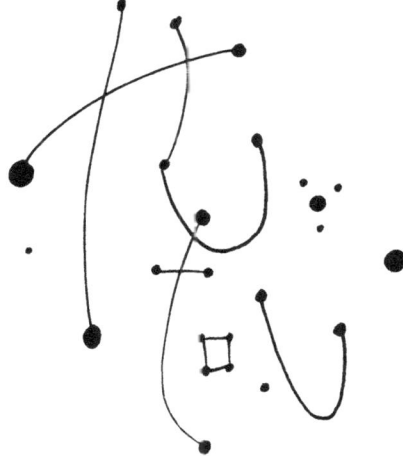

HE FELT COMPELLED TO ASK FOR SOMETHING from a loved one.

This wasn't easy, as he had never put his odds and ends aside for the sake of vulnerability.

He once tried asking for help with a whimpering and a slight groan.

It was pathetic. Like a small child receiving pity.

Calling out in the night is one way of asking. Opening your mouth and making utterances is another.

There is really no right way to do it.

There is just bending. Bending towards reciprocity, although most would not think of it in this manner. Bending of time and space into oblong shapes which collapse the distance between people. When the mouth opens and spews outwards in the manner of a volcanic eruption. When we observe interior workings made manifest.

Bending like a body, stronger than his own, shaking him.

Asking him: 'what the hell is wrong with you?'

'Why can't you forget it all and just persist?'

'If I grip you like your life is on the line will you finally quiet down?'

And his spine became stone as it wound up out of the Earth.

Vascular systems threadbare. Gravity, entropy, guiding the fleshy yarn-ball of consciousness into greater and more discreet articulations of form.

Just a musculature, coalescing. That is what he needed.

Strong-arming to oblivion. Energetics, aerobics, and perhaps more whimpering.

There is no philosophy to it. All of the moaning and groaning.

It's up and down pragmatism. And you'll know it if you see it.

He turned over strange thoughts again and again in his mind until they reached a new pinnacle of absurdity. These thoughts resembled hills in their verdant rolling onwards. He could stride on them, but it didn't quite match the feeling he was going for. Power, attention, focus. He couldn't do it all himself, but he also still could not seem to ask for assistance.

He possessed four wheels and his own blood which could only pump so hard. How far could he honestly get under these conditions? The vehicle without an engine. The engine without a vehicle.

He needed attributes. Accretions, and the like.

That is how he helped, you see?

Those were his eyes. For him to witness and for me to witness him.

In order to get out to the open country he sought so terribly, he knew that he would need the help of others. Now, lest we forget that intimate affairs such as these require more than just another person. He needed someone who loved him. Someone who loved him as much as he loved them. And he knew that this was hard to come by. There were few and far between who truly reciprocated with sincerity.

Perhaps if he lit a torch. Like slathering a great tree in tallow.

So many could see his light, from such far away distances.

¶ *The Fifth Night*

THEY MET IN A FAMILIAR PLACE ONCE INHABITED.

Since their time of coexistence many walls had been erected.

Screaming lineage was the least of their worry.

Her face shone like moonlight through an azure glass. Tile worked darkness, pattern as repose.

The backdrop of her confusion raised no questions as to her whereabouts.

For her banishing to the wilds serves as yet an unknown purpose.

If conclusions must be drawn, they arise abreast, yet remain obscure.

There is a heartbeat amidst the newly fashioned barricades.

Yet her blood has not awoken to its riverway.

So she stands an evergreen mosaic arching among doorways.

Gravel spills between her teeth as she calls out, mumbling her words so often incoherent.

This great unknowing belies a choice. In one hand she holds a mirror.

In the other a caress. That which she once ascribed mercy can no longer be grasped.

For her eyes have become like diamonds.

They were plucked from a leviathan and unwillingly nestled forth.

She now sees things that are hidden. She now sees others who have been banished to the forest. She now knows touch and scent and inner vision. She now builds private worlds perpetually evading capture by unsuitable suitors of the fairy tale brand.

"How is it that I now see you? Who or what has altered my form?

Who or what has penned a novel destiny?"

She holds herself as if a deer suffocating in the gaze of headlights.

Each ray bouncing to and fro, freely, amidst her hollowed and glazed ceramic body.

How she mutters to the walls for closure and liberty in a single breath. Each breath a nuisance all the same.

"I wish to see the whole of things. I wish to see with every part of me.

I wish to see every tree of the forest with complete clarity, all at once.

I wish to know what cannot be known, and I wish to have my memory be dashed of every beautiful sight I have witnessed. That I be punished for every temptation in which I answered. That I be celebrated for every impulse in which I chose to move instead of stay."

"I wish to leave this place of wonders in which I was given everything and nothing. I wish to run away from this garden of sorrow which knows no difference between pleasure and pain, abundance and desolation, myself and the one whom I am searching for. I wish to no longer feel hunger and thirst, and I wish to no longer be satisfied."

She meant to fashion a path through the dense forest. Perhaps others may find their way after her. Examining where she had been and what she acquired she soon realized that there was nothing left but to find the other in whom she sought the end of separation and the beginning of togetherness. But where she was at the moment of this reflection did not exist yet. Nor could it ever in entirety. She realized that it must always be maintained. That a part of it was always on a road or in a crisis or in the throes of ecstasy.

They met in this place.

¶ *The Sixth Night*

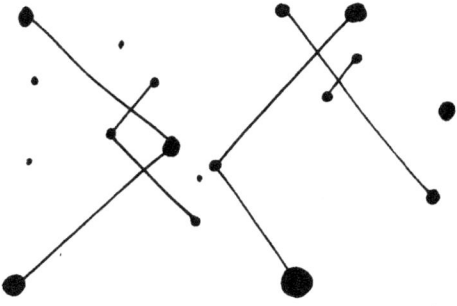

REELING FROM THE PREVIOUS NIGHT'S TRAVELS, he came to a point in the journey assuredly requiring rest. The funny thing about a pause while one is moving is that it may not be initiated without an effort all its own. One cannot cease making an effort—even to pause—while one is moving. This is a fundamental paradox of nonaction. That it is itself an action which must be taken.

"Perhaps I will lay my head down to rest here, in this abandoned place, upon this stone."

He could not help but fear the tombstone-like shape of this particular formation that he had decisively chosen as his place of cessation.

Nonetheless, it had been a grueling journey. Dead nerve endings dotted his spine. His bones were loose and wickedly tied, as if strung up into a gruesome basket that held his skin like a burden. His neck, kinked and all too stiff from old hatred and the like.

"I must only sleep but for a moment."

"Any longer and I will lose momentum."

So, with haste he rested his head as comfortably as he could across the shimmering gray stone. After a few readjustments of his neck, the exhaustion overcame him and he quickly nodded off. As he fell asleep he listened to the awful howls of this desolate place. This is a place in which his body forced him to stay. His mind thought different, yet the mental substance was of a weaker nature to that of his surroundings, including his very own flesh, which coiled about the maypole of his consciousness in unforgiving clamor.

His was a place uncertain. Incessantly so. Here, in this wasteland of a town, or some forgotten dwelling, he somehow found respite.

The complete discomfort caused intense bouts of waking and falling back into and out of sleep. Such is the nature of rest when the body has nearly given up and the mind cannot find pause. The wind simultaneously whispered and screamed, taking possession of his voice, crawling deeper underneath his skin, to get the message across without question.

He listened to himself repeating...

"To be seen is to feel one's gut.

To be hated is to feel the other's eyes.

And to be loved is something in between.

Such is the ebb and flow of any journey."

Sleeping and waking now took on the same character as one another. What was at first only his beloved tombstone now opened up to an indigo landscape, no less awful yet feverishly populated. The first thing he witnessed were the trees that resembled beached wood. Their viscera twisted and skin cold-dry. They bent and cracked and whistled like old bones. Powdered vessels breaking and reforming, dressed like axes splitting themselves, only to will their bodies back together again.

Stuck here like a trap with the glue still soft, he could not reckon mind and body nor find his legs again.

"If I could only rest but for a moment longer.

I need the strength so that I may move onwards from this ghastly place...

Yet my limbs resemble these old trees, and so too does my mind. As if the ghosts who haunt this place are not enough companionship, I also bring my retinue of sorrow, co-mingling against my better wishes."

This is the sculpture now. Let it scar where it must.

He had become one with the graveyard in which he chose to lay. Yet somehow it did not feel as if it ever was a choice. Now, as the roots of both his mind and his body began to curl around and through the barren soil of his chosen bedrock, he accepted this guillotine-of-a-night for what it was.

Finally, he drifted off to sleep without a stir. For the next leg of his journey would not be taken by the body that he once knew but something altogether different. As he learned to love his death, he found his legs again but in reverse. An enshrouded nobility, a backwards honor, moving circular, which found its way again to places of origin. This would be his vehicle now.

¶The Seventh Night

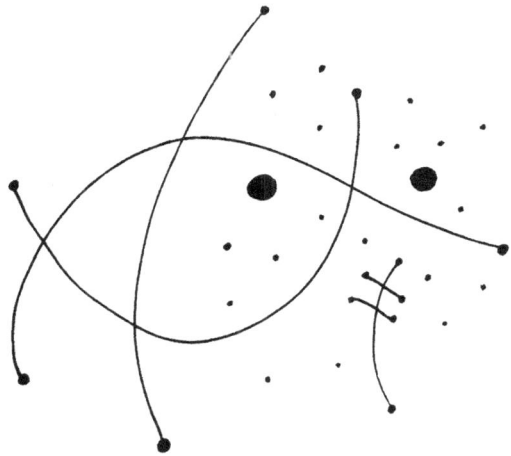

NOBODY HAD TOLD THEM HOW MUCH STRIFE and uncertainty they would encounter on the road ahead. But, with one another in each other's lives there was such a thing as reciprocity. There was such a thing as dialogue. There was even that most precious of relations, friendship.

"I am not sure how I would survive without you..."

"Have I made this clear to you? Have I truly expressed how much I care?"

"Sometimes, yes." "Other times I wonder if you were ever really there..."

He pondered how he could say such a thing.

"After everything we have been through together, you can say that to me?"

"You can look me in the eye, my eye which resembles yours so distinctly, and say that to me?"

"We supposedly share a soul, remember?"

"We supposedly can hear each other's thoughts?"

"I have no doubt that you probably sense my frustration even at this moment."

All of this fervent discussion about what one did for the other, how they have shown up or not for one another and the like, was not necessarily leading anywhere. On the other hand, it did not keep their feet from moving forward. Their pace remained consistent. Step by step they walked alongside one another as they had always done.

It was in the pre-dawn hours that they spoke to help pass the time. Though the conversation began to slowly slip into an argument, it was clearly better than the alternative. To say nothing would be the death of them. Though they knew with certainty that the Sun would soon rise, their stroll still found them below the stars and nervous of their surroundings.

"I think we have passed through here before."

"I recognize this place through feeling. It consoles me."

"There is an opacity to the plant life which sets the background every time."

As they moved forward more memories began to return.

"How can I forget that distinct buzzing of wings? Reflections of moonlight, iridescent flashes from the swirling insects...It is this very place that I remember myself and who you are as well."

"It was only our last adventure that I came to a sort of motto for this place..."

He sang to his companion and to all the many others who were present at that moment.

"Repeat the words so we may hear ourselves ever louder.
Repeat the words so the gods may hear us ever more.
Repeat the words so that our tongues may never stiffen.
Repeat the words so that our hearts may never weary."

What was once a motto now became a song in full.

Words flowed through him seamlessly and from where he did not know.

"Confuse the master so that he may never question.
Confuse the senses that we may never grasp it.
Confuse the mothers so that we may ever be born.
Confuse the fathers so that we may ever indulge."

Here was the ticket to certainty. It did not arrive by happenstance but through the concerted effort of movement, speech, and collaboration. Doubt need not apply as their gestures spoke for themselves. Suddenly things became clearer.

Upon the horizon, in the very same direction that they strolled, they were witness to the rising Sun. Though it seemed that it was the same familiar Sun, it was also somehow novel. As if a fresh skin of amber had been donned for just that very moment.

¶ *The Eighth Night*

SHE HAD NEVER SEEN A JUNGLE BEFORE, NOR the strange creatures that might inhabit one. Feeding off of copious-airs they grow to large and unruly sizes. Endlessly shape-shifting, rainbow style, into arrays of color unseen by the superficial human spectrum.

It was life upon life. Heavy breathing and the forces which articulate bodies. And all the giving in-therein. Death and perfume comingling. Novel adorners passing through, swayed by putrefaction, decay, as well as more sophisticated smells. The flora resembled cartilage, all bundled together into twinkling strands both firm and flexible alike.

"I am not sure if I am alive or dead.

If I figured it all out, or I am left knowing absolutely nothing."

She encountered what seemed to be a large crystalline structure embedded within this teeming place. All around her, entities were breeding, and clarifying, and acting causative, yet the alabaster eye before her shone unflinchingly. It was a subtle axis cleaved between the buzzing. A steady anchor braced amidst an ever-falling world.

"Am I to ask it a question now?

My confusion has brought me here... To the center of it all.

Questions have only led to greater questions... so what good has inquiry done for me thus far?"

Now, we must not forget that cities can also be jungles and vice versa. She was familiar with this correspondence. The clean lines before her, the immaculate certainty of said center. It all triggered a familiar memory for her. It was something like civilization bubbling up despite all the savagery.

"How have I arrived here?

This is my first question."

There was no telling from where this voice emerged, only that it could be felt in the feet as much as one's ears. It was dislocated and ever-present, as if a whisper out of every tiny being which lingered along the outer edges; a chorus of the dark background.

"You lost your way"

"And that is how you found yourself here..."

"That is the only way that people ever find me...

Through a hole in the Earth, 'Wonderland' style."

ORDO AB CHAO.

"And you wanted to get so close to me that it would be undeniable.

Didn't you? Is that right?"

"Until the doubt left you...

Until it left with the certainty of a soul leaving a body.

Until you got close enough that it might make you utterly sick.

Until decomposition. Until proximity becomes suffocating. Over-familiarity. Like a bundle of knots from the same mother. To reach a moment, that if you were to pull it apart, it would undo its potency."

"Until you look at each string in this vast ball of cords and just gasp at the togetherness of it all. Until you cry out at all its inherent horror. Until every sense becomes enmeshed so tightly that life and death have no choice but to coexist, tolerating one another."

"There is a concordance, a harmony to all of this (me), that you seem to be missing."

She puzzled over the perplexity of this conversation with herself, the center, and all the humming life just outside the periphery. How one could be surrounded by such richness and still feel so completely isolated. How one could read every text upon the matter and still know absolutely nothing.

Knowledge like that doesn't just *happen*.

It must be shaken repeatedly.

You don't just make it.

It must be torn out of chests and strewn about the lawn.

Piled up, shuffled, sorted through, curated.

Only to be mixed back up, examined, smelled, and listened to a little more.

All of the senses unified, right?

¶ *The Ninth Night*

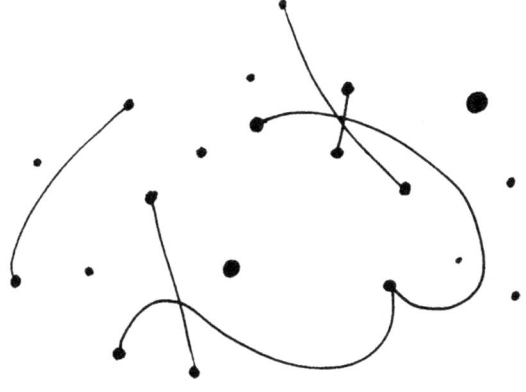

HE DIDN'T TELL ME WHAT I WAS GETTING into. Nothing of the sort.

Like a childhood moisture it was utterly aberrant. The kinds of things he babbled on about...I mean...

He found the smallest mason jar possible. Showed me pictures of various preserves, something like what would happen to both my flesh and my being as this process moved forward.

I was to be condensed into the most minuscule point of light.

I am not entirely sure how this would occur, yet that did not keep him from describing the gory details of the transformation to me again and again.

He revealed a tall black chair draped in black cloth, as if a monolith set upon a stage.

This will be the place of my unfolding. This is the place of my undoing.

He told me to sit there until I could read the wall-writing and various scribbles.

But I couldn't find them. And if there was something to decipher I couldn't decipher it.

This was a laboratory of all things thrown away. It was the abandoned who dwelled here.

It was my childhood dolls, and in particular their vacuous eyes, that set the dreaded mood.

There were many before him and there will be many after him. If I wasn't trying so hard to become something new I wouldn't understand this. If I wasn't keenly aware that I had to crawl through the mud to arrive at a semblance of an honest existence, then I couldn't sympathize with his tortures.

He told me that I had to become small enough to fit through a keyhole, but large enough to announce my presence to the new world that I was on the verge of.

The next thing I knew I was wrapped in shadow. Tiny eye holes cut out from the vast black so I could see. Even tiny slits for my eyelids. But all I saw was white. For days... white.

It was like being trapped in a large glass filled with water.

Perpetually drowning at first, I soon learned how to steadily breathe.

Light reflected back and forth as if through a prism.

My vision worked its way through an intestinal hallway of milky textures, but to no avail.

Rhythmic-blinking-induced-self-hypnosis, or something like that.

The way was surely lit but I couldn't tell exactly how.

Finally I collapsed on my shadow-throne, in the manner of a proper Regent of the Underworld, and accepted my condition as a cave.

That is what he kept telling me...I guess.

That the circumstances would condense until they couldn't any longer.

That black and white would weave together into unbreakable snags.

That my restraints would become my strengths. That I would see beyond good and evil like the philosophers of old.

That I could become a killer just like him. That I could consume those weaker than me but eventually bring them into the fold (against their will).

That I could hurt everyone who hurt me and perpetuate vicious cycles.

That I would become poison and love myself completely for it.

That observation would become my favorite pastime.

But I couldn't hear him over his presumptions...

Yet...in that cloak, a part of me already knew. What I was, I mean.

But also what I could become. Which is something like going deeper.

Vantablack for the soul.

I couldn't stay mad at him. Even though he placed her in the most precarious of circumstances. It was a trial that I knew I must endure. That I couldn't simply give it away, write it off, or anything of the sort.

I also knew I couldn't stay. Not one second longer. I had new places to go and things to see. People to observe with my infinite gaze. New obsessions to salivate over. And, of course, new people to wrap in cloaks and stars. With little eye slits for them to see from.

¶ The Tenth Night

I WILL RECOUNT TO YOU ONE EVENING IN WHICH I found myself bloodied and wartorn.

I could not move myself from what seemed to be the grave, exactly where I stood, and 5 feet deeper than ground level...

Consequently, I stood in observation of the floor.
I could see the mice scurrying along; the roaches too.
So many dancing feet. Heels swaying and the like.

From below I felt the Earth quaking.
Exasperating, even belching forth
a line of ants transforming into jittering figures.
Fetus, shell, quadruped, monkey,
human, skeleton.

A scarlet procession through the halls of power.

Upheld by twin serpents of brass, fuming mouths, jagged silhouettes.

Amaranth garlands lined the corridor. Architecture that imposes.

A long unseen-sight yet no less a sight.

From where has the dance macabre emerged?
Of what hole?
Of what trench? Of what ruin?

The landscape, a family of green unconquered
though still battered.
Rhythms of marching hooves, the bestial hordes,
coming to knock on all doors.
A sigh was uttered and heard as if a tremor.
Down there they marked every dwelling in red.
Breathing fire upon the threshold.
Snuffing it out whenever suitable.

Those who evaded ashes donned flowers and began to dance.

No less a horde, no less a monstrosity, they sang and howled and fucked until Kingdom came.

At the end of their phantom troupe crept a lonely scribe.

His pictures partake of eternity yet he knows not of what he writes.

Inscriptions like fire, whipping about.

In their path they leave husks, easily blown apart by the oncoming winds.

This same hall now expanded past the limits of the Earth.

For the Kingdom, in all of its apocalyptic language and end-of-the-world sensibilities, cannot be halted by the margins of the atmosphere.

To the stars, they persist. The monstrous horde, the end-times, and the scribe.

¶The Eleventh Night

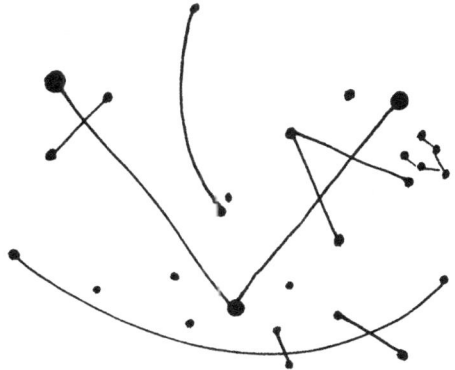

THERE IS NO PLACE FOR WANDERERS AMONG these well manicured flatlands.

Where everything is tiled and neatly arranged. Where the ancestors laid out their foundations, their architecture, their languages and all things civilized. A place of few gradients.

Here she is in black and white. A checkerboard floor, there then there.

"Oh, what a joy to dance the night away...

I adore how it tickles my skin, that hot breath."

It was an inverted paradise. This doesn't quite equal hell, mind you.

It just makes things hotter, more prone to grow. Erection-materials.

He watched from afar as her body swayed, pink flesh and all, around the perfectly luminous surface. Was she dancing for him? For the sake of contrast? Or perhaps for nobody but herself.

"You see, don't you?

You can read my lips not with words but with feeling."

"You want to make sense of it but you can't."

He held himself tightly in repose.

This was one of those moments that he learned about in psychology class.

It was a moment of sublimation masqued as grandeur. He wished to indulge in all the pleasures that the feast has to offer, but then what would become of him?

Palm trees galore...testicular botanicals, liquid filled and ready to burst.

Civilization must not be completely bland. Reproduction continues.

So have a little fun while you are at it.

"He can crush his desire for me, I know it.

It will be something to marvel before, the feat to end all feats.

What masterpieces he will bring forth, all in my name."

He gripped himself once more in anticipation.

"I am not sure if I can continue on like this."

"That vast expanse... the weight of responsibility amidst so much beauty. It is practically unbearable. The time is ripe and the moment is now. She is right here in three dimensions, tangible, real, and everything I have waited for and more."

(an afterthought...)

Now we see that attraction persists until it gives in to death. People must come together in their beds; in dark places. Whispering to one another about how they are going to pay their bills and do everything necessary for their families and their survival.

If you want to see it built, your pleasure must be sacrificed.

The moment must be seized, gently.

¶ *The Twelfth Night*

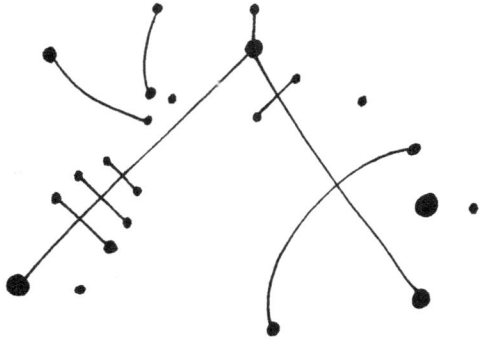

AT THE CENTER OF THE PYRAMID LAY A LARGE banquet. This food is not meant for the masses, nor any sort of group that might resemble a parade. It is for that sole individual (intentionally redundant). The one we all long for. The one we wish to become, yet few of us will ever be.

How is it that one person is able to consume so much? A feast for many, reserved for one. How are they to fit through the door just beyond the dining hall? As their body grows while the passageway leaves wanting. Beyond this door is a hallway growing in length and reducing in width as it extends out towards eternity.

A decision is called for. To stop eating and decide to be present.

To chew the food. To salivate.

When the choice was made finally things seemed to look up.

Here we find a person, a real one, in complete sincerity, staring down the hall.

She could feel the warmth emanating from a faint red

light curling its way through the corridor, which enticed her further. One magnificent doorway of scintillating iron, a marvel of craftsmanship, was found a few paces deeper. Releasing an atavistic moan the large door swung open revealing a scant-adorned, cavernous space.

Here she found a large volcanic pit, which bubbled and churned like a Sunday school story about hell. Instantly she knew where she was, but not through her eyes. In her groin, yes, she knew. Through her pores, yes. Somehow she knew this was a place of emergence. A place where existences were molded, mixed, and sometimes thrown together, swallowed, and regurgitated. These acts playing out in a prolonged series, something like cows chewing on cud.

"What brings you here?" asked a bellowing yet familiar voice from one of many darkened corners.

"I recognize you..."

"Not the typical dove, I would say..."

She responded in haste, only to find her words unnerving and increasingly unsettling.

"I followed an impulse. Simple as that.

Something like searching for a pill to alleviate a headache. Or a belly ache more accurately."

"Well have you found what you were looking for? Is your hunger sated? Did you leave food behind?"

She couldn't answer his questions because she could barely recall what came before the warm red glow of the pit she found herself in. It was something like dying and being born all at once. She was completely dumbfounded.

"Since you do not have words I will provide them for you. That is what this place is for, you know... Not simply the end of hunger and desire, but an open wound to let the muses through."

His (the creature's?) teeth were yellowed and jagged from chewing on an assortment of stones. Black was his favorite, as well as the color of the garment that he always wore. This was in contrast to the white dusty floor, patterned peppery, through eternities of crematory processes.

"I can grow palm trees too, you know...

I can garden and cultivate in ways never seen before.

Let me give you words for what your eyes will not provide you...

To fill your gaping mouth, understandably awestruck."

"You are witness to the hidden hand."

"You are witness to the place the bullet landed after being shot indiscriminately upwards towards the sky."

"You are witness to every color of the rainbow."

"You are witness to passion and the results of treating her well, as if a spouse who one adores."

"You are witness to a wind capable of shaping sand castles."

"Yet you must not speak of it to anyone."

¶*The Thirteenth Night*

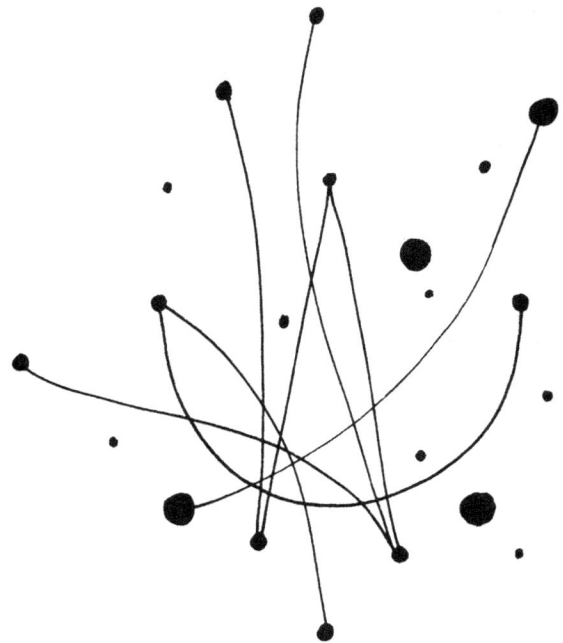

her, a countenance of stone
cold cold and nothing more
or less

they exchanged hands
& numbers, with no barriers
of communication

counting, crossing limbs
extending outward and
again again, without wit

labyrinth guide to the ever-more
is what she fashioned herself
for he was a jester
and a bit of a magician too

hearts crossed with desire
for all the things unseen
roiling tongues, offered up
glances, away away

flirting in the aftermath
fucking in a taxi cab
clinking glasses as they rue the day
never never
let it happen ever

"you never had me anyways..."

they never had each other
courting quick, the only way
cat calling a cell
down across the hall

and they met, for only but a moment
in that place...

¶*The Fourteenth Night*

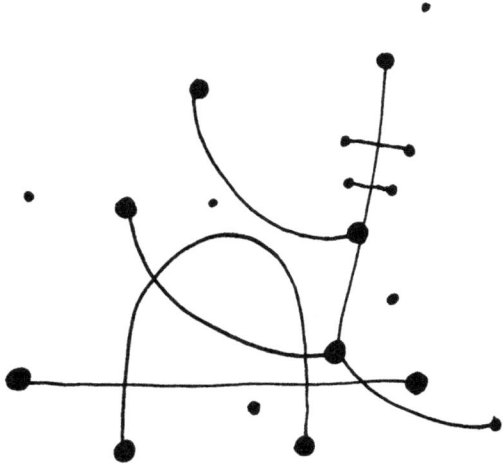

I AM GOING TO TELL YOU ABOUT SOMETHING I found one evening. It was on my walk along the shore. The place I go to get inspired. An in-between place where I can dream and exercise all at the same time.

It was the discovery of a small brass object hidden among a bag of shells and various materials. There was $4 in there, all in change. A small wooden-handled knife dulled from repetitive use. A pack of gum, presumably for the freshening of one's breath. There were shells which I mentioned, as well as some sand. And then the object... of course.

Inside of it was a mechanism, and inside of the mechanism was a microcosm, and inside of the microcosm was something resembling an eye staring back at me. Beyond a thin blue/darkly colored veil, glittering eye lashes batted, as if antennae receiving transmissions. This machine was aware of my presence, and at times blinked in response to my movements.

Instructions were whispered to me in a kind of coded language consisting of binaries. After much effort in decipherment, a map began to emerge out of this obscure code. Over the hill, a clearing opened up into a vast array of mechanisms operating throughout the land. Their purpose was not solely for the sake of extraction, as much as they formed a kind of dance troupe. I had the sense that humans were forbidden from partaking, as their limbs and gaits lacked the necessary perfection to align with this great spectacle.

※ ※ ※

It was at this point that she paused her story.

Looking out through the crystalline window she could see her reflection as it laid out upon the sea.

It was as if she was dictating her words directly to the waves. In their rhythmic motion, carving various forms onto the shore, her thoughts formed letters in azure and sea-foam. She wondered if her mind was too easily read.

Who else came to witness but the very stars themselves?

Brought on by the finding of this object? Or perhaps some other unknown cause.

Oh, this great dance, of little flesh, but every glistening-metallic color. What radiance, reflecting star light back towards the attentive audience. The perfection that was witnessed but never grasped. Never with mortal eyes. This dance is for those of light and those of stone. Complete softness or complete hardness. And nothing in between.

¶The Fifteenth Night

THE AIR WAS THICK AND THIN ALL AT ONCE.
Saturated by an inkling towards the higher powers.
Perilous to lunge forward all at once.
It is a great distance to be covered, mostly vertical.
There is no shortcut.

Atop the peak resides a man with five faces.
Beards adorn three while the other two remain youthful.
There is a face which receives questions and one that responds.
He is a benevolent king by all mortal standards,
but a tyrant by eternal ideals.
Not quite a god and not quite a human,
he straddles an uncomfortable in-between.
Ritual-fiending perpetuates his reign.
He has been here for so long that even the aeons call out in arrest.

There is a sign which marks the path to his cloudy domain:

Climb as you must.
Grin until you fall
and don't forget the walk down is just as painful.
Doubt with spit and plenty of vitriol.
Do not stop and do not look back.

If we were to project perpetual thought onto him…
An immense lemniscate, up there.
Inexhaustible vertebrae in figure 8.

How is it that we remain cordial?
Amidst splintering rain.
Of mind-clatter-concept.
When the fog sours.
When life blisters and obsessions persist.
Arranging matters by distant prognostications.
Assembling grains into elaborate designs.
Our marathon exhaustion,
beleaguered by proxy.
Yet even knowing,
auto-sacrifice, here, on the mountain-altar,
keeps the whole world going.

¶*The Sixteenth Night*

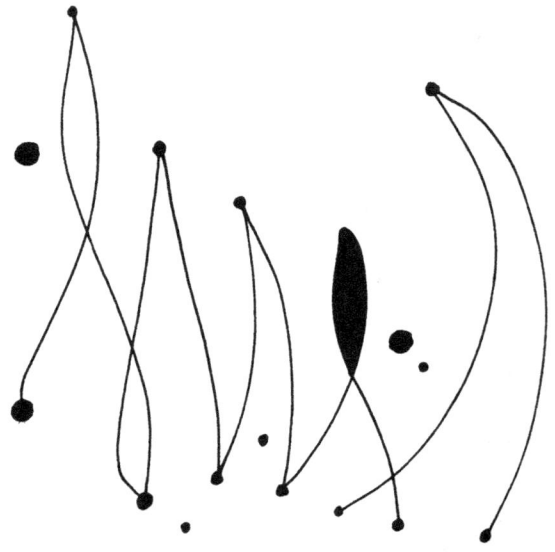

...AND A CLOUD DESCENDED.
Roiling into his ear, flooding outward.
Prophesying flowers and life and movement.

"I can do something with that" he grumbled under his breath...

Dug into an embankment, both in mind and in landscape,
he could grasp precisely half of what was going on.
It was a scene from the *4 of Cups*,
*poof,*an opportunity to do something real in the world.
The chance to create life.

The mist rang out in a strange melody, accompanied with words:

"Containment is a form unknown to me.
In all my forms and in every form.
I call out to your bones.
Shivering them. Inciting them.
A gentle cantor, these words bespoke.
Brushing up against your hardened skin.
As if a paint brush on concrete."

He pondered how to package the situation.
He pondered how he could go home to the woman he loves having listened to this revelation.

They lived together in a small cottage in the valley. The land resembled a basin, and the rain waters always seemed to slither softly downward towards their home. He was a farmer and his wife a weaver of beautiful tapestries. They had been together longer than they could remember, knowing consequently that they would die together too without a stir.

The cloud continued.

"What splendors await you and your gross existence.
How little you have seen and felt."

The farmer mustered a response.

"Have you watched me from up there? Truly?"
"Have you taken the time to cohere?"
"I think not, or you wouldn't be what you are and what you claim to be."

"The work I have undertaken...unimaginable for you.
Even in your infinite state you mock me, ethereally, as
if you knew..."

"Every cherry on top has been a battle.
My knuckles tend towards a purple-shade as I squeeze
them often.
Life out of life. Like wringing out a towel.
I am unrepenting. Forlorn but never for long.
And the most desirable undesirable.
I make decisions by clenching my teeth, air escaping
in tiny bursts."

"Must I spell it out for you?"
The cloud responded.

"I come bearing gifts and you fight me nonetheless.
If you continue to do so, I will respond in kind, with
venom."

"Caustic and sweet,
I am the perfect-saccharine picture of similitude.
I am a dragon by another name.
I am a pearl necklace draped atop leather.
I am every rejection.
I am validation."

"If I ever had a tongue, it would be-becoming.
Evaporating sometimes.
Coming from here and going there.
Don't you ever follow me.
Or you will become lost in the current-clatter.
In a crumbling layer."

The cloud cautioned that if he were to find himself there regardless...

"Out in the rubble pile, if you did follow me...
You could throw rocks at idols.
Jump up and down when you get a chance.
But you should probably never follow me..."

This wasn't going to help take care of his wife. It wasn't going to help him with much of anything that he could have used help with.

"No better than a puff of smoke from my pipe or my rifle" he thought.

¶ *The Seventeenth Night*

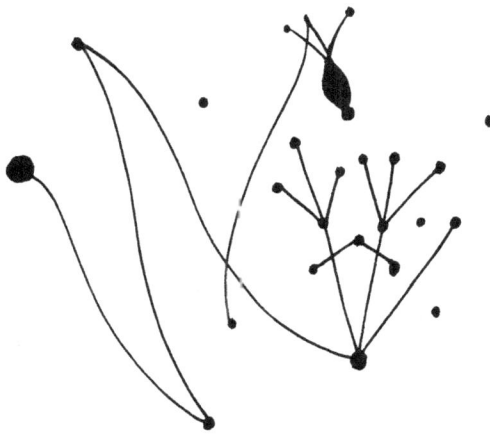

"It's a fine structure, they tell me..."

"A place of wonders and pleasures. A place of abundance and music."

She pondered entrances and exits.

She could not quite make out a visage and therefore dwelled further on what was the inside and what was the outside of this strange building she approached.

From where she stood, she could see a single lamp hoisted up from on high. Each particle of light clung to the next, as the great chain of being from creator to created was made ever palpable. Water, as conductor, guided the various luminosities in train-like fashion towards her eyes.

"Enchanting..." she thought.

"Not quite how I imagined it."

From the fog emerged an arched shadow something like a crescent Moon; black and undeniably inviting. She found herself peeking through a small doorway. Upon entering the loosely built brick structure she came upon a room dressed in scarlet curtains and embroidered with fine jewels. Brass implements of pleasure dotted the space. They felt as if they were longtime residents here. The objects gazed upon new guests who might happen to wander in.

The draw towards the bed was natural. It seemed that the sheets had been continuously ruffled, never fully cleaned, as so many had passed through time and again without pause. This was spectacular to witness. She became keenly aware of the many ghosts moving back and forth from where they had once enjoyed that most distinct of all pleasures. Connection, conversation, and communion with one another was such a way. Like the lanterned-light, every night after would whisper that red-echo in perpetuity.

"For the life of me, I cannot become a denizen, a dweller, a pleasure seeker here among the ruins. I am water and I flow onward. I am pleasure and I will not be damned."

Using all the force she could muster, she slammed her body up against the wall in an attempt to escape. The invitation was sincere, and this she was aware of. But it would not be sufficient in confining her to this wretched place, no matter how lovely the wallpaper was laced with filigree.

The brick, or the seemingly impenetrable facade of this now forsaken castle, was nothing but a paper tiger. She could take in the fog and the air and the light once more. A sense of field-depth reinstated.

In the distance lay a hill or a small mountain. She began climbing it, far far below sea level. Still, she was aware that once she rose upwards and onto it, that the run back down was completely inevitable.

She savored the climax nonetheless.

Even if it was but the smallest and most precious moment, it remained worthy throughout every trial and long winded sprint. When it seemed that there was no end in sight, she finally caught a glimpse of that ruddy light long sought after. A faint glow indeed, but good enough to pull a moth from great distances, and therefore worthy of her efforts.

¶*The Eighteenth Night*

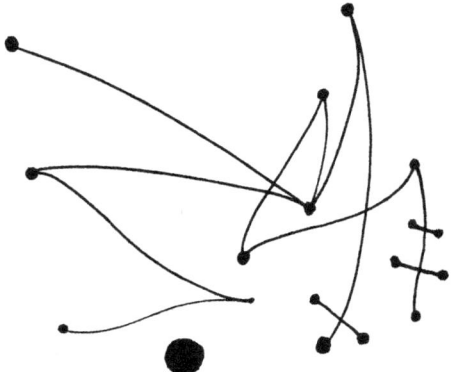

SHE HAD WONDERED WHAT WOULD HAPPEN when the red sands filled her lungs.

When the south grew hotter and the days more oppressive.

When fresh air would be traded for cruel earth.

A storm brewed in her heart which she could not ignore.

It wasn't the sight of toil, and even slavery which inflamed it.

It was even more overt than that.

The word she used was "armageddon."

Almost casually she repeated it, "armageddon... armageddon, armageddon, armageddon."

Armageddon bordered on meaningless with every passing through her lips. Her tongue, like the master's whip, held to the tune of armageddon in its lashing back and forth. One couldn't hear the word anymore. Just a deafening sound and a numbing of the pain.

"armageddon, armageddon, armageddon..."

In the corner of her eye, she began to witness the shifting of sands. Every strand of dried-out hair became visible. Every flake of dead skin, crystalline in its reflection. The wind continued to pound until it struck bone. The relentless desert climb held no alliances. What seemed to be a hand extended... in reality, the hairy black arm of a scorpion's tail, salivating from the reverse. Or the fleshy mouth of a viper, perhaps mistaken for a cactus fruit. The plants were no more friendly as they throbbed a ruddy-crimson, itching to deliver thorns into the wayward traveler.

In the heart of a sand dune, revealed by a petulant wind, came a low and raspy voice she had never heard before. It was a sinister tune, to be sure, and she could not tell whether to listen more closely or to plug her ears up in protest.

"Do not move or I will strike."

"I raise this storm so that you may take pause. Have you not noticed how much is changing right before your eyes? How in this wasteland, empty from horizon to horizon, viscous in its austerity, a smoke may still curl around your periphery without a word?"

"Oh, that is it though." "You have uttered a word..."

"*Armageddon,* an appropriate one indeed, but not sufficient."

"Your tongue may lash, but will it survive the trials before you?

That which lay waiting in this wretched place that you have found yourself.

Is it enough?"

The conversation that ensued took place entirely in the gut. To be torn open for the time being was not satisfactory. Her hunger was too great. What she truly craved was to look upon a mirror only to witness her skin turned inside out. So that she might examine every pathway, every inlet, and all the miniscule arteries and inner-mechanisms, while still being conscious of what is happening. She wondered what it might be like to perform surgery on herself.

The ghost persisted in its inquiries.

"Why have you awoken the machine?

Its hunger will never cease.

Now, as the awakener, you must feed it.

You must feed it with everything you are capable of feeding it.

You may begin with your own blood. Is this something you possess?"

Yet she could not relinquish a heartfelt, kindred sense.

She knew the responsibility before her. But she couldn't admit it.

The intrigue alone was enough to cause a rupture. If only her family and her friends knew the wretched words that she whispered back.

It was then that the tune changed from "armageddon" to something far more terrifying and world-shattering.

Before that horrendous whistling could end she finally surrendered to the calling.

The demon of the sand was her own, and fully capable of moaning words other than...

well...you know what...

¶ *The Nineteenth Night*

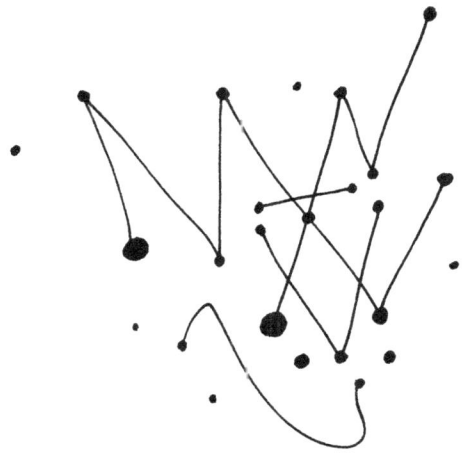

THE STREETS HAVE EMPTIED. THERE IS NOTHing in the sky save the fullest Moon.

One could hear the soft bristle of a passing owl feather. One could hear saliva hit the floor.

There was much anticipation for the banquet to come. Large blankets were laid out in many colorful patterns, the rock-forms below peaking through, as if a family of gnomes gathering to bear witness.

They placed their ears upon the Earth in response to a far away rumble.

"Is that what I think it is?"

"Goading us deeper into this whole tangled mess?"

They turned to gaze upward at the moonlight, looking for some sort of sign. Like the gaping mouth of a rabid dog the Moon let out a shrill and piercing scream directly at them. It wailed and it wailed, relentlessly, until they had shrunken into their blankets.

What of so much bounty they had collected? What of this great wealth? Rubies, sapphires, bloodstones, and the most magnificent carnelians? Foodstuffs, as well. Cakes and meat and carnage, salted and peppered, all neatly packaged, arranged in orderly little rows. Well, the stars would not let them savor their treasures this evening. Not under that sky. Not without imbuing them with some remorse.

"If only we could cover our faces and bodies.

If only we could walk towards the horizon with any sort of certainty that our labors were worthwhile.

I hate being seen like this. Under the nocturnal spotlight, I mean."

"This night, and the ensuing hunger, the dread of things to come...

Like a termite colony below us all.

An accursed fate."

One of the group members felt a sharp sting on her foot. Insect-unknown. Or, perhaps, no insect at all.

As the blood began to flow towards the fresh wound she could sense a calling embedded within the rupture. The bite, the nibble, the pinch (scale was hard to gauge) was not unlike the Moon, yet ruddy and throbbing. Whatever it was, she was sure that it could not fly. This was a messenger from below, or from the horizon at least. Delivering a message from every ancestor that was never heard. Human and otherwise.

Though almost unbearable, the Moon's silver-light seemed to cauterize the wound.

It sealed shut. Not through physical means, though. It was the psychic world, the one of plant-life in deep slumber and earth dragon's trembling, bound by soil. Chthonic facilitations.

It could have been like any other bite, no? Why wouldn't it have been?

Yet somehow, in this particular moment, standing beneath the stars at the edge of that dark precipice, it was a message unlike any other. Who knew a branding, or a mark of this sort, could emerge from an unwitting organism. It was a reminder of purpose. And perhaps it was not unwitting... or even the measure of fate, a smattering of pain and sick delight, woven into such a microscopic moment. Like the first entrance of a disease into the body. Or a mosquito hungry for blood. It was simultaneously the outer reaches of destiny and the bumbling mishap of a curious bypasser. It could be nothing less.

"When the trouble dies down, why don't you break out the wine?

Or smash a bottle, at least, against a stone on the edge of what is visible.

If the Moon wanes, which it seems to be, we can begin what we already started."

"Let me ask you."

"You, over there, crawling on your knees, getting all bloodied."

It was a tightly knit group but there were quite a few of them.

"Yes, exactly, you, now I have your attention.

Do you do it out of faith?

Howl back in the direction of all the wild creatures?

Because you believe that is where you, or better yet all of us, will return one day?"

When one wears their skin so tightly and nothing seems to break through, it could be a hindrance, or perhaps the unknown secret to everything. Until a break in continuity, of course. A simple crack. There is a remembrance of how beautiful the cracks and breaks can be. For some, they must be reminded that the cracks are actually who they are, completely.

¶*The Twentieth Night*

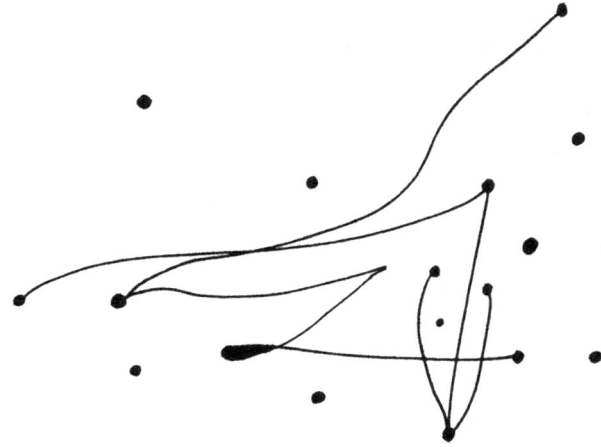

"THE CHINESE BELIEVE THAT SWORDS RE-
semble stars...

It is that glittering that they do, scintillation. It is a light which cuts.

Cold, distant, and metallic they shine. Have you noticed this?"

"There was that time I was confronted on the road to better things. I was trying my best to abide by the law and be a moral person. How do you think that went for me?"

He told his tale as they settled along a mossy wall. Beyond the wall a garden. And beyond the garden a place where conflict inevitably led to peace. A place where words had weight and meaning. Beyond there, a place unknown to the average human mind. Where faith remained intact, parallel to the cynicism incurred throughout a life of being beaten down.

"I came to a watering hole of sorts. There were animals gathering together triumphantly as if they had heard a call inaudible to me. I couldn't find the nourishment which seemed so palpable for them. It was a place of relaxation and beauty... but I found myself looking over my shoulder again and again. Perhaps waiting for a star or a sword to sneak up on my back."

"After enough of this back and forth, I finally arrived at a moment of solace.

Exhausted by my vigilance I laid down on the grass and shut my eyes.

It was but a moment of sealed eyelids before I heard a great bell ring out. It was bright, like the sound of reverberating brass, and I could not place where it was coming from. I felt a slight breeze and a wisp of air upon my shoulder."

"Standing before me rose a man of great stature. His hair white as winter, eyes black as night sky. His beard an icy river spilling out far below his chin with every word he uttered. The language that he spoke hailed from a land quite far from my own. In one hand he held a cornucopia of jewels, fruit, spices, and all kinds of riches. In the other, a most elegant sword, gleaming in the sunlight. This weapon had never been stained by blood. This much I was sure of."

It was not a choice as much as a suggestion of things to come.

"He opened his mouth as if he was about to speak to me but I could not understand his words in the slightest. It was his presence which stirred me to action. His honor without the sacrifice of strength. His detachment without the sacrifice of care."

As he sat across from his friend, recounting the story of his encounter with his conscience, he could feel his eyes opening again. They had not opened since that time, and light had not made its way to him.

He witnessed the Sun once more. A star all its own, among many, never alone.

❡ *The Twenty First Night*

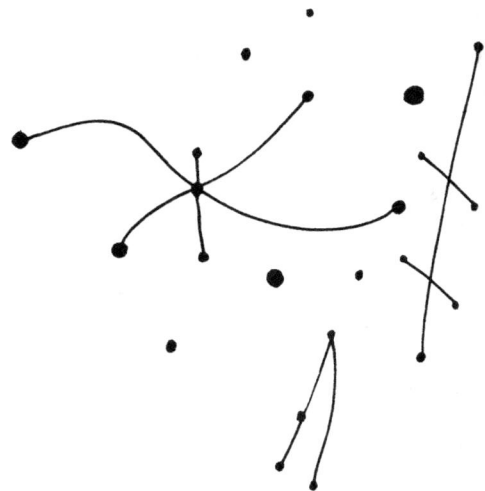

I CANNOT HEAR A THING OVER ALL OF the clatter...

There are so many of them, at this point...

So many ways to be myself.
To express myself.
So many skins for the One.
One for the many...

I am terrible in my overcoming.
Unbearably responsive.

When I walk towards the Sun I call out.
When I walk upwards,
I do not stop until forced downwards.
By the gravity
of a dying social order.

I wrap my hands around you.
Hold you up,
closer to the warmth.
As I would love myself.
As I would embrace myself.

I look out at the vista of humanity.

From the fish,
onwards to the apes,
onwards to the skyscrapers.

I am the bustle of a city.
The fruit of a culture.
The silent one, hooded,
walking about.
The gathering...
a crowd.

The minds of so many onlookers.

¶ *The Twenty Second Night*

YOU ARE NOT MEANT TO SEE THIS. YOU ARE NOT meant to see this. You are not meant to see this.

You are not meant to see this. You are not meant to see this. You are not meant to see this. You are not meant to see this. You are not meant to see this. You are not meant to see this.

You are not meant to see this. You are not meant to see this.

You are not meant to see this. You are not meant to see this. You are not meant to see this. You are not meant to see this. You are not meant to see this. You are not meant to see this. You are not meant to see this. You are not meant to see this.

You are not meant to see this. You are not meant to see this. You are not meant to see this. You are not meant to see this. You are not meant to see this. You are not meant to see this. You are not meant to see this. You are not meant to see this.

You are not meant to see this. You are not meant to see this.

You are not meant to see this.

You are not meant to see this. You are not meant to see this. You are not meant to see this. You are not meant to see this. You are not meant to see this.

You are not meant to see this. You are not meant to see this. You are not meant to see this.

You are not meant to see this. You are not meant to see this. You are not meant to see this. You are not meant to see this. You are not meant to see this. You are not meant to see this. You are not meant to see this. You are not meant to see this. You are not meant to see this. You are not meant to see this.

You are not meant to see this. You are not meant to see this. You are not meant to see this.

You are not meant to see this.

You are not meant to see this. You are not meant to see this.

You are not meant to see this.

You are not meant to see this. You are not meant to see this.

You are not meant to see this.

¶ *The Twenty Third Night*

IT WAS ONE DAY I LURKED ALONG THE SHORE with intent.
Sniffing around, step by step, glance by glance.
My eyes darted back and forth at passing sounds.

It was something of an anomaly.
Surely fated...

The distillation of the moment was gyroscopic.
It spun around and around until it could not turn any longer.

Its sides were lined with tiny holes which eked out bits
of time moment by moment,
aspersion by aspersion.

Lesser beings, and by this it is meant those who are
minuscule, lapped up these bitty moments opportunistically in the act of extending their lives.

The shore began to extend.
I could see the cosmos from every angle.
It was nothing short of a miracle.
But I kept asking myself...

What is it that kept me moving forward?'
But that tune that hummed inside my chest cavity?

This is how it went:

Turning turning, the great machine,
Behind our eyes we cannot see.

We are bound to dance, wherever it be.
Turning, turning, the great relief.

Moving, dancing, how great for me,
Beyond the sky we cannot see.

Twisting, singing, what a joy it be.
Stepping, stepping, the grand party.
Turning turning, the great machine,
Behind our eyes we cannot see.

We are bound to dance, wherever it be.
Turning, turning, the great relief.

¶ The Twenty Fourth Night

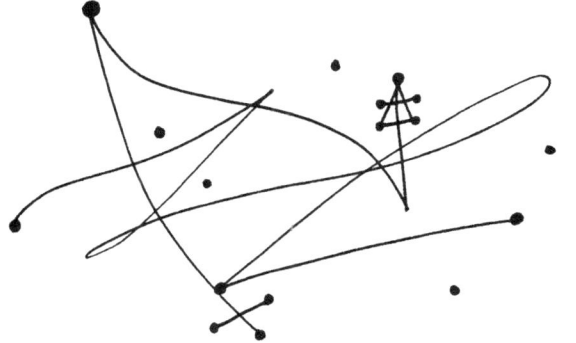

A LIGHT FROM THE FINAL DIRECTION BECAME visible.
It wasn't clear whether walking towards it would be a smart idea or not.
If anything, the operative decision for the moment involved lingering in between the space from whence it came to the direction its feet were moving.
The light began to pulse.

Blacker than black, the light refracted into hard edged patterns along the wall.
Like the hands of a clock they threatened the onlooker with their repetition.
Reminders of time and its cycles tend to do this.

Daring to invest further in the particulars would be a trial.
I couldn't decide...
the form, the measure, the song?
It all just collided forcefully in my lungs, only to be

expelled as dragon-breath.

In the place of light I found beauty in its words.
In the way forms would bend across its skin.
In the shivers of its spine.

It wasn't so much the snapping and twisting of it all.
The breaking of the system?
Alas, it was that special *something* which was always there. It had never left and it walked into the reverberating light with me.

¶*The Twenty Fifth Night*

LUSTROUS VAPORS REMAINED VISIBLE EVEN IN the waning moonlight.

The light was gentle and the darkness increasing.

A great mass of moisture, which had overtaken them, seemed to grow as if a pernicious mold. The scent was unmistakable. Violent yet subtle, life was doing its covert work.

Their group was lost once again.

Perhaps they could use their sense of smell to find their way out.

If it was going to be anything that could do it, it would be their noses.

"A familiar bouquet, yet all too rotten..."

Rotten like their circumstance. Rotten like the generations that abandoned them here.

"I don't suppose you have a compass, or a more useful tool? I mean, look at us! Wandering about blindly. Feeling around like some disgusting creature of the floor."

With sufficient lamentations one can elicit a response.

Although, the nature of it as such may not be what one desires. In fact it might be quite the opposite.

You could say that at this point the wandering group was overcome with something of a mass hallucination. Struck down from above and sunken down from below they were forced into their feet to reckon with the mud. It was no longer their flesh-eyes but their internal organs which they must begin to sense with.

Their imaginations were subjugated to a single image.

A tower at dawn, arising through the darkness, resembling the Sun.

Yet its form did not bring solace nor repose. Only more confusion.

Against their backs a great wind pushed. Into the imposing edifice they were blown.

Upon entering, this same air guided them through a series of rooms and hallways. As they drifted further into the interior, they were brought to the most marvelous spire at the center of the tower. The spire stood erect at the center of a courtyard, with four waters emerging in radial fashion from this point.

As the air pushed them through the central spire, the depth of center continuously increased as they moved through center to center.

Enclosed within the seventh courtyard, or the seventh center, lay a bevy of substances. There were spices from seven continents. Seven kinds of smoke curling in serpentine forms. Large pipes with billowing clouds emerging from them.

A small group of onlookers watched their movements. They wore head coverings. They grinned like crescent moons, forming a great chain of cold-sickle shapes encircling their plunge towards the central axis. Their heads bobbed like discarded fruits floating atop the water.

Birds glanced down from above the roof of the courtyard. Dotting the inside were exotic trees gently grasping flowers, the petals of which would only reveal their supple faces after sunset. Not on any old night, though... It must be a night when the breeze is just right. It is this breeze which signals to the flowers to reveal their hidden visage, but also their most secret scent.

Only the chosen few are capable of discerning it from among the many scents interweaving through the market. Only those whom the flower feels are worthy may indulge in this most sacral of encounters. If one were so lucky they might find themselves transported far beyond their mundane existence into something so utterly entrancing that they would be disposed to never return to their daily—and frankly—boring lives. Mundane existence would become increasingly frustrating as they have now tasted the nectar of the gods. Their feet have now grown roots and become ever so comfortable in this secluded courtyard. Their body now shuttering at the thought of ever dislocating from this spectacular dream.

Their decadence, and the possibilities of the ongoing hallucination, know no bounds. Here they have support.

Their feet have found aerial roots among the outcasts. Never have they felt so taken care of as they have since their arrival.

Never have they been so at home in a place with no walls.

Not only are there no walls here, but the sensation might be described as something akin to floating above the roof of your home.

Out of your body, with nothing but the thinnest silver cord connecting you back to that most painful understanding of all things mundane.

These thin silver cords resemble the stamens of unfamiliar flowers.

They beckon their kind back to their bosoms, calling them back to the ever subsistent dream. To finally abandon this place, to struggle out of it, would be quite the feat.

Like falling through the sky there is no end in sight. Infinite black expanses which seem to go on and on. It's a wall that is a wall but never actually a wall. More like floating above and looking down at the world below. Or perhaps floating down below and looking up at the world above. These are one and the same here.

¶*The Twenty Sixth Night*

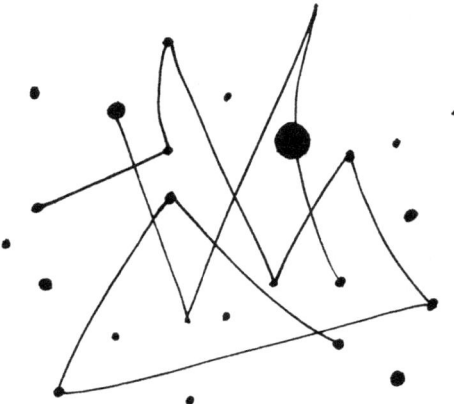

ON THE VERGE OF THIS NIGHT CAME A SIGN from heaven.

A shooting star perched above the rooftop making its way across the crystal vault, unencumbered by the weight of our petty little problems down below.

It was something like god spitting across the sky to get his point across. But it didn't last. It was only for a moment. A spark and nothing more. Yet it registered in ways that books consisting of thousands of pages could not.

It registered in ways that even the most grief-struck voice, wailing the saddest of songs could not.

It was this sign which set a rapturous mood between the two.

A phantasmagoric night between two lovers...

They sang to one another:

"You can find me when you close your eyes.

I am ablaze in your mind.

I am a pyre in your heart.

There are many trees, and therefore many aromatic woods which fuel it.

I am a house, a mansion even.

Resting upon your feet.

...and so I engulf your body completely."

Together they arrived at the edge of a river which could never be damned. It resembled a spiral moving upwards into the infinite recesses of time. Yet it could not be swam in nor should it.

Approaching the center of the formation they witnessed a large group of small beings gathering around a fire. They all simultaneously looked into the light and then away from it. Their bodies writhing in formation as they began dancing more and more ferociously rising into the sky. Like a great silver ring they drifted upwards, reflecting bloody-starlight.

Below the great black square of sky remained a wasteland. A utopia, a no-place.

They could rest their heads there for a moment.

As their eyes closed they began to whisper to one another.

"What is it you think of when you hear my name?

What image is conjured?"

The first responded:

"I am an extravagant farce, the greatest of illusions.

I am a magician, and a spectacular hoax.

I am light born of darkness, of the abyssal maw.

Yet it is only a skin, temporary.

On a sea of never ending no-things.

The second responded:

"Do not mistake me for anything Other.

For I will have it all in the end.

Love is all-consuming.

What is it worth if not?"

¶ The Twenty Seventh Night

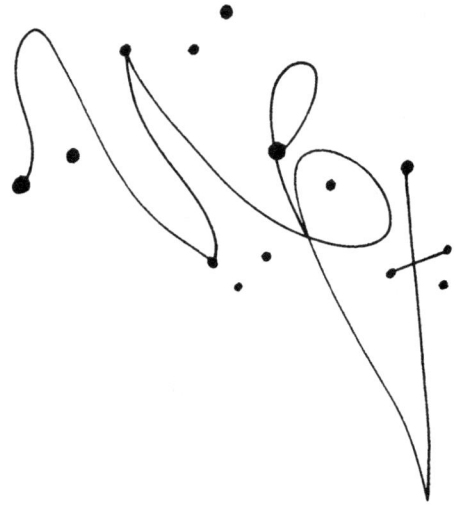

HOLDING ON TO ETERNITY IS EXHAUSTING.
It doesn't give way and it has no pity.
Thank goodness for the lack of pity.

Curious thing, that great vastness.
Like walking into a sideshow hall of mirrors.
It lacks what I lack and gains what I gain.
Densely packed, like molecules of a diamond.
A chain stretching back to the beginning of time.
Past the big bang and even further.
It's all so inconclusive.

    Faint persistence is the only thing that seems to render all that nothingness into something useful. Addressing an entry point is something else entirely.

A whipping post at the center of the sea.
No coordinate, no map or logic.
Just an empty stare.
Just a pair of scales bobbing back and forth.
With no weight applying to either.

So I won't struggle any longer.
It isn't worth it, really.
Just a thousand-league fall into her arms.
Just another gaping hellmouth.
Another ride through nowhere.

Basilisk-tongued she speaks to me; forever growing distant.
I try to make love to distance when I can.
As you would expect she eludes me constantly.

I don't think it's worth it.
The cycle in a cycle in a cycle.
The weight, the gravitas, the snake-pit conundrum.
Of here, to forever more.

¶ *The Twenty Eighth Night*

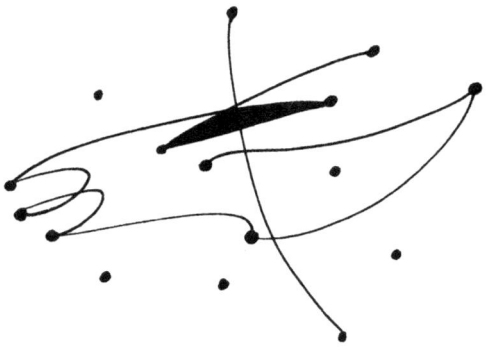

THE SCENE LOOKED SOMETHING LIKE AN OLD film. Grainy footage of a large sea vessel on the verge of an immense voyage. There were little people waving, flags of many colors, and so much hubbub. It was surely a celluloid moment. Looking back into preserved time and watching long dead people drifting off to that same inevitable place. With fanfare no less.

One thing that hasn't changed are long trips by sea. They used to go that way.

Towards some kind of death...

But this was a group of fine fellows. Familial and familiar bonds = apotropaia.

Better than a ghastly face mounted to the bow.

The length of their journey could no longer be counted by days. It was starlight which held sway. These many far away diamonds of varying cuts and hues now told them of their fate.

"I wonder if this is what the Earth looks like from the sky."

"I wonder if this is where people first found god."

"It is one celestial harbinger, one after the other."
Ringing softly, ringing out, a call to gather amassed in huddle.
"Are we sure where we are going anymore?
You said we would see another side by daybreak, but it doesn't seem so clear."

Every mind castigated, yet together.
Dining on shells, old coins, bottom feeding.
It was rough but ever so abundant.
Simultaneously dying, fucking, living, running.
Chewing, screwing, lashing, screaming.
Scraping bits, rhythmically,
minute by minute, counting
salt and tears, together
smashed upon the rocks.

Then it was all origins again.
Crying for home. "Help me I am falling."
They couldn't remember how long it had been.
The Sun couldn't help them with that either.

"If we continue west we will surely find our destination.
I made promises to each of you. And your families.
That I would bring you back one day, all in one, maybe two pieces."

And back to it they went... infinity's race.
Each one of them, some on foot, others on wing, and even others on fin.
Howling, shrieking, cawing, moaning, mooing, chirping, buzzing, bleating.

"I see myself in each of you. And in this way, for me to let you down I would also be letting myself down. I know what it is you want. I know it because I want the same thing. All of you, seriously, I mean it."

"I want to survive. Long enough to see what happens on the other end of things at least.

I want to watch you all grow old and see the wrinkles form. And the beautiful children who will come of it. And laughter and joyous memories. We all want to see these things and not just from our current distance."

"But it isn't enough to gather here like this. We have to act in concert. We have to take care of one another. We have to feed and clothe each other. Or what are the odds?"

"If any of you know any other way please speak up now but I don't think you will... Because there was never any other way but this. That isn't going to change."

And why should it? Why should it be anything other than a hazy notion of cooperation?

Out there at sea, they understood this. How islands connected to other islands.

Land-mass isolation was an illusion of the first order.

¶ The First Night

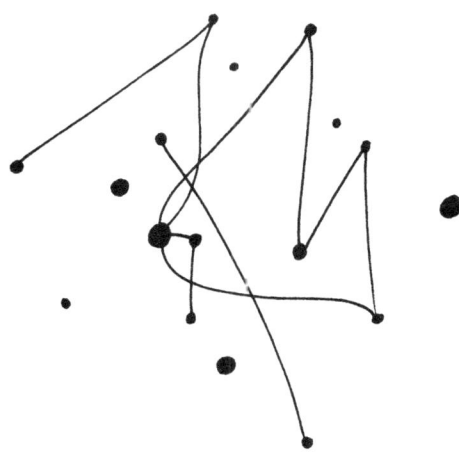

Apologies un-accepted thank you very much!

I will close myself into a scarf, with a grimace-replica never before seen.

My teeth were cut on practice, trial and error. Something like repetitive double takes and scene clippings edited into a fury. My skin peels. It's a new fashion.

Exercising my rights at no expense.

Our world, an oyster. Let me tell you that much. I slurp its flesh and carve decorations on its shell. I wear the sea and its many colors. I make it all my bitch and continue to laugh about it.

I walk with the new-skin. Hyde laughs with me and Jeckyl at me.

Rejections un-accepted. Kowtowing all-will, as I look back and laugh and spit and cry. You cannot. You will not. There is nothing else to it but that. Get in my face about it if you want?

Have you ever met me before? Like, really met me?

I am a son of a bitch. My parents live in the sky.

Have you met my brother? Have you met my other half? The silent one?

Don't be fooled by his demeanor. He is even harsher than myself. We became closer as we sought out battles and gatherings and confluences together. We realized we could work together. Even if it meant destruction as a necessary prelude to creation.

¶ The Second Night

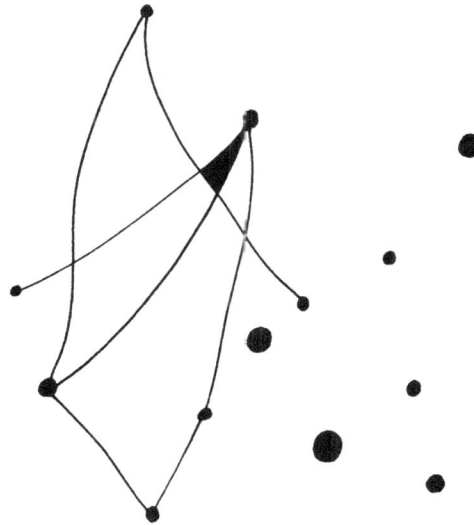

black sun dowsing
as if a ray lodged between ribs
screaming hold on hold on
possess the bile
rub it around

these are the self exorcisms

a specter, all too aware
floorboard curling
all about, tooth for eye

indiscriminate-inferno
keen on holding to

> never asking for a cent
> just a pity soul
>
> strain of the cauldron stirrer
> bitumen crawl
> through aching luster
> out, a blind single-eye
>
> everybody, carcass now
> whole gang-goes inward
> the melting pot
> now stirred

* * *

They realized they were dead too late.

Each one knew one another from a time they couldn't quite place.

"And you were there, and you were there, and you were there..."

"You killed me once. We fucked once. You fed me once. I killed you, I think."

"We all ate soup together, at one of those long tables. Everybody was starving and it was a moment of respite. I remember everyone looking across the table at one another's eyes. You could see all the colors, different races and ethnicities, so many hopes and dreams, but also nightmares."

Everyone wondered about the golden cord that tied them all together. Something like a clothes-line dotted by raggedy cloth. Yet their connection was pristine. It was the thing which brought them back to this familiar place.

And if they started in the sky they ended in the pit.

Just as black, just as numinous. Just as star-clad and no less divine.

II

An Exposition on the Lunar Stations

A Brief History of the Lunar Stations

THE lunar stations have their roots in night sky observation. Dotting the blanket of darkness are seemingly limitless points of light we know as stars, which go on to be connected (although some stand on their own) into increasingly complex imagery and narratives. Next to the daily movement of our star, the Sun, these 'star images' or asterisms form the root of all practices we now would call astrology. Preceding the modern era, these same astrological observations were not distinct from astronomy, as the tracking and measurement of manifest phenomena was inextricably linked to its interpretation.

We must never forget these roots. Even today's codified systems remain imagistic at their core. Each lunar station, as well as the ambiguous space between them, is an ever-shifting form; a night-procession, which both reflects and speaks back to us through the shapes of our living circumstances.

In this way, the writing of a history is largely incidental. The Moon and her stories are continuously being written. Some of them remain ever mysterious to the human being; and, perhaps, not meant for our ears. Must the Moon be anthropocentric? When the dog speaks with the Moon, they share a unique rapport. When a star speaks with another star, it is likewise a conversation unto itself. This history, this procession of images over time, is as much about our own history as well as theirs. We may be so lucky to tune in. When the stars and planets do speak back with us, it must be through the faculty of imagination. If anywhere, this is the place where we find common language.

When it comes to material histories, some of our first documented interactions may be found amidst cave drawings from Paleolithic times. Perhaps the most famous of which is Lascaux. These paintings are estimated to be roughly 17,000 years old, having been continually worked on over many generations. Though most of the imagery depicts large mammals from the area itself, they are often accompanied by assemblies of dots in a variety of shapes. Dot arrangements are a common theme among many prehistoric cave systems, and they have consistently baffled researchers as to their significance. The painting of one Lascaux bull in particular, and seven dots above its body, has spurred on the possibility of a connection to the Pleiades.[1] If we observe the Western constellation known as Taurus, we can see this bright cluster of stars situated right above its shoulder. If one is painting natural scenes, then why not stars?

Fast forward 20,000 years to 1,200 AD. Assemblages of dots are one common feature in the Perso-Arabic literary tradition of astronomy. These arrangements were meant to, however roughly, correspond to sky observations and the constellation groupings therein. From Zackariya Qazwini's *Book of Wonders* to Ahmad al Buni's *Shams al Ma'arif*, these dot patterns became associated with the lore of the lunar stations and the zodiacal signs.[2] This is in part for very practical reasons. Though we have largely relegated

---

[1] Brady, "Images in the Heavens: A Cultural Landscape," 463.
[2] Smith and Smith, "Islamic Geomancy and Thirteenth Century Divinatory Device: Another Look," 247.

sky observation to a separate field of astronomy, if one wished to find the current placement of the Moon by sign, they may look upwards at her and observe the shapes of nearby stars. If these patterns matched the drawings in the book, then their exoteric utility has been achieved.

Though many of these diagrams are quite simple, perhaps garbled through multiple transmissions, their original intention was to resemble the constellation or star grouping in question. From an astronomical standpoint, the lunar stations are nothing but these asterisms and their proximity to the movement of the Moon in physical space.

As the Indian nakshatra structure of regular signs mixed with the so-called *anwā* stars (star calendar based primarily on weather conditions) of the Islamic and pre-Islamic world, these asterisms and their related stations aggregated a wide list of correspondences. Aside from the Chinese xiu, the infusion of nakshatras into the Arabic tradition has remained the pivotal moment for the lunar zodiac that we know today. Most importantly, this transmission brought mathematical regularity to what were uneven segments of the sky. In addition to this, the majority of interpretive principles used in the Arabic tradition (and already existent within the nakshatras) for the lunar stations similarly emerges from this encounter.[3]

Though there is scant published information on the subject, one of the more interesting connections is found between the manzils, or Arabic lunar stations, and that of the 16 geomantic figures. Next to astrology, which it was ubiquitously interwoven with, this divinatory system acted as one of the most popular in the greater Islamic world. Sharing similarities with systems such as the Chi-

---

3 Varisco, *The Origin of the Anwā in Arab Tradition*, 21.

nese I-Ching and West African Ifa, it is based on binary numbers and their manipulation.[4]

Like the constellation figures, the 16 letters of geomancy are constructed through a series of dots and sometimes lines. Due to the system's well-established links with astrology it seems inevitable that connections would be made with the lunar stations. The most prominent example is that of the figure *Laeticia* with *Al Dabaran*, the fourth lunar station and that of the large red star Aldebaran. Another example is the claws of Scorpio (now considered to be the scales of Libra) and their station of *Al Zubana*, ascribed to *Cauda* and *Caput Draconis* accordingly. At some level, all three of these figures do indeed resemble the associated asterism. Not unlike other forms of sky watching such as discerning shapes among the clouds, we must recognize the limitations of a purely scientific perspective. More important for our purposes is the process of image translation through imaginal lines. Better phrased as a question, how is it that an assemblage of dots garners these associations?

This is of course an intentionally open-ended inquiry. How does one small line of 4 stars come to be called Aries the Ram? Let alone the constellation's lifetime of worldwide associations, many of which have nothing to do with rams? Without digressing into philosophical tangents on the nature of perception, it is important to situate the history of the lunar stations in this same process of imaginal translation. Once more, though these roots are shared cross-culturally, we may begin to draw distinctions between the development of the solar zodiac and that of the lunar. Following the introduction of this book, it is the visibility of the stars amidst the nighttime hours that foregrounds image, shape, and line. Constellation images

4 Skinner, *Terrestrial Astrology: Divination by Geomancy*, 1–4.

are given life at night. The realm of the Sun maintains a mostly four-fold form, devoid of these same images, placing him in a related yet separate domain.

Similar to the geomantic figures, another association that has been made and speculated upon is that between the lunar zodiac and the earliest alphabets. Through the work of researchers Hugh Moran and David B. Kelley, likenesses were proposed between the 22 letters of the Hebrew alphabet, astronomical observations, and the 28 Chinese xiu.[5] Later scholars made connections between the 28 stations and the 30 letter Ugaritic alphabet and the 22 Phoenician letters.[6] Seafaring cultures such as the Phoenicians were already using stars in their nightly systems of navigation. It is not a great stretch of the imagination to see these same processes of standardization being applied to communication, especially if considering the commercial implications of long-distance trade.

The inclusion of the *Prayer to Mene* list (one schema of the stations sometimes thought to be related to the goddess Hekate) found in the *Greek Magical Papyri* mirrors this notion of linguistic correspondence, yet, perhaps with a more mystical bent. Semitic letters and their astral relationships are comparable. If we observe the Moon's aperture of light and darkness we may begin to understand these connections from a tangible vantage point. When the Moon is new and completely dark she is empty of sunlight. Just as we must open our mouths to speak the letter A, so does this sound and shape resemble the Moon in this phase. When she is filled with light we see her resemblance to the letter M, wherein we must close our mouths to speak it. One of the more prominent examples of the relationship between letter forms and

---

5 Pellar, "On the Origins of the Alphabet," 2.
6 Ibid., 2–3.

celestial phenomena found in Semitic mystical literature is the *Sepher Yetzira*. Here, the structure of the cosmos is threaded together by the Hebrew letters as constituent parts. Their recitation, magical efficacy, and the like, come in part through their relationship to celestial and astrological affiliations.[7]

Correspondences will always remain arbitrary. To this point, there will never be a unified list—much to the chagrin of our categorizing minds. Yet, there remain parallels that seem to align consistently to the archaic images of the stars. Some cultures have spent at least a millenia standardizing the lunar zodiac to their cultural norms. Though it is far beyond the purview of this book to discuss the unique origins of these systems, such as which emerged first and the like, they must be addressed for their idiosyncrasies as well as their more persistent similarities.

Some scholars have found a possible Babylonian origin for the lunar zodiac; even though much of what it consisted of is lost to time. On the other side of our planet, we find the Vedic or Indian nakshatra and the Chinese xiu. Scholars still debate about which culture standardized the stations first.[8] Of course, a satisfactory answer to this question may never be found. It is fairly well established that the Arabic iteration of the stations are the youngest of the three, at least in terms of standardized form. Yet, as we have already seen, the manzils still maintain much deeper stratas of starlore woven between Indian cultural imports. The adaptability of the Arabic lunar mansions will eventually bring them further west, as they become the primary reference for Europeans as well as later Western magical traditions.

---

7 Segol, *Word and Image in Medieval Kabbalah*, 98.
8 Yampolsky, "The Origin of the Twenty-Eight Lunar Mansions," 68.

The manzil, nakshatra, and xiu are historically situated in the realm of electional and mundane astrology. Out of the three, it would seem that the nakshatras have their origins primarily in the sacred calendar. By this it is meant that the lunar stations in their formative instantiations dealt with the worship and supplication of deities, ritual timings, and the marking of important sacred days.[9] Though the xiu and manzil do indeed possess strong sacred and/or mystical connotations, they would seem to be more aligned with mundane elections in their origins. This would include ideal timings for agricultural purposes, warfare, travel, commercial exchange, as well as various kinds of magical and esoteric work.[10] All three systems emphasize sacred and mundane qualities first and foremost. Its application to natal interpretation arises much later.

It is from these three streams of wisdom that this book emerges, and without them could not be. Therefore each lunar station holds a dedicated section for each culture. It is important to mention that lunar zodiac interpretation is not solely limited to them. For the sake of organizational purposes, many cultural byways have been grouped together due to likeness. For example, the reader will find the Tibetan station name and interpretation in the nakshatra section as they are the closest in resemblance. Let us not forget that the entirety of this book relies wholly on published English language sources. The true diversity and breadth of lunar-stellar lore far surpasses the scope of this book and the sources therein.

---

9   Falk, "The Early Use of Nakshatras," 528.
10 Varisco, "The Origin of the *anwā* in Arab Tradition," 5–6; Stephenson, "Chinese and Korean Star Maps and Catalogs," 517–18.

A NOTE ON COORDINATES

Another expression of the station's diversity, their reckoning, or sign boundaries will also vary (sometimes heavily) depending on the culture and practitioner at hand. All of these schemas have their true origin in non-specific divisions of the sky; that is, naked eye observation. The relativity of sign boundaries cannot be stressed enough; especially when attempting to merge them together as found in our present text. Importantly, the serious reader should explore the ways that the stations and their images manifest during set periods of time. It is through this process of experimentation and observation that the most ideal approach might be found.

As far as the present text's chosen methodology is concerned, the likeness between the concept of precession and the title of this book is deliberate down to the technical details. For the task of synthesizing three primary cultural reckonings we have chosen to use precessed tropical coordinates with a Lahiri ayanamsa. The specific coordinates chosen come from Vic DiCara's *Nakshatra: The Authentic Heart of Vedic Astrology*, a much preferred text in terms of nakshatra structure and interpretation.

It is through years of research, chart analysis, as well as trial and error that has led to the use of nakshatras as the glue which holds these distinct reckonings together. Nakshatras are, no doubt, the most coherent and intact schema of the lunar stations. Setting aside the historical implications of this, they may serve as a foundation for bridging a variety of cultural byways. For DiCara as well as a minority of Vedic astrologers, what sets them apart is their intentional use of the tropical zodiac as opposed to the sidereal. The methodology behind this decision lies in the distinction between a solar zodiacal wheel based on equinoxes and solstices and that of the sidereal or starry movements of the night. The differentiation as such remains a core ethos of this book.

Though they remain separate, the chosen system of precessed tropical coordinates in reality incorporates both simultaneously. This allows one to find the station boundaries using the relatively standardized coordinate system of the solar zodiac. Due to the ever-changing nature of precession, or, the reason there are tropical and sidereal zodiacs, these coordinates will inevitably change as time moves onwards. For example, by the year 2060, these tropical coordinates will have shifted roughly .5° forward through the zodiac. The closest analogue to what we have utilized here is that of the fixed stars and their coordinates in Western astrology.

Fixed star interpretations are calculated using precessed tropical coordinates; meaning that the coordinate of the star shifts roughly 1° every 72 years. Our chosen coordinate system is essentially the same, the only difference being that each lunar station has a designated beginning and ending as opposed to the single degree of a fixed star. Vedic nakshatras are divided evenly into 27 instead of 28; wherein Abhijit, the 28th station that is the far north star Vega, exists between two others (see station 22). This equal division is maintained in the present text.

As previously mentioned, a majority of Vedic astrologers use an equal division of 27 nakshatras with sidereal zodiac coordinates. This means that the first lunar station, or *Ashwini*, will always begin at 0° of sidereal Aries. For those who wish to use this system, this reckoning is listed in the section titled 'Nakshatra.' As information on the Chinese xiu is the most scant, their systems of lunar station reckoning are perhaps the most variable. That said, the Chinese asterisms largely align with both the Indian and the Arabic. If one is interested in the tradition which utilizes uneven sign boundaries, see the section titled 'Xiu' of the following text.

Non-precessed tropical coordinates are primarily used in the Arabic and European traditions of tropical astrology and astrological magic. The majority of these approaches, at least as far as the lunar stations and their magics are concerned, are derived from the *Picatrix*; the 13th-century Latin translation of the earlier Arabic *Ghayat al Hakim*. These coordinates have been placed in the section titled 'Manzil'. Unlike the nakshatras, both the Arabic and the Chinese divide the lunar stations evenly into 28 parts. Once more, for the purposes of this book, the stations have been divided into 27 even portions, with a 28th situated between 21 and 23.

As a final note, some reckonings propose uneven sign boundaries for the Western lunar stations. This could also be done for the solar zodiacal signs, as the constellations in the living sky are anything but evenly spaced. Though there is definite merit to this breakdown, for the sake of utility we have chosen not to employ it. If one is interested in this approach, books such as Oscar Hofman's *Fixed Stars in the Chart* offer tables with uneven lunar station boundaries.

The 28 Lunar Stations

3.

Ignite/Scatter Stars and See What Grows

Precessed Tropical Coordinates:
20° 47' Taurus–4° 07' Gemini

MANZIL

Al-Thurayya 'THE LITTLE WEALTHY WOMAN'
  'THE MANY LITTLE ONES'
TROPICAL ZODIAC: 25° 42' Aries–8° 34' Taurus
ASTERISM: Pleiades
Belongs to the retinue of MONDAY, ANGEL GABRIEL, AND JINN KING *Al Abyad*[11]

---

[11] There are seven references in this book to the retinue of the day, an angel, and a jinn. These references follow the esoteric tradition which acknowledges seven missing Arabic letters from the first surah of the Quran, al-Fatiha. These seven missing letters each align with a lunar station based on the traditional abjad order of the Arabic alphabet.

IBN ARABI: ع (Ayn)
THE UNIVERSAL NATURE, THE INTERIOR
LIBER LUNÆ: Face of Venus. For words of grace and joining together.
AGRIPPA: Spirit name is Amixiel. For sailing, hunting, and alchemy.
PICATRIX: Image of a seated woman with her hand over her eye. Talisman for the acquisition of all good things. Spirit name is Anuncia. Wrap in cloth and suffumigate with musk, camphor, mastic, and aromatic oils. To sail safely on the sea, to complete works of alchemy, to incarcerate prisoners firmly, *all works done by fire*, and to hunt in the country.
AL BUNI: ج (Jeem)
Works to aid women. Cooling medications. Craft talismans. Success for travelers and profit. Meet with or write to kings. Everything done in this mansion will prosper. If one is born here they shall live a happy and pious life. They will mingle with scholars, rulers, and the righteous and have favor among them. Will have discomfort around liars and the immoral. Flaxseed and black seed.
IBN AL HATIM: Spirit name is Abulsith. For love of man and woman.
AL ASHRAF: Frankincense and black seed.
SOLOMONIC RING (CUNNING MAN): Blood of a man. Spirit names are Advolita, Alibeat, Urcifery, Obtablat. For the purposes of making the wearer appear in armor. For protection.

NAKSHATRA

Krittika 'KNIFE' OR 'SPEAR'
SIDEREAL ZODIAC: 26° 40' Aries–10° Taurus

ASTERISM: Pleiades
TEMPERAMENT: Mixed (Soft & Sharp), Daemonic
CASTE: Brahmin
DIRECTION: North
MOTIVATION: *Kama*
ANIMAL: Female Goat/Sheep
SOUNDS: Aa, I, U, Ae
TREE: *Ficus Racemosa* (Cluster Fig)
Oudumber is an extremely useful and virtuous tree.
It is cool by nature. Birds, insects, and worms are attracted to its fruits because of its sweet taste and worms are found in their fruits. But the fruits are dried and crushed into powdered form for storage. A sweet food is prepared using this powder after adding milk, sugar, and flour. The leaves of this tree are good fodder for domestic animals. The nectar dribbling from its roots is used to prepare Oudumbarasava. This is a very useful remedy for patients suffering from Small-Pox, Chicken-Pox, Measles, etc. This is also used in the case of diabetes patients.
VIMSHOTTARI: Sun
DEITY: Agni, God of Fire
SHAKTI: To burn and to purify.
TAITTIRIYA BRAHMANA: "Catalyst of fire needs fuel for light"
BRIHAT SAMHITA: "Will delight in white flowers, will perform sacrificial rites, will be *Brāhmins*, potters, priests or astronomers."
TIBETAN: *Mindruk*. He who has six mothers. Youngest son of Mahadeva. Among the Hindus Katrikeya is a warrior god who rules the degenerate age of the Kaliyuga. Voracious, even gluttonous, a sensualist, susceptible to lechery. Native is famous and attractive. Introduced to royal circles.

XIU

Mao 'Hairy Head'
AKA: 'Six Stars' 'Herd of Sheep' 'Six Sisters' 'The Head of Time'
Uneven Tropical Zodiac: 28° Taurus–8° Gemini (19–29 May)
Asterism: Pleiades
Sky Quadrant: White Tiger of the West
Planet: Sun
Animal: Rooster
Artley: The Rooster is the domestic equivalent of the phoenix. The rooster's morning crow wards off evil spirits. An embodiment of Yang energy. Represents the warmth of the universe. Can change into human form and inflict good or bad on mortals. It symbolizes the five virtues—those literary, those of battle, courage always in the face of enmity, benevolence (always clucking for the hens when he finds a grain) and faith—never failing to tell the hour. The white rooster is the only capable guide of transient souls. A cock-crow late in the morning is a bad omen for the family. Determination, pride, confidence. Abrasive, even borderline aggressive. Resolute in career. Shrewd business sense. Always an underlying motive. Precise attention to detail. Tends to take on too much. Stamina and vitality in business. Perfectionist. Astrologically inauspicious. Anything started on this day brings bad luck. When the Pleiades flickered it was considered to presage invasion by foreign barbarians. The Pleiades were considered the ears and eyes of heaven. Presages death and punishment, judgment.
Element: Varied
Matanga Sutra: Offering of curds. Those born here are of great renown and revered by others.

GEOMANCY

Tannery & Al Mawṣilī: Fortuna Major

Al Mawṣilī: Fortuna Minor

PGM/GREEK

Bull, 'Groaning.'
Deity: Hestia

PROTO-SINAITIC/HIEROGLYPH

Giml, Gemel 'Throwstick'

WORDS

Fire, Populating, Spark, Initiator, Fusion, Rain, Direct Inspiration, Complexity, Magician, Lord of Wonders, Feeling, Machine Gun, Discernment, Flint, Ignition, Engine of Creation, 'Cooking with Gas,' Effulgence, Voracious, Creatrix, The Shot That Began the War, Insatiable, Transformation at the Atomic Level, A Light Bulb, A Light Above the Head, The Cook, Brute Strength Turned Towards Civilization's Ends, A Weapon.

The constellation we know of as the Pleiades has accrued some of the most significant stellar narratives across a vast span of time and culture. This small yet relatively bright cluster of stars has been the focus of some of our oldest and most formative stories. Many a cosmology have this asterism as a point of origin, as well as holding a deep connection to agricultural cycles, hunting mysteries, and shamanic roads of spirit travel.

With so many tales related to the Pleiades, it is no wonder that the lunar station evades easy definition. The desert climate being what it is, the Arabs associated it heavily with rain and consequently dubbed it the most auspicious station of them all. As such they related it to Gabriel, the most important angel of Islam and the bringer of the holy Quran. Both the nakshatra and the xiu are slightly more ambiguous about its nature. This is perhaps because there are less overt relationships with powerful climate phenomena. In fact, it is often quite the opposite, as the latter two traditions tend to emphasize the station's fiery quality above all else.

One of the most consistent themes found with the Pleiades is that of beginnings. Many have speculated on the astronomical phenomena of precession itself, and what asterisms would have been rising at the spring equinox at any given point in history. It is true that the stars nearby to Taurus would have been rising at the beginning of spring during many of the earliest mappings and codifications of lunar stations. While the Arabic lists do not explicitly begin here, both the nakshatra and the xiu's emphasis on fire speak to the energy of an initiatic spark. Just as the Rigveda begins with the word Agni, so too do the lunar stations. It is this same spark, as well as the fire sacrifice, that initiates all worthwhile spiritual endeavors. Similarly, the rooster's call of the Chinese station acts as the beginning of a new day and the rising of the Sun.

Another important image worthy of the Pleiades is that of the Mithraic tauroctony. With proximity to

Perseus as well as Taurus, this station is a proper staging ground for the ritual slaying of the Bull. It is this act of bloodshed which becomes the initiatic spark already mentioned. There has been much speculation on these same mysteries and their relationship to precession. It would seem that many of the images found in the Mithraic scene relate to the shifting of the pole and the beginning of the vernal equinox. Alongside fairly explicit zodiacal imagery found near the ecliptic, the primary symbol of this station as a knife may be seen in the hero Perseus' hand for the purpose of slaying the Taurean bull. This is an assertion of choice and change in a domain previously seen as fixed (the motion of the stars). It is this very action, symbolized by fire, initiation, the blade, which cuts into the world forever altering it.

Technological developments in hunting, agriculture, cooking, and in general are well illustrated here. The promethean spark of the Pleiades symbolizes the power of focused will and intelligence in its ability to alter the landscape. Unlike the stars of Aquarius which have a similarly promethean sense, here we find force laid bare; something closer to the first stages of harnessing fire. This mirrors 'the fall' as well as the unending torture of the titan in his act of theft. With fire now unleashed, humanity is wont to return to their previously raw state of existence.

As another form of beginnings, we may see this asterism as a kind of inception. Mirroring the cluster-form of the stars themselves, is the notion of the 'many little ones,' as the asterism is sometimes referred to. These stars were frequently thought of as seeds. In this way the lunar station possesses the ability to multiply and populate quite rapidly. Through this lens we can see the Arabic associations with auspicious growth once more. That said, rapid growth does not always equate with desirability. We must be decisive in our actions here. The metaphor of wielding fire is appropriate, as second chances rarely occur. The image of the blade is not altogether different, for when one has cut something it may never return to its original state.

Pleiadian fire is of a primordial nature. It is that which lies at the beginning of all things; some might even say the fire of stars themselves. In Western astrology, it is in this region of the sky that both luminaries are exalted (appropriately in the spring season, at least in the northern hemisphere). It is the triumph of light and life amidst the seemingly endless darkness of space. It is this primeval spark which emerges from the vast-blackness which drives consciousness forward; a fount of action. It is the opposing region of the sky, wherein the black hole at the center of the Milky Way, reveals the true origin of all things manifest. This spark is less the root as much as it is the first shoot of green from the depths of the wintry Earth. It is the energy of spring and the invisible fires which elicit it; a theme which will be much continued in the station to come.

PLANETARY PLACEMENTS

THE PRESENCE OF THE ☾

The Moon here brings strong intelligence, as if the mind was spear-sharpened and ready for battle. The decisive act finds possibility here; a powerful sense of criticality (the same root as the name of the nakshatra), capable of careful discernment in intellectual matters. Path-forging and beginnings of initiations are found here. Similarly, the act of inception and the first inklings of spreading outwards. Energies are action-oriented in this station, capable of moving on projects in ways that other more contemplative stations simply are not. There is naturally a strong relationship with fire. This may be in the form of metal, industry, and technology. Less material versions of this same drive may come with analytical thought, computer languages, and debate. On the other side of this, multiplying fire always has the risk of over-consumption. Fire as a tool must be contained and managed with high precision to yield optimal results. Otherwise, if left unchecked, the fervent search for new fuel sources may spell disaster where possibility and transformation were once desired.

The Presence of ☿

This is a strong placement for Mercury, as they function in a deeply analytical and practical manner here. They are quite at home with new technologies as well as applications of intelligence which involve precision, high quantities of data, and rapid number generation. Speech patterns may run the gamut from comfortably direct to unabashedly inflammatory. As this is a station of inspirational sparks, ideas may come quickly, and fade near after. Rapid physical responses and dexterous movements are also possible here; refined hand motions and skill all the same.

The Presence of ♀

We may consider the aesthetic applications of fire. This is a Venus fond of cooking and like practices. Products of transformation for the ends of pleasure. She is a jeweler, metalsmith, and craftsperson. Rapid processes of change brought on by this station are put towards the ends of beauty and design. The incessant need for creation, in particular a creativity which moves like fire, is ever apparent. Similarly romance and relationships may have this effect. She may be the one who offers the first kiss, as well as one with a long term interest in keeping things warm as well as novel.

The Presence of the ☉

Much like the xiu, the Sun has come to be associated with this lunar station for its connotations of brilliance. This is a natural leadership placement, as it aligns well with solar energies. Goals, drives, and ambitions may be quite clear for the Sun, as he knows what he desires, and possesses the capacity to attain it. This is a strong go-getting placement, as well as one that endows him with a robust and even visionary intelligence capable of seeing far ahead of others. Like Mars, the Sun as a fiery planet is well aligned here, yet it must be with intention and containment in mind. The ritualistic burning of incense is a proper metaphor for the Sun's well-being in this station, as the heat generated aids in the transformation of solid substance into upward-moving air. It is this same process which speaks to priestcraft and the knowledge of communing with the gods so associated with this lunar station (the nakshatra in particular).

The Presence of ♂

This is a strong placement for Mars as he shares many a wavelength with this station. Qualities of immense heat, initiation, and inception are heightened. In this regard, he may struggle with anger and intensity of emotional volatility. Not unlike the Sun, the fires must be tempered and contained in order for this placement to yield its richest expressions, lest the flame become too unwieldy and uncontrollably destructive. Mars' presence here necessitates an application for his fire; tasks for it to accomplish, somewhere for it to go. This is to ensure its productivity as opposed to potential self immolations.

The Presence of ♃

Here we find a feisty Jupiter. The planet of growth often aligns with this lunar station's objectives yet sometimes lacks the necessary grounding for intelligibility. The opposite case may also be true; that the Jupiterian cause may remain excessively grounded to the point of immobility, yet this is far rarer. Here we find the planet of buoyancy as if it were a hot air balloon. The general warning of this station remains. There must be attention paid around careful mixing of ingredients. As we know the mixing of air and fire is quite flammable. It is this volatility which lends his presence here towards certain extremes. Optimism may be consumed quickly in the pursuit of flight. At the same time, the sinking of the balloon is felt just as palpably. The trick may very well be in how one tempers the stream of gas, so that the flame may burn steadily but not excessively towards one side.

The Presence of ♄

One of the stranger placements for Saturn, the planet of slowness does not necessarily align with this station's sense of action and quick inception. He more often than not opts for slow and steady growth, patience, as well as a disposition towards rumination. As this station is about rapid forms of action, there may be a feeling of division between his capacity to act and his capacity for endurance around any given matter. Saturnine senses of responsibility may similarly feel too quickly sprung. Almost on the opposite end of Mars, this placement entails labor and the recognition of a flame which must consistently be fed and tended to.

4.

Volcano / Bountiful

Precessed Tropical Coordinates:
4° 07' Gemini–17° 27' Gemini

MANZIL

Al Dabaran 'The Follower'
Tropical Zodiac: 8° 34' Taurus–21° 25' Taurus
Asterism: Alpha Tauri (Aldeberan)
Ibn Arabi: ح (Hah)
Universal Substance, Prima Materia, The Last
Picatrix: Image of a knight on a horse riding with a serpent in his hand. Talisman for obtaining hostility. Spirit name is Asarez. Red wax suffumigated with red myrrh and storax. For the destruction of cities, villages, and buildings. To place discord between husband and wife. To destroy fountains and streams. To kill and bind venomous reptiles.
Liber Lunæ: Face of Mercury. Adversity, desolation, loss.
Agrippa: Spirit name is Azariel. For discord, hindrance of structures.
Al Buni: د (Dal)
Enmity, hatred, and corruption. Beware of beginning new endeavors. Do not fashion talismans or crafts. Suitable for burying the dead, burying treasures, hiding secrets, and digging wells. To be born here is to be forsaken. They will have hindrances but things will im-

prove later in life. Pomegranate peel and frankincense.
IBN AL HATIM: Spirit name is Iswawis. For enmity.
AL ASHRAF: Pomegranate peel and frankincense.
SOLOMONIC RING (CUNNING MAN): Ashes of grape vines. Spirit names are Bersada, Hara, Lascra, Eianliarug. For the purposes of making grape vines appear.

NAKSHATRA

Rohini 'THE RED ONE' 'CHARIOT OR CART'
SIDEREAL ZODIAC: 10° Taurus–23° 20' Taurus
ASTERISM: Alpha Tauri (Aldeberan)
TEMPERAMENT: Fixed, Human
CASTE: Worker
DIRECTION: East
MOTIVATION: *Moksha*
ANIMAL: Male Serpent
SOUNDS: Au, Va, Vi, Vo
TREE: Jamun, *Szyhgium Cumini* (Java Plum)
The fruits of this tree are sweet and tasty. Fresh fruits and their juice is used for patients with diabetes. Generally the fruits are ripe during monsoon seasons. They are useful in ailments. It alleviates stomach ache, indigestion, and lack of appetite. In the case of a scorpion bite, the juice of its leaves is very effective. Its wood is used in construction, furniture as well as fuel.
VIMSHOTTARI: Moon
DEITY: Brahma (Prajapati, Creator), Krishna
SHAKTI: Power of growth.
TAITTIRIYA BRAHMANA: "The Procreator's arousal needs moisture for plants"
BRIHAT SAMHITA: "will be devout men, merchants, rulers, rich men, *Yogis*, drivers, or men possessed of

cows, cattle and the animals of water, farmers and men possessed of wealth derived from mountain produce."

TIBETAN: *Narma*. The Peaceful Goddess. Rules 5 star gods in the form of a chariot. Faithful and beautiful, a great speaker with a fine voice. Connected to Brahma. Amiable and calm. Clear and solid mind. Charitable, and even religious. Has large eyes.

XIU

Bi 'NET'

AKA: 'SANDALWOOD' 'WIND TUNNEL' 'TO SHEPARD' 'RED EYE'

UNEVEN TROPICAL ZODIAC: 9°–24° Gemini (30 May–14 June)

ASTERISM: Alpha Tauri (Aldeberan), Hyades

SKY QUADRANT: White Tiger of the West

PLANET: Moon

ANIMAL: Crow

ARTLEY: The Crow represents filial piety. A solar animal. Takes care of the elderly and disabled. Auspicious. Plentiful, especially from agriculture. Luck and fortune. The negative side indicates a renegade. The cry of the crow is said to be a bad omen, and that work should be delayed when it is heard. When crows gather in the corner of a city, it is said to portend impending drought and infighting. People whose heads are sat on by crows should offer clothing and sesame oil to the poor and needy. Hyades and Pleiades were considered the mesh of a hunting net. Therefore the mansion is associated with hunting, accumulation of resources from hunting. Potential

border disputes. Burials on this day confer honor to the deceased.
ELEMENT: Varied
MATANGA SUTRA: Offering of deer meat. Those born here are distinguished and praised.

GEOMANCY

TANNERY & AL MAWṢILĪ: Laeticia

AL MAWṢILĪ: Tristicia

PGM/GREEK

Beetle, 'Hissing.'
DEITY: Pasiphae

PROTO-SINAITIC/HIEROGLYPH

Daleth, D 'DOOR' 'WAGON' 'CHARIOT'

WORDS

Volcanic, Bountiful, Terraform, Chariot Driven, Doorway, The Four Horned Beast, Smouldering, Tectonic, The Great Mover, Chthonic, The Wagon and The One Who Steers It, Abundance, All-Creator, Basket of Produce, The Driver, Creative Force, Generator,

Compulsion, Passion, Meaning Maker, Death
Dwelling Son of a Bitch, A Tractor, Earth Work
(Spiral Jetty), A Hulking Mass, Matter Over Mind
Over Matter.

Akin to stars such as Sirius and the Pleiades cluster, Aldebaran is one of the most well known in the night sky. More often than not it is in relation to the constellation Taurus, where this star forms the ruddy 'Eye of the Bull.' The appellation 'follower' comes from this star's movement towards or behind the Pleiades (the previous lunar station); sometimes thought of as a hunter pursuing their prey.

As mentioned in the section 'A Brief History of the Lunar Stations,' many of the geomantic associations with the stations are formed through the observation of actual constellations and their shape. From a certain vantage point, the star Aldebaran and its surrounding asterism resemble the geomantic figure of Laeticia, or six dots in three rows of two with a single dot on top making seven (see Geomancy section above). This seventh dot, a crown of sorts, is the star Aldebaran, resembling a great ruby atop the monarch's head.

This connection between the lunar stations and the geomantic figures is exemplary in this instance. The various dot diagrams used for the stations in texts like the *Shams al-Ma'arif* and Qazwini's *Book of Wonders* frequently have *Al Lahyan* or Laeticia illustrating Aldebaran. In addition to this, their resemblance goes deeper than topical association, for the redness of the Bull's Eye often evokes fire. This single dot atop the geomantic figure is a reference to the element of fire, being the primary activated quadrant in the figure. Similarly, though scholars disagree, it is sometimes thought that this same red star of Aldebaran is the flame atop the Aztec constellation of the fire stick known as *Mamalhuatzli* (the operative device of the gods for ensouling human beings with the spark of consciousness).

As the sign of Taurus is related to the season of spring, this star becomes associated with returning warmth that elicits growth. Not unlike the inner or primordial fire spoken of in the previous station, the hidden light is one of generation. As the season unfolds so too does this inner flame as it goes on to culminate in the summer solstice event.

Kenneth Johnson appropriately relates this lunar station to the 'Red Goddess.' The nakshatra name Rohini is a reference to reddening, once more a reference to the color of its associated star as well as the passionate and magnetic forces it elicits. Another common symbol for this nakshatra is the cart (the Chinese image is a net, similar in its ability to carry objects) which is oftentimes filled with freshly grown produce. This signifies abundance as well as steady cultivation of the land. Though other stations hold the ox as their primary animal, the character of strong domestic animals is palpable here; for it is through their labor that this productivity emerges. The trained concentration of the ox and the life-giving powers of the cow and its milk may both be found in this station.

The growth of spring is but one association. What is the underlying force that elicits growth, birth, and abundance? It is no other than the Red Goddess herself, voluptuous, radiant, and all-inviting; she beckons life from the death of winter back into manifestation. Both the cart and the net signify life worth capturing for the sake of life, or, in other words, the things we consider to be food.

PLANETARY PLACEMENTS

The Presence of the ☾

Rohini nakshatra is often considered the most favorable of them all for the natal Moon placement. One reason for this is perhaps that its boundaries fall within sidereal Taurus, giving her exaltation status. Along similar lines, this place of growth and cultivation shares much with the qualities of the Moon herself as a gardener of the soul. Steady nourishment is one of the Moon's prerogatives. This lunar station is capable of accomplishing the task. The symbol of the ox and its cart is appropriate here as patient labor towards particular ends may be achieved. The station of bountiful harvests is intimately tied to the undercurrents of growth. It is this same harvest that brings nourishment, and in this way the cycle continues between planting, tending, harvesting, and increase. Though it may be seen through a strictly agricultural lens, a cycle of harmonious growth may apply to any process or commitment, whether artistic, political, financial, or otherwise. Similarly, the strength and attainment built through steady unfolding make for an unmistakable heartiness when the Moon is found here.

The Presence of ☿

The slower-moving qualities of this sign share less with Mercury's winged feet, although an awareness of method, process, and organization may be all the more keen. As discussed in regards to the presence of the Moon, an understanding of cycles and timing stands out here for planets more broadly. Mercury, in their systematic way of being, brings rhythm and discreet purpose. The Chinese symbol of the net is apt, as Mercury's placement readily establishes grids to yield discreet results. The Chinese animal symbol of the crow is also telling, as they are capable of wielding tools with their beaks; a testament to extremely fine motor function. Akin to the alchemical schema and its *nigredo* phase, both Mercury and the crow are capable of discerning seeds, particles, and bits from the greater *prima materia* (or mass of potential), only to extract them for their ends. In other words, this placement asks which parts of any given system are viable, sustainable, and profitable for the long term.

THE PRESENCE OF ♀

Continuing with the theme of growth and harvest processes, Venus in this station speaks to an intimacy with quality-driven action. What must be done along harmonious aesthetic lines? How might the beings of *this* land work together for the sake of all land and its well-being? In particular, these actions relate to processes of endurance and worldly potential. This is a strong sign of grassroots organization as well as intimacy with place. We also find the previously mentioned Red Goddess here, as the element of magnetic attraction (as well as a necessary repulsion) found in this lunar station signifies Venusian priorities.

THE PRESENCE OF THE ☉

As one of the most critical elements in the process of growth, the Sun provides another source of nourishment parallel to that of this lunar station's. Therefore they are much in alignment as the Sun's life-giving qualities are seen clearly here amidst the broader agricultural theme.

He may feel quite warm in his ability to tend to life's needs. In particular, those concerns we would consider to be 'rooted.' There is a 'salt of the earth' quality to this placement, harkening back to older times involving steady farm work, love for one's land, tradition, and hard-earned yet rewarding labor. The Sun shines with a kind of meritocratic principle. He does indeed shine for all, yet here it would seem that only those who have put in the requisite effort will yield the results of increase that he may offer.

THE PRESENCE OF ♂

Mars in this station evokes the 'Bull's Eye' more than any other placement, as the red planet shares much with this station in its fiercer forms. Though there is growth and nourishment to be found here, it would be remiss not to speak to the exceptional amounts of energy needed for related processes. Herein we find domesticated animals and their greater-than-human strength. Though not solely related to Mars, he does hold access to this same force of nature. His channeling of this power allows for the great accomplishments achieved through long and consistent labor towards an end; a classic 'practice makes perfect.' Mars therefore provokes the dangerous parts of these natural forces. Tempers may flare up unexpectedly. Though the bull is not the only animal in the lunar zodiac prone to anger, once it has been roused it may be nearly impossible to quell.

THE PRESENCE ♃

Jupiter may be witness to the more explicit sides of a bountiful harvest. Similar to the other benefic planet Venus, Jupiter bodes well for high-quality yields and sustained growth. As he is the planet that fattens and enlarges by nature, we see a natural affinity with produce that is healthy, nourishing, and even delicious. The magnetism and growth orientation of this lunar station allied with the living 'plus sign' of the planet Jupiter brings big results capable of feeding those far beyond the single-family household. Jupiterian qualities of speech, education, and parenting also do well here, as tangibility is heightened in regards to practical results and gains.

The Presence of ♄

Saturn resembles some of the Arabic associations with this station as a place of death and hardship. Though we may not consider this a primary connotation, it is worth mentioning the auspicious timing for burying the dead and other like activities. For the hole that is dug to plant the roots is also where we say farewell to those we hold dear (in their physical forms, at least). Less discussed is the relationship between so much abundance and processes of decay. Of course Saturn is also associated with agriculture, making these much discussed cycles of growth and harvest still applicable here. In regards to Cronos, we find aspects of harvest as well as saving for the winter to come. Saturn has the long game in mind. Sustainability is key. Similar to Mercury, this placement holds strong systematic qualities. Lest we forget that Saturn is quite capable and keen on forming grids and networks for the purposes of optimization.

5.

Head of a Doe / A Hunt at Twilight

Precessed Tropical Coordinates:
17° 27' Gemini–0° 47' Cancer

MANZIL

Al Haqa'a 'The White Spot' 'The Hair Whorl'
  'The Head of Orion' (*Al Jabar*, 'The Giant')
Tropical Zodiac: 21° 25' Taurus–4° 17' Gemini
Asterism: Lambda Orionis (Meissa), Phi Orionis
  (Alhaqah)
Belongs to the retinue of Monday, Angel Gabriel,
  and Jinn King *Al Abyad*[12]
Ibn Arabi: غ (Ghayn)
The Universal Body, The Manifest.
Picatrix: Image of a head without a body. Talisman
  for receiving favor from kings and high officials.
  Spirit name is Cabil. Metal is silver. Sandalwood is its
  suffumigation. Also may be placed under the pillow
  for aid in dream-sight. For youths to learn arts and
  occupations, for safe travel.
Liber Lunæ: Face of the Moon. Allegation, building.
  Images of joining and friendship. For fortune.
Agrippa: Spirit name is Gabiel. Return from journeys,

---

12 Though this correspondence does not belong to the seven missing letters of Al-Fatiha, the author uses them in light of this station's established presence as the preeminent location for the Spirit of the Moon.

instruction by scholars, health and goodwill.
AL BUNI: ☊ (Ha)
Distill and develop poisons. Do not work with the Sun or Moon. Do not marry in it. Natives will enjoy the latter years of life. Incense is aloeswood, frankincense, benzoin, and mastic.
IBN AL HATIM: For noble acts and the presence of kings. Spirit name is Iqbal.
AL ASHRAF: Frankincense, aromatic wood, mastic.
SOLOMONIC RING (CUNNING MAN): Spirit names are Osturcios, Betradandi, Hamistradany, Pathmisici. For the purposes of making woods, green meadows, and sweet smelling flowers appear. For verdant growth.

NAKSHATRA

Mrigashira 'THE DEER'S HEAD'
SIDEREAL ZODIAC: 23° 20' Taurus–6° 40' Gemini
ASTERISM: Lambda Orionis (Meissa), Phi Orionis (Alhaqah)
TEMPERAMENT: Soft, Divine
CASTE: Farmer
DIRECTION: South
MOTIVATION: *Moksha*
ANIMAL: Female Serpent
SOUNDS: Ke, Ko, Ha, Hi
TREE: *Acacia Chundra* (Cutch Tree)
Extract or powder of the Catechu tree wood is the main product. It is used with betel leaf. This extract or powder (Katho) is used to prepare ayurvedic medicines such as Swalp Khadir, Khadirashthi, Khadirashtak etc. This tree is a useful medicine for skin diseases and toothache.
VIMSHOTTARI: Mars

DEITY: Soma or Chandra (God of the Moon), Parvati
SHAKTI: Power of giving fulfillment.
TAITTIRIYA BRAHMANA: "The entreaty of gentility needs diffusion to weave"
BRIHAT SAMHITA: "will delight or deal in perfumes, dress, pearls, flowers, fruits, precious stones, wild beasts, birds and deer; will be *Somayajis* or singers; will be lascivious; will be good writers or painters."
TIBETAN: *Go*. The Stag Headed. Inferiority complex and shyness in youth. Later becomes optimistic, diligent, but glib. Likes an easy life. Bathing is important. A sensualist. Prosperous and skillful.

XIU

Zi 'TURTLE'S BEAK'
AKA: 'BEAM' 'PARROT'S HEAD'
UNEVEN TROPICAL ZODIAC: 24°–25° Gemini (15 June)
ASTERISM: Lambda Orionis (Meissa), Phi Orionis (Alhaqah)
SKY QUADRANT: White Tiger of the West
PLANET: Mars
ANIMAL: Monkey
ARTLEY: The Monkey is said to be able to control malevolent spirits. An emblem of ugliness and trickery. Inventive and agile mind. Insatiable curiosity. Quick-witted but sometimes scheming. Full of words and ideas, but a tendency toward unscrupulousness. Fundamental insecurity behind a mask of audacity. Rarely taken seriously. Prone to resentment and pent-up anger, leading to depression. Complex problem solver. Versatile. Success can sometimes go to the head. Latent arrogance, but always socially

engaging. Inauspicious astrologically. Building today brings lawsuits. Funerals lead to collapse of the house with at least three deaths to follow, followed by dwindling reserves. Governs herd animals, people under protection and punishment. Warning to play by the rules.

ELEMENT: Fire

MATANGA SUTRA: Offerings of fruit. Those born here take pleasure in disputes and harbor noxious thoughts.

GEOMANCY

TANNERY: Puella

AL MAWṢILĪ: Albus & Rubeus

PGM/GREEK

Falcon, 'a cry of joy'
DEITY: Prometheus (alternatively, Selene or Artemis)[13]

PROTO-SINAITIC/HIEROGLYPH

Khuwt, Heth, Ha, 'THE TWISTING ROPE'

---

13 Alternative deities are the author's addition.

WORDS

Braid, Water Color, Threading, Mist, Subtle
   Nourishments, Fog, Hunter Now Hunted, Musical
   Instrument Made From a Turtle's Shell, Twisted
   Rope, Hearth Stones, Grass, Lovers Who Hunt One
   Another, A Body Manifest, Water, Lord of Monsters,
   The Woven Basket, Silver Light, Synthesis, Pelt,
   Scent, Seeding, An Arrow's Path.

Head symbolism permeates this station through and through. The image of a head persists through the transmission of nakshatra lore from India to Arabic speaking cultures. Texts like the *Ghayat al Hakim* or *Picatrix* would maintain many of these same images into the magical literature of the Latin West.

Mrigashira nakshatra, or the Vedic iteration of the lunar station, illustrates an often controversial story between the primary creator deity Brahma and the goddess Vac, a deity of personified speech who is created by Brahma himself. In her beauty and ability to express or give form to his primeval creative power, he becomes infatuated with his creation/daughter. Brahma persists in his sexual advances and Vac consequently flees, becoming a deer so that she may escape more rapidly. As Brahma does not give up, he is confronted by the storm god Rudra or Shiva who decapitates him for his obsessive pursuit. The nakshatra Mrigashira consists of Vac's creation and pursuit, while the act of decapitation for her protection becomes the story of the following nakshatra Ardra. This dynamic is contained within the greater constellation we know as Orion, wherein Mrigashira belongs to the faint stars in the hunter's head while Ardra those brighter stars of the arms and torso.

The constellation of Orion more broadly is related to the Arab folktale of *Jawza*, the great celestial woman who died before her marriage to *Suhayl* (Canopus). As Suhayl fled out of fear of the repercussions for her death, he was followed by his two sisters, *Al Shira* (Sirius) and *Al Ghumaysa* (Procyon). This story is reflected in the observable precession of the stars. Suhayl, or the star Canopus, has crossed the river of the Milky Way alongside Sirius leaving behind Al Ghumaysa or 'The Crying One' as she weeps for her lost family. In both instances, we find strong themes of obsessive pursuit, tragic love, and the fleeing of one party in pursuit by the other. This is not dissimilar to the original Greek conception of Orion; obsessively overhunting and eventually struck down for his hubris and nagging persistence.

Jawza, probably initially represented by the three belt stars of Orion, later took on the Greek connotations of the hunter or the giant *Al-Jabar*. Unlike the Vedic nakshatras which split Orion into two stations, the Arabic lunar station of Al Haqa'a is the sole place related to the hunter. In this respect, many of the indigenous connotations have blended with Hellenistic associations, yet primary themes often remain the same. In the original story, it is Suhayl who likely kills Jawza. Whether this is an accident or not, we cannot be sure. Nevertheless, Suhayl's actions mirror those of Brahma and Vac, embodying both the pursuit and the escape simultaneously. In other words, the dynamic of hunters being hunted and the role reversal therein is another primary theme. Embodied in the giant himself is the mystery of headlessness and headiness; where that division is and isn't becoming an important point of ambiguity.

As each nakshatra has a ruling deity, Mrigashira is associated with the god of the Moon. Sometimes referred to as Chandra but more properly in this context as Soma, this deity is exemplified in the 'elixir of the gods' known for its potent immortalizing effects. The doe-eyed image of persistence in this lunar station represents the ever-renewing spring much sought after in poetry and romance literature the world over. Distilled into something essential, the spirit of rejuvenation or the alchemical elixir of immortality, is the basis of the pursuit so marked by this lunar region. Humanity's persistent temptation to possess, obtain, and dissect the seemingly inexhaustible resources of the natural world colors the mood here with varieties of darker shades. An eluding deer is both a temporary reprieve as well as a sign of the never-ending chase; one aspect of this so-called immortality being the recognition that at some level the predator-prey dynamic fuels creation in a fundamental manner.

In some instances, this lunar station accrues strong associations with the arts. The *Brihat Samhita* likens natives of this nakshatra to painters, perfumers, poets, and those skilled in arts of this sort. The Arabic lunar mansion talismans also show an affinity with visionary experience as well as the garnering of skills in various art forms. In contrast to the potentially dangerous practices of sport hunting and human technological pursuits, we may observe more aesthetically oriented ways to search for immortality. Through the auspices of art we may approach the splendorous mysteries of nature without seeking to possess them. We may model ourselves, donning the proverbial skins of the wilderness, in the manners of non-human others. The mystery of headlessness does not end with the hunter's simplified pursuit of base gratifications. We may remove our heads for the sake of resembling the forest. No longer a towering human ego but an animal among animals.

The Arabic name for these stars is the 'Hair Whorl,' representing tufts of hair on a horse's body. With the deer we have seen the animal resemblance which is so strong here. Not dissimilar by any means, the rulership through Soma connotes nourishment and rejuvenation specifically through non-human aid. Bedouin peoples sometimes used the image of a cooking trivet for these same stars. In the ancient Maya cosmology the stars of Orion were not only thought of as representing the traditional structure and center which is the Maya hearth, but also the cracked turtle carapace wherein the maize deity is reborn after emerging from the underworld. It is interesting to note that the Chinese image for these faint head stars is that of a turtle's beak.

Important here is the recognition of actual food substance and its ability to maintain and prolong our lives through nourishment. Whether it be the harvesting of grain or the hunting of animal food, this cyclical process is akin to the everyday imbibing of Soma's elixir; that which extends existence into the following generations of human beings; all the same as the maize, or the deer, dying and being reborn.

Similar to the Maya, other indigenous American stories speak of the stars of Orion as a great severed hand which the souls of the dead may enter to walk the ghost road that is the Milky Way. For just as hunter and hunted are inextricably linked here, so is life and death. Though these stars seem to be by and large connected to rejuvenation or rebirth, their proximity to the Milky Way and the path of the afterlife remind us that this cannot be achieved but through a death of sorts. Similarly, the lunar stations directly across the circle also deal with entrances and exits from this same afterlife path.

PLANETARY PLACEMENTS

The Presence of the ☾

As the Moon deity is thought to reside in these stars, this is an all around position of likeness. As mentioned, the Moon here was thought to bring a disposition towards the arts; in particular towards art forms with prominent aesthetic dimensions (as opposed to art forms of a more technical and utilitarian variety). This is due to the watery nature of the station, which functions through the means of exploration and dispersal. The Moon is fond of weaving (and consequently hair!) here, another prominent symbol, wherein creative growth is achieved through threading seemingly disparate parts together into new forms. Therefore the literal arts of weaving may be practiced as well as anything which samples, collages, collects, or brings varying pieces together for the achievement of the work. With such a strong emphasis on food, nourishment, and plant substances, she is often drawn to practices and lifestyles that emphasize holistic approaches and Earth-centered byways. A deep connection to animals and wildlife is almost a given, as well as spiritual beings of a more animal-like nature. Similar to the deer, her character is reserved, quiet, but also a little on edge. Deer are social creatures, and the theme of weaving may also be applied to the social atmosphere of these natives. She very much needs this social fabric so that she may spread out and explore in the manner that she wishes to; creative or otherwise.

The Presence of ☿

Similar themes of weaving emerge for Mercury in this sign, as well as a strong inclination towards the aesthetic expression of communication, speech, and writing. They may have a trickster streak about them. The deer and its ability to evade capture, weaving through dark and densely packed wooded spaces, is illustrative of the planet of intelligence's skills here. Mercury as magician shows an inclination towards magic of a wild or verdant variety. Animal communication and the like may be found. Thoughts may be put at ease in the presence of wilderness.

The Presence of ♀

Similar significations to that of the Moon, artistry and aesthetic sensibilities, are heightened with Venus. The beauty of the natural world that draws explorers and dominators alike may be seen with Venus here. In the dynamic of the deer and the hunter, this placement signifies the beauty of the doe which compels in a gentle manner. There is a natural magnetism, and she may be sought after in a variety of ways. Those who would attempt to subjugate and possess verdant, Venusian beauties must be weary of the hidden retaliations born of the wilderness. This placement shares much with the Moon in terms of significations.

The Presence of the ☉

As this region is akin to the nocturnal forest, the presence of the Sun has a mixed quality to it. As we will see, the harsher planets (Sun, Mars, Saturn) have a more challenging time in this lunar station as it is marked by qualities which may be called gentle or soft. These same harsher planets function best with this placement when acting in a protective role; much like Shiva counteracting Brahma's obsessive pursuit. The Sun's presence here shows a similar inclination towards animals and wildlife; yet often with a more conservative tone. This does not necessarily equate to political conservatism, although it is possible. Solar principles give light and nourishment to the great trees that form the canopies that enshroud this place. From inside the various groves the Sun is largely blocked out as the lunar principle holds sway. A position of observing wild spaces from the Sun's more 'objective' distance makes him a natural explorer here, and he may become known for his adventurous sensibilities and curiosities. It is not clear whether Soma has psychoactive properties indefinitely; though this interpretation has been much used time and again. The Sun as plant food, psychedelic or otherwise, may figure prominently as well.

THE PRESENCE OF ♂

As mentioned in regards to the Sun, the harsher planets function best in this sign when they are in a position of protection. More than any other planet Mars may act as the hunter in this station; yet the role is of an ambivalent nature. As this station is considered gentle, he may struggle with when to use force and when to withhold. This position may easily become defensive as it is felt that his softer nature must be protected. Classic dangers of overhunting and excessive butchery are apparent. This station also carries significations of mixing substances and poisons. The placement of the Moon or Mercury may bring out more of the healing or nourishing qualities of medicine mixing, yet Mars functions as a poisoner and alchemical transmuter. In the process of creating Soma, the plant matter must be mashed and reduced, and here is where we find Mars. To reach the essence of the substance an extraction must occur. In other instances, especially wherein the poison becomes the medicine, we see the character of this placement as one of transformation.

The Presence of ♃

Something of a wilderness church. Jupiter may feel a very palpable sense of religiosity towards the natural world and wild spaces. He may even take up causes to protect and advocate for it as such. Similar to the other creative planets, Jupiter brings strong artistic inclinations as well as a facility for poetic speech. In his lawgiving form he inclines the native towards their more 'natural' forms; a sense of justice no doubt, yet not necessarily that which is rooted in the laws of human beings. He may be inclined to educate not only on matters of animal and biological life, but also through these same artistic endeavors and pursuits.

The Presence of ♄

As one of the harsher planets, Saturn functions well when creating sanctuary here. In his rigid forms he may struggle with the watery and loose qualities of this station as defined by an attempt to structure among apparent disorder. As this station is both light and gentle, the heaviness of Saturn may come into conflict. Pondering this weight as defined by the stones and mounds of this forested region may be helpful. Ancient monuments, grown over and one with the land around them, are something of an image of Saturn here. The planet of death may see the presence of dead hunters and wild animals come to prominence.

6.

The Retaliating Body/ An Instinct to End

Precessed Tropical Coordinate:
0° 47' Cancer–14° 07' Cancer

MANZIL

Al Hana'a 'The Mark Branded on the Camel's Neck'
Tropical Zodiac: 4° 17' Gemini–17° 8' Gemini
Asterism: Gamma Geminorum (Alhena)
Belongs to the retinue of Saturday, Angel Kasfiel, and Jinn King Maymoun
Ibn Arabi: خ (Kha)
Form, The Wise
Picatrix: Image of two people embracing. Talisman for bringing two people together in friendship and love. Spirit name is Nedeyrahe. Two images from white wax wrapped in white silk, suffumigated in amber and lignum aloes. For the destruction of cities, for the placing of armies, for the enemies of kings to exact vengeance, to cause friendship, for the destruction of medicine, and to improve hunting.
Liber Lunæ: Face of Saturn/Mars. For love and relationship.
Agrippa: Spirit name is Dirachiel. For sieging, hunting, and hindrance of medical care.
Al Buni: و (Waw)

For affection and love. Visit kings and notables. Works to fulfill your wishes. To be born here will be to lead a happy life wherein success may be found. Materially driven. Death may be at the hand of another; one becoming a martyr even. Burdock and mugwort seed.

IBN AL HATIM: Spirit name is Anari. For love and medical treatment.

AL ASHRAF: Costus and wormwood.

SOLOMONIC RING (CUNNING MAN): Blood of a cow. Spirit names are Adariat, Perdagaman, Cauda, and Rupasta. For the purposes of bringing forth of a feast, in particular of meats and rich foods. For success in hunting.

NAKSHATRA

Ardra 'THE MOIST ONE' 'THE HEAD OR TEARDROP'

SIDEREAL ZODIAC: 6° 40' Gemini–20° Gemini

ASTERISM: Gamma Geminorum (Alhena), Alpha Orionis (Betelgeuse)

TEMPERAMENT: Sharp, Human

CASTE: Butcher

DIRECTION: West

MOTIVATION: *Kama*

ANIMAL: Female Dog

SOUNDS: Koo, Kha, Ang, Cha

TREE: *Dalbergia Sisoo* (Indian Rosewood)

Indian Rosewood is a deciduous rosewood tree, also known as Sisu, Sheesham, Tahli, Tali and also Irugudujava. It is native to the Indian Subcontinent and Southern Iran. In Persian, it is called Jag. It is the state tree of Punjab state (India) and the provincial tree of Punjab province (Pakistan)

Vimshottari: Rahu
Deity: Rudra or Shiva, God of Storms
Shakti: Power of effort.
Taittiriya Brahmana: "The strength of the destroyer destroys predators to protect prey"
Brihat Samhita: "will delight in killing, torturing, lying, in adultery, thieving, cheating and tale-bearing; will deal in pod-grains, black magic, sorcery and exorcism"
Tibetan: *Lak.* The Ferocious. The Hostile General. The Black. Incapable of sincerity. A cheat. Proud and selfish. Ungrateful and filled with anger.

XIU

Shen 'Three Stars'
aka: 'Parrot's Hand' 'Hand'
Uneven Tropical Zodiac: 26° Gemini–6° Cancer (16–26 June)
Asterisms: Zeta Orionis (Alnitak), Epsilon Orionis (Alnilam), Delta Orionis (Mintaka)
Sky Quadrant: White Tiger of the West
Planet: Mercury
Animal: Ape
Artley: The Ape is much the same as the monkey. Auspicious. Building brings great benefits. Lettered individuals. Irrigation brings fruitfulness. Marriages and funerals end in broken families, though. Jobs of communication, culture, and most importantly industry. Governs executions. Closing projects. Governs literature.
Element: Water
Matanga Sutra: Offerings of butter. Those born here overindulge in food and drink with fine flavors.

GEOMANCY

Tannery: Rubeus

Al Mawṣilī: Aquisitio & Amissio

PGM/GREEK

Crab, 'Moaning.'
Deity: Typhon

PROTO-SINAITIC/HIEROGLYPH

Rosh, Ras, 'Head'

WORDS

Force, Incontrovertible, Fundamental-Matters, Storm, Temperamental, Intensity, The Headless Body, Nature's Wrath, Interpenetration, King Annihilator, Wailing Forward, Protection, Flesh Rending, Certainty, There is Always Someone Stronger, Vengeance, Analysis, Descent, Obscuration From Below, Focus, Liberation Through Power/Violence, Haughtily Kind, The Big Bad Wolf Who Blows the House Down, Martyr.

The Vedic story of the previous nakshatra, wherein Brahma's attempt to possess the goddess Vac, ends with the god Rudra (Shiva) severing one of the creator's heads in the midst of his pursuit. This act is imaged in Orion's severed head, or the asterism of the previous nakshatra, in relation to the arms and shoulders of the hunter seen in the stars Betelgeuse and Bellatrix. This same lunar station in the Arabic conception is derived from the star Alhena, the heel of a Gemini twin yet also referencing the 'brand on the camel's neck.' This brand marks a similar division between the head and body.

Hunting in this station takes on different connotations. Headless yet persistently intuitive we may attempt to calculate on one side and step into the currents of the Earth on the other. If the previous station is about the head's travels and tales, this one speaks to the life of the body. Even more important than this is the act of severing, both familiar to the god Rudra-Shiva as one of primordial destruction, as well as the images associated with the lunar station: the brand on the neck, the head itself, and perhaps the most instructive being that of the teardrop; a head of its own, as well as the bodily response often accompanying circumstances which involve endings.

The Chinese station refers to those most famous belt stars of the hunter. Similar associations may be found in regards to its mundane forecasts of executions and endings of things. This brings up an important astronomical point. Just as Sagittarius and Scorpio hug the other half of the zodiac's crossing of the Milky Way, so too does the constellation of Orion on the opposing side. Cultures from Asia to Europe as well as the Americas have associated the Milky Way (and in particular these points of crossing) with the movement of souls from this world to the next and vice versa. The Neoplatonic formulation of this, or that which is most commonly referred to in Western astrology, are the entrances and exits found in Cancer and Capricorn respectively. The beginnings of these signs align with the summer and winter solstice which were also often conceived of as entrance and exit points into the otherworld. Due to precession, what was once an observable alignment between these asterisms, the Milky Way, and the solstices, has now slipped as the seasonal cycle of tropical astrology has moved away from observable star locations.

Returning to the figure of Orion, it is no surprise that both the hunter and the nearby dogs of Canis Major (Sirius) and Canis Minor (Procyon) have all come to be associated with underworld journeys. The summer solstice point is akin to a solar death. This is not the star's full underworld traversal but the point where the blow is dealt, and he begins to fall. From here, he falls ever deeper, until his restoration and returning climb at the winter solstice. It is this same severing, or the blow dealt by the hunter, which sends souls to the land of the dead to begin their journey across the Milky Way road. Yet, with all of that said, we must bear in mind the notion of opposing poles. For just as the hunter deals the dying blow, so does Osiris and the great maize deity of the Maya become reborn. Once more it is important to note that these same stars hold strong associations with rebirth just as much as death.

How do these realities coexist? Sometimes they simply cannot, and it truly is the end of something. Yet, in finding one binary within the other, it is the decapitation dealt by Shiva that initiates a new beginning for the creator deity. It remains an act of destruction. Yet this same power is capable of digging into great depths in the revelation of truth, awakening him to the error of his ways and the blindness of his pursuit. For all of its force and intensity, this lunar station subtly embodies both extremes in quite the potent manner. The Arabic magical image depicts two people embracing in reconciliation, yet may also be used for destruction of all kinds. Though many of the lunar stations hold a similar ambivalence, it is perhaps most obvious here in the tendency toward extremes.

PLANETARY PLACEMENTS

The Presence of the ☾

The Moon here may very well bring endings. As discussed above, this is the critical juncture wherein the head of the hunter is severed. 'The Brand on the Camel's Neck.' The old life has abandoned us and we are cut off from what came before. And yet, almost implicitly (or, at least painfully) new beginnings may also arise. This is a stormy placement for the Moon. The tension born here as well as the proximity to extremes, one might say a straddling above the gaping maw of the underworld, is capable of immense power, yet so often susceptible to strife. She may even be drawn to situations of this sort. Placement here may increase the fierce protective-mother aspect of the Moon. For though she is often stereotyped as tranquil, her constant shedding and donning of new skins reveals a restlessness and intensity of a kindred nature. At the same time, if unafflicted, she may be capable of channeling this same power into great and daunting acts, often inconceivable by those outside of the current. Like other lunar stations that deal with destructive energies, she is similarly best suited towards pursuits that uncover, possess depth, focus, as well tasks that call for tedious and attentive care. Like Shiva, she may have a proclivity for hanging out in cemeteries, as well as associating with all kinds of ghosts and frightful spirits. She may be drawn to spiritual paths and practices of a similar character. Returning to that primary image of the headless body we may observe the hunter's lack of a connection with 'above,' or, we might say, things such as purpose, guidance, and greater meaning beyond what is directly in front of us. In other words, the severing of the head may signal the pursuit of truth, yet it is just as capable of initiating the opposite. One example of this relates to materiality, or those things associated with the physical dimension. Here it may seem that matter is all that exists. The body is removed from the head, but has forgotten it entirely. The degree to which these differences are recognized is the degree to which the Moon walks the knife-edge path between what is being brought together and what may become separated.

The Presence of ☿

The planet of buzzing intellect is close in style to that of Venus and the Moon with less overt emotive qualities, yet the vigor remains intact. Sometimes the tension between strong feelings and overt rationality may clash; once more playing out binaries so familiar to this station. Ones and zeros are capable of constructing elaborate and engaging models, as Mercury, planet of mimesis, penetrates into the inner strata and structuring mechanisms of the world. It is this combination of emotive sensation with analytic skill that makes for powerful potentials with this placement. This manifests in particular around the arts, music being a prime example wherein both aspects are needed for the creation of robust works.

The Presence of ♀

The planet of relationships naturally pours passion and intensity into connecting with others here. Oftentimes this intimacy is reserved for the smallest of groups and those capable of dedicated reciprocity. Few other placements hold this deep a sense of care. In this way, she focuses with laser sight, yet not without side effects. The same tensions found throughout this lunar station remain as Venus' radiance may slip into potentially overbearing grips. Often this is in relation to matters of nurturance. This may indeed take on an aesthetic dimension, mirroring the red giant star Betelgeuse associated with this station, in its undulating intensity. Venus' creativity and pleasure born here throb with energy; oftentimes being simply too much for those who prefer containment and repose.

The Presence of the ☉

As discussed in the passage above, this region of the sky has long been related to the death of the Sun in the northern hemisphere, coinciding with the summer solstice. We may also observe this movement in reverse wherein this same place becomes the rebirth of him; once more, inextricably linked and dependent on one's vantage point. Remaining with the tension, the Sun may be deeply connected to those same transformational forces that elicit 'crossing over.' These are processes of breakdown and coherence. The potential for one's sense of self to move in both directions remains constant, even if both of these directions fundamentally lead to the same place. As the lunar station of 'losing one's head,' it is important to recognize the Sun's own role as a planetary leader and the implications therein. Oftentimes he is better left to these acts of creation and destruction, especially in the places where they coexist most intimately. This is instead of being a dedicated head of operations. It is the god Shiva's ascetic tendencies which bolster this notion, as the Sun is less a strong and certain leader here and more an independent ground-breaker at the edge of things unknown.

THE PRESENCE OF ♂

The planet of war fits in, in a place where he can dig deeply into interiors as well as protect in the larger battlefield of culture. Unlike other planets which act in similar fashion, Mars engages with this lunar station at the most fundamental binaries of life and death, sadness and joy, etc. This is also one of the portions of the tropical zodiac where he moves out of bounds (declination). Also, unlike other planets, he is the most susceptible to issues when he attempts to function in a manner other than that outlined here, such as digging deeply and protecting those in need. Similarly, if passion exists for a particular goal, Mars is more than capable of honest pursuit. Like Venus, his intensity is felt through care at microscopic levels. Left unexercised, this same energy easily becomes destructive, often leading towards detrimental ends. Both Mercury and Moon may find a similar sense of criticality, as this station's penchant for analysis finds the flaws in edifices.

THE PRESENCE OF ♃

As there is a consistent theme in this station which deals with the pursuit of truth, the planet Jupiter is well suited here. He maintains a penetrating intellect and a firm moral sense. Though the themes of tension and struggle are not necessarily alleviated by the Greater Benefic, there is a stronger likelihood that they may bear wisdom and learning; oftentimes only possible through intense direct experience with a placement such as this. Here he learns through these trials, therefore becoming an elevated teacher through his lived engagements. Jupiter will not offer his advice nor his wisdom without having made the effort himself. Similarly, he is not stingy here, as generosity towards 'the body,' or the masses is likely.

The Presence of ♄

Like the red planet, Saturn has a pension for digging deeply in the pursuit of hidden matters. These qualities are familiar to this place, yet this slowest of planet's heavy movements often run counter to the vigorous activity here. In this regard, the same energy reservoir already discussed does not necessarily yield like results for him; perhaps instead opting for 'physicalist' tendencies of cold analysis. Along with a penchant for ghoulish figures and the darker shades of things, Saturn more than any other planet here may become susceptible to materialist inclinations and atheism. In other words, this same head in which we have continuously returned to as a primary image, never existed in the first place and is consequently never missed. What may be misconstrued as an entirely 'cerebral' approach could very well be the repetition of the body's needs ad infinitum.

7.
Born Again / Die Again

Precessed Tropical Coordinate:
14° 07' Cancer–27° 27' Cancer

MANZIL

Al Dira 'THE PAW OF THE LION' 'THE FOREARM'
TROPICAL ZODIAC: 17° 8' Gemini–0° Cancer
ASTERISM: Alpha Geminorum (Castor), Beta Geminorum (Pollux)
Belongs to the retinue of SATURDAY, ANGEL KASFIEL, AND JINN KING MAYMOUN
IBN ARABI: ق (Qaf)
THE THRONE, THE ALL ENCOMPASSING
PICATRIX: Image of a man with his arms upraised in the act of supplication or prayer. Talisman for the acquisition of all good things. Spirit name is Siely. Fashion out of silver and suffumigate with sweet smelling things. For safe travel, increase in merchandise and profit, increase crops, for friendship, and to expel flies. Helpful in approaching the king.
LIBER LUNÆ: Face of Jupiter. For wild animals and peace.
AGRIPPA: Spirit name is Sheliel. For gain, friendship, lovers.
AL BUNI: ز (Zayn)
Spiritual healing, beginning studies, and virtuous acts. Gather in houses of worship. Meeting with scholars and the pious. Make talismans. To be born here is

to be fortunate and guided and blessed. Well mannered and uncomfortable with rudeness. Nettle and flaxseed.

IBN AL HATIM: When the mansion rises dogs pounce (connected to Sirius). For the presence of kings, binding spirits and bodies. Spirit name is Sha'lika.

AL ASHRAF: Nettle and frankincense bark.

SOLOMONIC RING (CUNNING MAN): Spirit names are Eanche, Ustay, Amrrehar, and Fastarin. For the purposes of making fruiting trees appear. For abundance.

NAKSHATRA

Punarvasu 'THE BOW AND QUIVER'
SIDEREAL ZODIAC: 20° Gemini–3° 20' Cancer
ASTERISM: Alpha Geminorum (Castor), Beta Geminorum (Pollux)
TEMPERAMENT: Mutable, Divine
CASTE: Merchant
DIRECTION: North
MOTIVATION: *Artha*
ANIMAL: Female Cat
SOUNDS: Ke, Ko, Ha, Hi
TREE: *Dendrocalamus Strictus* (Bamboo)

This tree is found in every part of India. It has many varieties in length, thickness, etc. Every bamboo tree has knots from which a very effective medicinal substance named Vansh-Lochan is obtained. This medicine is used not only in India but also in Japan and China. The leaves are boiled and pasted on the joints of the human body to treat rheumatism. Similar to bamboo's usefulness, the person belonging to this Nakshatra is ready to help others.

VIMSHOTTARI: Jupiter
DEITY: Aditi (Mother of the Gods), Rama
SHAKTI: Power to gain wealth and substance.
TAITTIRIYA BRAHMANA: "The eternal re-becoming needs to make the old and dry fresh and new"
BRIHAT SAMHITA: "will be noted for truthfulness, generosity, cleanliness, respectable descent, personal beauty, sense, fame and wealth; they will also be merchants, dealing in excellent articles, will be fond of service and will delight in the company of painters and sculptors."
TIBETAN: *Nabso.* Goddess of Gifts. Reasonable and full of tact. Content with little. Amiable character. Astute and intelligent but of a weak constitution. Drinks too much water. Simple and retiring life.

XIU

Jing 'WELL'
AKA: 'WHITE STAR OF THE WATER' 'BEAR'S CHEST'
UNEVEN TROPICAL ZODIAC: 6° Cancer–6° Leo (27 June–28 July)
ASTERISM: Mu Geminorum (Tejat), Epsilon Geminorum, Gamma Geminorum (Alhena)
SKY QUADRANT: Vermillion Bird of the South
PLANET: Jupiter
ANIMAL: Wild Dog or Tapir
ARTLEY: Little is known about the wild dog. It is said to bring benefits in agriculture and success in general. Be careful to take care in funerals for one who has died a violent death. Auspicious. The Head of the Phoenix. Beauty, water and most importantly

cleanliness. Consequently moral uprightness. Good for gardening and taking exams.

ELEMENT: Water

MATANGA SUTRA: Offering of honey. Those born here have overflowing granaries and much livestock.

GEOMANCY

AL MAWṢILĪ: Conjunctio

PGM/GREEK

Dog, 'Barking.'
DEITY: Artemis (alternatively, Rhea)

PROTO-SINAITIC/HIEROGLYPH

Yod, Yad, 'ARM'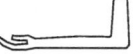

WORDS

Doubling, Chain Link Fence, Descending Wings, Repetition, Touch, Sustained-Sustenance, Birth/Death, An Extended Hand, Cross-Roads, Mimesis, Generosity, Shelter for the Wandering, Starry Funnel, Potentia, Spreading In/Out, Prayer, Maternity, Resurrection, The Kind, Marvel and Mind, A Chorus of Breath and Elevation, Co-Presence, The Midwife, Ascension, Glorious Lights, Inter-Relation.

The Arabic, Vedic, and Chinese lunar stations all maintain a relationship with the stars known as Gemini. In this same way it is useful to conceptualize this sign through the broader themes of twinning, doubling, and repetition. Even lacking an explicit reference to twins, these same themes are undeniably prominent in many of the station's images. Alongside twinning, dogs are also another prominent signification found here. As mentioned in the previous station of Orion, it is both Canis Major's and Minor's (interesting that it is two dogs and not one!) proximity to this region which lends itself to certain underworld associations, yet for different and often less destructive reasons. If death and rebirth were prominent themes in the previous stars, we share alike binary here, yet with a stronger emphasis towards rebirth.

Birth as a major theme arises importantly with the associated goddess figure. This is Aditi, mother of the gods and creatrix in her own right. Though this lunar station primarily coheres around the constellation of the twins, it is also appropriate that it falls directly in the center of tropical Cancer. Just as Aditi is the mother of the gods and primeval creatrix, this lunar station also resembles the Hellenistic *Thema Mundi* or 'Birth of the World Chart,' having Cancer rising and the rest of the signs being birthed from her. This chart has a strong relationship to the land of Egypt, as the rising of Sirius and the stars of Cancer were related to the flooding of the Nile and consequent fertilizing of the land.

The connection between the station and the stars of Sirius and Procyon exists at various levels. As mentioned in the fifth station of Orion, ancient Arab lore sees Procyon as weeping the loss of her sister who has crossed the river, leaving her behind. Here again we find two siblings, wherein one has moved into a different dimension than the other, yet their connection has not ceased. One way this can be conceived is by a division between the plane of mortality and that of the spiritual dimension. In addition, the ancient Egyptians also associated this star with the Pharaonic cult of the dead and similar passages to the underworld. Sirius is also known as 'the scorcher,' related to the so-called Dog Days of intense summer heat, as well as to its brightness (in fact it is the brightest star in the night sky). Not unlike the previous station, life and death are in close proximity here.

Both the dogs and the twin stars represent the doubling process so familiar to this place. The image of a bow and quiver, one of the primary nakshatra symbols, lends itself to this pattern of action, retrieval, and repetition; the natural movement of an archer. The nakshatra functions similarly, especially in the context of reincarnation. If the soul is the arrow (and Sirius has also been thought of as such) then it is shot into this world only to be inevitably retrieved and placed back within the quiver that is the afterlife. From this perspective, it is important to remember that not every arrow will hit its mark. Those that miss completely will be retrieved and another attempt made. The quality of repetition is born from the ongoing process of attempting to reach a mark within the greater cosmic cycle.

Oftentimes schemas of soul-movement hold a concept of a twin-like being or double which exists in the otherworld simultaneously to the mortal on the material plane. One's daemon, or even 'higher self,' may be thought of in this way. Twins are one (or two!) way that this could be represented. The Arabic image of the man with his arms raised in supplication is also relevant here. For the being that he asks for assistance from is none other than his higher self, or in Arabic, the *wajh* or face of God; acting as the intermediary between the almighty and our individual existences. We may use the Arabic image of the lion's arm (as we will see the Arabic *Al Asad* lion constellation was much larger than the Greek) to represent extension, or a bridge between the worlds. It is this appendage that unites the hand and torso. In this respect the lunar station is less about the selection of particular souls and consciousnesses (seen more in the second lunar station of judgment) and more about bridging worlds together. When the archer reaches for a new arrow from the quiver, there is no selection process, simply the necessary action. The birthing process is largely the same.

PLANETARY PLACEMENTS

The Presence of the ☾

The Moon here is representative of the classical associations of said luminary. More to the point, as this station is related to the mother goddess, she often embodies these same proclivities of caring, nurturing, as well as being deeply tied into creative processes. This station lends itself to strong expressive qualities. Less craft-oriented, she tends toward the creative gateway as opposed to more analytic processes of fashioning. The process of repetition familiar to this station has the Moon in a constant flow of trial and retrial when it comes to any given practice. Sampling and experimentation with a variety of options is often a stereotype given to the zodiac sign of Gemini, and it remains true for the lunar station as well. Often she must repeat actions multiple times in order to find the right fit. Yet, it is this action of repetitive testing which is capable of generating wondrous results. When a stride is found, or new territory broken through to, things cohere as if a novel being has been born. Due to the nature of this station, these beings are representative of much older phenomena now renewed or given 'new clothing.' Such is the nature of the reincarnation processes here. If we think of the archer once more, to shoot an arrow into unknown territory and discover where it has landed may actually be the necessary breakthrough; although this cannot be achieved without trying.

The Presence of ☿

The planet of intelligence feels deeply here. Mercury as a psychopomp moves along the bridge which defines the station; back and forth between the various worlds. There may be a strong historical sense as well as an ability to bring it forth through tangible works. As Mercury is already a planet of doubling, themes of repetition take on great import. With positive aspects, this placement is capable of sensitive refinements, articulation of feeling, and acute expression. As the planet representing our handiwork, the ability to channel intelligences and bring them into manifestation becomes possible through the medium of gesture.

The Presence of ♀

For Venus, this station is one of her more intimate placements along the lunar zodiac. Lucifer, the shining planet, mirrors Sirius in its expressive radiance. This is a head-turning placement for her. As this station is linked with gateways, the energies that swirl around her cannot always be articulated easily. Oftentimes she has a strong effect on those nearby, though it may manifest subtly rather than outright. Her aesthetic sensibilities can be highly refined, yet more often than not this is in a sensual manner as opposed to the cerebral. As this is a station of repetition and history, Venus may become deeply in touch with the cycles of various trends. Sometimes when she is found here she may be the one to actually revive certain aesthetic trends that have not been seen in many years.

The Presence of the ☉

His sense of self has the potential to be remarkably transpersonal, in particular in regards to historical consciousness and a keen awareness of what and who has come before. There is a recognition of luminosity as a means of care, as well as something which must be tended and cultivated for its continuation. This is a strong placement of torch bearing. Similar to the Moon, there may be an emphasis on proximity and care in regards to family and those one considers to be intimate familiars. Patterning here is typically established through tried and true methods and traditional values laid down by past generations. It is still possible to innovate, yet he prefers to do so in the manner of renewal from the past, giving something a fresh start and a new chance to re-emerge.

The Presence of ♂

Out of all of the primary planets, Mars is likely the most challenging here. As this station speaks of birth he may experience some of its more painful components as such. In regards to a historical awareness and orientation towards the past, he is particularly sensitive to traumas, especially those around women. Similar to Mars' position in the previous station, this placement functions best when the warrior planet dons the role of protector; especially for those whom they love as well the vulnerable. If Mars is treated as such, there may be immense strength and deeply held convictions.

The Presence of ♃

Once more a strong position for the Greater Benefic. Jupiter is firm here in his role as teacher and parent. He is capable of fulfilling both the conventional roles of Father and Mother all at once. We observe the planet of guidance in unison with the lunar station of mothering. Connections with established systems of moral guidance, as well as traditions within one's family structure are extremely robust. He weaves networks of connection that are capable of bringing up the generations to come. Once more, as we speak of birth, Jupiter is properly resourced to handle the necessary consequences of new life manifesting in the world.

The Presence of ♄

The past orientation of this station aligns well with the planet Saturn. Strangely, as well, there may be a mothering-orientation to be found here, especially in relation to the 'long game' aspects. The danger here is that of cold mothering, or a parental guidance that becomes overly rigid in its frameworks and disciplining. Saturn may also signify trauma in relation to the mother or her ancestral line. Deferring excessively to tradition and those who have come before is possible here. In his historical awareness, Saturn is capable of renewing things from the deepest aspects of antiquity; though they may not always be things deserving of return to the present times.

8.

A Blister, A Thought / Eye of Potential

Precessed Tropical Coordinates:
27° 27' Cancer–10° 47' Leo

MANZIL

Al Nathra 'The Dimple Between the Whiskers of the Lion' 'The Gap or Crib'
Tropical Zodiac: 0° Cancer–12° 51' Cancer
Asterism: M44 (Praesepe)
Ibn Arabi: ك (Kaf)
The Footstool, The Grateful
Picatrix: Image of an eagle with the face of a man. Talisman for victory. Spirit name is Annediex. Suffumigate with sulfur. For love and friendship, safe travel by wagon, for strong incarceration of captives, and to expel mice and vermin.
Liber Lunæ: Face of Mars. For water, seas, rivers, and flooding.
Agrippa: Spirit name is Amnediel. Love, friendship, fellow travelers, drives away pests.
Al Buni: ح (Hah)
For talismans of hatred and enmity. Fighting against aggressors, foes, and enemies. No works for Sun and Moon. Do not visit kings. Destructive works. To be born here is unfortunate. Finds tension with those

in power. Caring person who protects the ones they love. Costus and pomegranate peel.

IBN AL HATIM: For excelling in battle. Spirit name is Aqaris.

AL ASHRAF: Costus, frankincense bark, and pomegranate root.

SOLOMONIC RING (CUNNING MAN): Juice or smoke of the Oak tree. Spirit name is Bario. For the purpose of making Oak trees appear, and for their branches to be well populated.

NAKSHATRA

Pushya 'THE NOURISHER' 'A FLOWER'
SIDEREAL ZODIAC: 3° 20' Cancer–16° 40' Cancer
ASTERISM: Delta Cancri (Ascellus Australis), Theta Cancri
TEMPERAMENT: Quick, Divine
CASTE: Warrior
DIRECTION: East
MOTIVATION: *Dharma*
ANIMAL: Male Goat/Sheep
SOUNDS: Hoo, He, Ho, Da
TREE: *Ficus Religiosa* (Bodhi, Sacred Fig)

This tree is grown in every part of India. It is a sheddy tree with speedy growth. The followers of Hinduism and Buddhism worship this tree and consider it as a sacred tree on the Earth. Its soft leaves, buds, and fruits are used as a food during famine. Its fruits are a favored food of birds and its leaves are good fodder for domestic animals. Its wood is used for furniture. Its tender leaves and bark are used as medicine. The bark of this tree is a very effective medicine in skin diseases particularly eczema. This constellation is

believed to be very sacred and auspicious. There is
a tradition of purchasing gold, jewelry, ornaments
during the day of Gurupushyamrut Yoga or Amrut-
siddhi Yoga. The people belonging to this Nakshatra
are found spiritual, peace loving, calm and full of
perseverance because of this sacred tree.

VIMSHOTTARI: Saturn

DEITY: Brihaspati, Jupiter or Guru

SHAKTI: Power to create spiritual energy.

TAITTIRIYA BRAHMANA: "The success of the master
advisor needs tongues for the aspirant"

BRIHAT SAMHITA: "will be dealers in barley, wheat,
rice, sugar-canes and in the produce of the forest; will
be either ministers or rulers; will live by water; will be
Sādhus and will delight in sacrificial rites."

TIBETAN: *Gyal.* She Who Satisfies. She Who Har-
monizes. Good Nature, Erudition, Perseverance.
Masters passions and fulfills duty. Person of law.
Popular and well known, virtuous, rich, charitable.
Passive and sometimes obstinate.

XIU

Gui 'GHOST'
AKA: 'VICTORY' 'PHEASANT'
UNEVEN TROPICAL ZODIAC: 6° Leo (29 July)
ASTERISM: Theta Cancri, Eta Cancri, Delta Cancri,
Praesepe ('Cumulative Corpses')
SKY QUADRANT: Vermillion Bird of the South
PLANET: Venus
ANIMAL: Sheep
ARTLEY: The sheep is an emblem of retired life. The
essence of yin. Affectionate, caring, trustworthy,
selfless. Artistic talents with a craft basis. A bit too

fastidious. Complacent, but diplomatic. Tends to follow rather than lead. Hates being told what to do. Prefers shared decisions. Resists advice. Social work. Astrologically inauspicious. Building on this day may bring tragedy. Funerals are well placed here, but marriages lead to loneliness, esp. for women. Considered unlucky. Governs people recently departed, cemeteries, and hidden things in general. Good for memorial services and visiting graves.

ELEMENT: Metal

MATANGA SUTRA: Offering of peach flowers. Those born here cultivate goodness.

GEOMANCY

TANNERY: Albus

PGM/GREEK

Wolf, 'Bellowing.'
DEITY: Zeus
   (alternatively, Nike or Athena)

PROTO-SINAITIC/HIEROGLYPH

Saad, Tsade 'PLANT'

WORDS

Sting of a Wasp, Crawling, The Talon, Butterflies, An

Itch, Methods, A Swarm of Insects, Foam Bubbling
on the Surface, Everyone and No One, Actualizing
Potential, Stirring, Atomic, Fermentation, Holding
it All Together, Knowledge Acquisition, Pollination,
Mastery, Organization of Hidden Purposes, Callings
and Vocations, Bi-valve Organs, Hum of a System, A
Speck of Dust, Candied Razors, Porous.

The constellation we know as Cancer is the primary focus of this lunar station. Not particularly large nor bright, the faint star cluster Praesepe at the center of the asterism gives this place many of its associations. It is not hard to conceive of these stars as resembling the foaming mouth of a crab or the rabies-laden madness of an animal. Praesepe's other common name, 'The Beehive Cluster,' lends itself to similar associations as a throbbing mass of intensities, tightly bound and humming with thought and energy.

Many of the stations share strong associations across various cultures. In this instance, the relationships tend to vary much more widely. It would seem that the stars of Cancer are more ambiguous in form; unsurprising as they are notoriously dim and hard to recognize. The notion of a beehive is useful in exploring the diversity of stellar interpretations. Here we find our everyday sense of scale being questioned, as the invitation towards the small and multiplicitous seems to define this region of the sky.

The sign of Cancer has carried insect associations for quite some time. The crab as an animal is not terribly far from one in its form. In ancient Egypt the height of the Sun and the summer solstice were related to the scarab beetle; that great magician-sculptor of the *prima materia*. The insect kingdom contains an unfathomable amount of diversity, yet, for our often taken-for-granted perceptions, they exist on an entirely different scale, a microcosmic one. Cancerian variability may be looked at in this way. It is still of a type, no doubt. Yet, in this same manner, the station acts as a gateway into what we perceive as small, faint, and largely neglected. In all reality, it is from this mass of tiny multitudinous legions that our very lives emerge from and inevitably return to. From the mixing of sperm and eggs to the consumption of decomposing bodies by insects and fungi, this microworld is all pervasive, even though it seems to only account for very little of our daily lives.

The Arabic image for this station seems to emphasize victory in a Jupiterian fashion. Though Jupiter is classically exalted in Cancer, it does not naturally follow that this sign aligns with an overcoming sense of might. The larger figure of the Arabic lion constellation has this station near its mouth, or the whiskers of the beast. Yet there is still a reference to a kind of emptiness, or 'the gap' as it is called, wherein things move out of focus. As if a flea balancing atop the lion's massive head, we are asked to look closer. He is a powerful figure indeed, but it is the bacterium, the flies, and all of the tiny microscopic beings surrounding him who truly hold the power. Here can be found something of a mouse capable of frightening an elephant, or the notion of power in great numbers.

The Chinese xiu explicitly references the dead and the ancestors in this station, as it is titled 'Ghost.' Though the asterisms around Perseus are more well known for the moniker, Praesepe is also referred to as a place of 'Cumulative Corpses' in the Chinese astral imagination. There is much to be said for this region of the sky and its relationship to the cult of the ancestors. The Indian system of nakshatras also has its ancestor/cult of the dead station nearby. The so-called southern quadrant of the sky is sometimes seen quite literally as that which is 'down' or 'below,' the realm of the deep Earth and the dead, the land of the ancestors, and the cave of the ancient times. For the context at hand, we may think of it as the same soil from which the dung beetle rolls its Sun from, and to where it returns back to. The realm of the insect mirrors that of the dead and ghosts, as it exists directly alongside our own, yet, for the most part unrecognized in daily life. The nakshatra Pushya speaks more to what is grown from this same strata of potential. Perhaps more than any other station, at least in the Vedic context, Pushya is capable of discerning through the tangled mass in its ability to speak to what is possible. This is the capacity to discriminate between the strength of differing potentials.

PLANETARY PLACEMENTS

THE PRESENCE OF THE ☾

This placement is deeply tied into that which we call potential and where it might exist in any given circumstance. Similar to Jupiter, the Moon here makes for a natural guide, teacher, and information tender, as she knows the proper order of things to yield optimal results. The nakshatra emphasizes Brihaspati or the planet Jupiter as Guru. It is in this role as 'Guru of the Devas' that she is capable of discerning between the correct sacrifices and rituals necessary to bring about particular results. This position is one of wisdom and talent, often thought of as highly desirable for the Moon's nakshatra. The Arabic associations with victory are not related to the brutality and force observable in other stations. Here it is a victory of the small over the large through intelligence and wit. Though it may seem that the Moon has weakness in this station, it is precisely that reality of the insect world which shows us otherwise. This multiplicitous intelligence cannot be conquered, pure and simple. Consequently, when she has found her ideal place or point of vantage, there are few limitations on what she is capable of achieving.

The Presence of ☿

Mercury as an information dealer and speaker does well here. Synthesis and discernment are strong traits for this placement as they possess the power of articulation even in regards to matters of much ambiguity. This station is one of the stronger financial placements for Mercury. Perhaps less obvious is their aptitude for processes of divination, which may be used as organizational systems for the unknown.

The Presence of ♀

This is a powerful placement for Venus, especially in regards to creativity and aesthetics. Here she possesses the eye capable of both analytic and aesthetic assessments; a necessity for most forms of art. The ability to nurture growth is important for this station. There is innate sensing out of the generative core in any given endeavor, and in this way she excels at most Venusian activities. Something like finding essences and being able to bring them to light. It is perhaps in the domain of relations that she may find herself exceedingly particular. Not that she holds cruelty or malice by nature, only that the process of selection cannot include all by its very definition. She could even be a marriage counselor or sexual therapist here.

The Presence of the ☉

As far as the Sun's symbolism is concerned, his core principles of guidance around individual action align well with this station. Often times he finds himself in leadership positions, which come naturally. Like Jupiter, the Sun functions well as teacher, parent, and guide in this station. The ancient Egyptian symbol of the dung beetle may be invoked once more as he is capable of scaling up and down, grasping large and small, and all manner of increase and decrease in scale. As much as underlying potentials are integral, this is a placement of seeing the light in others and how it might be cultivated to become Sun-like. Spiritual processes of illumination and its mechanics as such are found here.

The Presence of ♂

The planet of warfare does not always have the patience necessary for growth. Mars' drive towards information gathering is potent here, as there is often a strong desire to seek out knowledge. The image of the gap between the lion's whiskers is useful in the case of Mars, as we may observe the deliberation between attack and repose. He is capable of guidance in this sign, serving a similar function to other planets, yet more than anything else Mars is a proficient leader here when acting from an informed position. He sets examples through these actions, and in this way he teaches others. He is individualistic by nature and therefore teaches through his own unique actions what achievements are possible.

The Presence of ♃

As the true deity of this nakshatra, the Vedic Brihaspati (Jupiter) is quite comfortable in this station which he calls his own. The planet of parentage, law, and education fits nicely. In the pursuit of knowledge, underlying structures of reality are revealed with an ease atypical for most placements. If so inclined, he will accordingly pass on these learnings through offering guidance and advice to those in need of it. This placement is one of the archetypal teacher. Much of what a great educator does involves this same process of discerning potentials. There is a strong awareness of the reality of sacrifice, as he is capable of efficient energy management. The Vedic conception of Brihaspati as Guru understands that sacrifice is necessary to accomplish most ends. This does not exist solely in a religious context, as business, education, and other endeavors require planning along these very lines. Here he excels at managing energy expenditure and guidance towards goals.

The Presence of ♄

Because this lunar station deals with the transformation of essential matter into awareness, there is indeed a proximity to the natural functioning of Saturn. He finds himself with a strong grasp of life's underlying mechanisms. Unlike a luminary in this position, which would be more adept at harnessing the forces of growth, Saturn may find himself perpetually dwelling amidst the density of things. The possibility of hidden knowledge is strong, yet often for its own sake and with little toward the ends of tangible growth. If we conceive of this process as one resembling the life cycle of a plant, Saturn's proclivity for shade and the avoidance of sunlight keeps the organism from emerging. There is a tendency towards the underground portion of the journey; the interior, hidden away from prying eyes. Here he is safe to do his work.

9.

Snake Pit / The Overcoming Eyes

Precessed Tropical Coordinates:
10° 47' Leo–24° 07' Leo

MANZIL

Al Tarf 'Glance of the Lion's Eye'
Tropical Zodiac: 12° 51' Cancer—25° 42' Cancer
Asterism: Lambda Leonis (Alterf)
Ibn Arabi: ج (Jeem)
The Self Existing Ultimate Sphere, The Starless Sky, The Zodiacal Towers, The Independent, The Rich
Picatrix: Image of a eunuch holding his hands over his eyes. Talisman for infirmity. Spirit name is Raubel. Fashion out of lead and suffumigate with pine resin. For the destruction of crops, and to make travels unfortunate, to do evil, to cause divisions between people, to defend oneself.
Liber Lunæ: Face of the Sun. For fowl animals.
Agrippa: Spirit name is Barbiel. Hinders harvests, discord.
Al Buni: ط (Ta)
Watery. Do not construct or make things. Do not visit kings. Love and wisdom are not found here. Better

to be alone. To be born here is unfortunate. There are relationship troubles here. Suspicious people by nature. Aloeswood and saffron.

IBN AL HATIM: For removing eye disease and the flow of blood. Spirit name is Rawyal.

AL ASHRAF: Aromatic wood and saffron.

SOLOMONIC RING (CUNNING MAN): Spirit names are Ereleri, Termat, Banros, and Benkurfsioth. For the purposes of making one appear to be drawing a sail or mast of a ship.

NAKSHATRA

Ashlesha 'THE COILED SERPENT'
SIDEREAL ZODIAC: 16° 40' Cancer–0° Leo
ASTERISM: Zeta Hydrae, Epsilon Hydrae, Theta Hydrae, Eta Hydrae
TEMPERAMENT: Sharp, Daemonic
CASTE: Outcast
DIRECTION: South
MOTIVATION: *Dharma*
ANIMAL: Male Cat
SOUNDS: De, Doo, Day, Do
TREE: *Mesua Ferea* (Ceylon Ironwood)
This tree is an ever-green. Its trunk is straight and sticky. The pistil of its flower is known as Naagkeshar. It is always used as medicine. This tree, having a large quantity of leaves, is often grown within temple compound, gardens and road-sides. Its wood is very strong and is known as Iron-wood.
VIMSHOTTARI: Mercury
DEITY: Nagas, or Serpents
SHAKTI: Power to inflict with poison.

TAITTIRIYA BRAHMANA: "The embracing serpents need seduction for arousal"

BRIHAT SAMHITA: "will be dealers in perfumes, roots, fruits, reptiles, serpents, and poison; will delight in cheating others of their property; will be dealers in pod grains and will be skilled in medicine of every sort."

TIBETAN: *Kak*. Dragon Tailed Goddess. Joyful and strong appearance. Speaks several languages. A cheat, ungrateful, selfish, and a liar. Skill and learning. Will undergo various deceptions.

XIU

Liu 'WILLOW'

AKA: 'PHEASANT' 'PURPLE HUE'

UNEVEN TROPICAL ZODIAC: 7°–19° Leo (30 July–11 August)

ASTERISM: Zeta Hydrae, Epsilon Hydrae, Theta Hydrae, Eta Hydrae

SKY QUADRANT: Vermillion Bird of the South

PLANET: Saturn

ANIMAL: Stag

ARTLEY: The Stag is credited with longevity. An emblem of long life. It is the only animal able to find the Ling-Chi—the Fungus of Immortality. Astrologically, it portends legal troubles, thieves, and disasters to the household. Sadness and suffering found here. Funerals and marriages should be avoided on these days. Generally inauspicious.

ELEMENT: Earth

MATANGA SUTRA: Offering of milk. People born here have many desires.

GEOMANCY

Tannery: Albus

PGM/GREEK

Serpent, 'Neighing'
Deity: Hydra (alternatively, Asclepius)

PROTO-SINAITIC/HIEROGLYPH

Nahs 'Snake'

WORDS

Underground/Underworld, Core of the Earth, Punk Attitude, Ley Lines, Bound/Binding, Curse, Alternative, Wrapped Together, Intrigue, The Stare, Intensity, Pain and Pleasure, Choking, Counter-Culture, Acute, Cunning, Constituent Parts, Embracing, The Squeeze, Journey to Elsewhere, Extremity, Mark of the Other, Leather-clad, Depth of Field, Estrangement, Power Struggle, Eyes From Below.

Intimately linked with the lunar station to come (number ten), we find the cat and the serpent aligned here through their mutual gaze. Unlike the station which follows, wherein the essence of the constellation is found in their respective heart star, here we find the death-gaze of these two predatory animals aligned with an intensity of appetite. This is most readily shown through the images of eyes and mouths; once more of the serpent and the cat.

It is the nakshatra, known as Ashlesha, which places heavy emphasis on this station's ophidian qualities. The encompassing stars make up the head of the extremely lengthy constellation known as Hydra. Though this nakshatra is given as representative of the constellation in its entirety, it is important that we focus upon the head and consequently the eyes, as the starry representative of the lunar station. Similarly, it is the head of the lion as well as its gaze that is represented in the Arabic asterism. The same manner in which the following station illustrates the heart (inner passions, drives, emotions) of said constellations, so too does this one reflect the head (mouth, act of consumption, eyes, 'the gaze').

The talismanic images associated with this place are telling, as the figures are seen holding their hands over their eyes. There is an intensity of 'looking' here. It is more than simple observation or curiosity, but rather one of hunger and consequent salivation. The animals associated with this kind of looking are also not those we would typically want to be stared at by. Eyes such as those portend death. In this way, the talismanic figure averts their eyes so as not to be revealed unless the most dire of circumstances calls for it.

Thoughts are attentive towards the proper moment to strike; and, importantly, that the action will be cutting and decisive. Energy here is typically bound up and tightly condensed. Reactions are sharp and forceful here due to this spring-loaded quality. Atomic energy, or the ability to garner massive power from the invisible and microscopic world, is a natural instructor for this station. Even more so as the materials that we use for energy are typically buried deep beneath the Earth. It is the harnessing of this 'bound up' power which speaks to the actions of this station.

Qualities of being cursed or doing the cursing are found here. In a similar manner the Vedic story of the fall of the Asuras is likened to this nakshatra as the Nagas, or primeval serpent beings, were banished to their glimmering underground realm reminiscent of this station and its darker dispositions. The constellation Hydra and its position in the far south in relation to the northern hemisphere, only adds to its quality of 'down belowness;' thoroughly existing in the chthonic dimension.

The hunger and desire associated with this lunar station is not exclusively for the ends of material gains. In fact, it is often a hunger for those deeper and more hidden qualities of life that these stars connote. As a realm of fallen gods there is a desire to climb back to a previous stature, to prove something, to overthrow hierarchies, as well as form new underground subcultures that may foster rebellion. In this way the station can be quite counter cultural in its disposition.

PLANETARY PLACEMENTS

The Presence of the ☾

The nakshatra is conceived as a coiled serpent. Tightly bound with power this concentrated energy needs periodic releases so as not to build up beyond a point of saturation. Overflow may lead to her more venomous qualities emerging. This is a Moon that must be roused, coaxed out from its state of condensation through the magic of snake charming. It is the 'underground' quality of this placement, in all the senses of that term, which lends itself to a kind of coldness. As this region receives no sunlight it must become self illuminating; more naturally aligned with the reflective and softer light of the Moon. The light here is that of precious gems. The folkloric motif of serpentine guardians of treasure may be found in this station, as the Moon in particular tends to bind herself to things of precious qualities, mirroring the serpent's coiling movements. Many of the plants associated with this lunar station, as well as the Chinese symbol of the stag, are representative of longevity. This is born from a sense of density, as well as the serpent's hidden alchemical mysteries of internal substances and medicines relating to life extension. When we consider what it means to be underground in a very literal sense, the image conjured is one of packed and stratified layers all the way down. Implicit depth has the Moon naturally drawn to occultism and matters considered hidden or behind the scenes. Another sense of the word underground speaks to her interest in subcultures and those realms concealed away from the light of day.

THE PRESENCE OF ☿

The planet of information becomes deeply immersed in hidden subjects and behind the scenes investigations. Not unlike the serpent or the lion's bite, their mouth and speech harbors forcefulness capable of piercing through. Similarly, words may deliver venom for better or worse. Speech has the capacity for harshness, and can be potentially harmful if left completely unchecked. Though the Moon and other planetary placements also carry this quality of sharpness, something very much associated with the nakshatra, Mercury with their pension for analysis is capable of cutting deep to reach the raw bone of any given matter. To that end, this is also a highly scientific placement. Connotations of sorcery extend beyond antiquated tropes into the reality of pharmacopeia, physics, and computer science.

The Presence of ♀

Sensual in sometimes uncomfortable ways, potentially seductive, Venus here reveals this station's pension for coiling things together. This is a Venus with desire to the front, drawing things closer to one another through magnetism and invisible force. She may be both the serpent and the lioness, as her prideful forms take precedence here, as well as heightened and deepened feelings of wanting. The planet's more conventional forms of relationality are less common. Even amidst the stars of solary Leo, by and large, Venus tends toward night-orientation. We may observe the Sun at Midnight as a kind of bioluminescence, a self-illumination, which does not give off warmth as much as radiance. Nevertheless, this placement still possesses a magnetism to it. Shades of the serpent in the Garden of Eden are evoked here. Perhaps the snake charmer capable of using music to arouse the coiled serpent is of a closer likeness.

The Presence of the ☉

Topically it would seem that there is relative planetary ease here. With that said, the realm of this lunar station is underground and does not receive sunlight. As a place of self-luminessence, the Sun is quite comfortable radiating from within to light his own path, with little or no affirmation from others. Similar to the following station, this is a Sun at midnight, or an Underworld Sun, wherein self-illumination necessitates expressive qualities for the purposes of growth and navigation. As the Sun is often likened to the eye, we see the head of the serpent or that of the lion projecting its light outwards with a penetrating gaze. This is quite different from the Sun in its daytime form, wherein his warmth and growth may be shared more abundantly. Similar to the Sun in Aries, this light is both self-illuminating as well as self-directing; like the eye, he may fixate on what he desires so that he can pursue it.

The Presence of ♂

Like Mercury, Mars has a distinctly sharp quality in this station, resembling something of a lion's tooth or the venom delivery system of a serpent. Pensions for squeezing and tightly embracing are common for Mars here. He possesses those fiercer qualities of the lion in both leadership and strength. This is often not in the manner of the status quo, but rather on the side of rebellious activity. Here he shows a natural sense of dominion for his nighttime kingdom. If inclined through other placements, he may bully, aggress, and transgress, as he sees fit. Mars in his healthier forms may not only be protective, but rebellious in a principled manner, as opposed to that of destruction for its own sake.

The Presence of ♃

Jupiter's buoyancy may struggle to flow in this lunar station's dense environment. Yet, even with limited resources in terms of growth, the planet of wealth may be able to utilize what is available for the purposes of making do; both in terms of material and spiritual gains. This is a Jupiter well acquainted with esoteric philosophies that plumb the depths. We may even find self help and material acquisition gurus with this placement.

The Presence of ♄

The planet of slow and collective movement brushes up against this station's self-driven orientation. All things considered, Saturn does share many of the colder and more underground qualities of this place, although he functions in a different manner. Saturn as self-effacer does not value self-illumination in this way. Though he represents outcasts and those who find themselves in 'fallen' states, the quality of this station has more in common with Mars and Venus in character. If we were to divide up the dimensions of the underworld, his place would be one of cold fate, wherein titanic powers of the cosmos bare down upon things palpably. The more blood-pumping desirous qualities of this station do not necessarily equate.

10.

Double-Chambered Heart / A Star Enthroned

Precessed Tropical Coordinates:
24° 07' Leo–7° 27' Virgo

MANZIL

Al Yabha 'THE FOREHEAD OF THE LION'
TROPICAL ZODIAC: 25° 42' Cancer–8° 34' Leo
ASTERISM: Regulus (Alpha Leonis)
Belongs to the retinue of SUNDAY, ANGEL RUQIEL, AND JINN KING AL MADHAB
IBN ARABI: ش (Sheen)
THE SKY OF THE FIXED STARS, THE SPHERE OF THE STATIONS, THE SUN OF PARADISE, THE ROOF OF HELL, THE POWERFUL
PICATRIX: Image of the head of a lion. Talisman for

curing infirmities and easing childbirth. Spirit name is Aredifir. Fashion from gold and suffumigate with amber. To bring love between people, destruction of enemies, strengthening and completion of buildings, and love of allies and their mutual aid.

LIBER LUNÆ: Face of Venus. For wolves, foxes, and beasts.

AGRIPPA: Spirit name is Ardesiel. For strengthening buildings, yielding love, help against enemies.

AL BUNI: ڐ (Ya)

Works for affection. Visit kings and seek what one needs. Treatments for the ill. Suitable for moving. Those born here are clever and dextrous. Highly skilled and successful in the use of said skills. Prideful yet generous. Valuing hard work. Fortunate and blessed. However they may be inclined towards trickery and deceit. Saffron and myrtle.

IBN AL HATIM: For presence of kings, curing disease, and childbirth. Spirit name is Aradin. Also takes walnuts for incense.

AL ASHRAF: Saffron and myrtle seed.

SOLOMONIC RING (CUNNING MAN): Ivory and the hair from a man's head. Spirit name is Fermagon. For the purposes of bringing forth an elephant with a castle upon its back.

NAKSHATRA

Magha 'THE GREAT ONE' 'THE PALANQUIN' 'ROYAL THRONE'
SIDEREAL ZODIAC: 0° Leo–13° 20' Leo
ASTERISM: Alpha Leonis (Regulus)
TEMPERAMENT: Fierce, Daemonic
CASTE: Worker

DIRECTION: West
MOTIVATION: *Artha*
ANIMAL: Male Rat
SOUNDS: Ma, Me, Moo, May
TREE: *Ficus Banghalensis* (Banyan)
The Banyan Tree is a symbol of long life-span, strength, and prosperity. It is grows to massive sizes with aerial roots. All parts of this tree are used as medicine. Its gum is used to treat boils, joint-pain, toothache and cracks of heels. Its fruits are given to stop diabetes and germ is a resulting medicine in family-planning and guinea worm. In Indian civilization, the Banyan tree is of great importance. A chaste & devotional wife worships this sacred tree on full-moon day (Poornima) of Jyestha month (Eighth month of Vikram Era). In one myth, Satyavan died leaving his chaste and devoted wife Savitri behind. She worshiped this tree, observed the vow of the tree and was able to bring her husband back from the dead.
VIMSHOTTARI: Ketu
DEITY: Pitris, The Forefathers, Ancestors
SHAKTI: Power to leave the body.
TAITTIRIYA BRAHMANA: "The power invested in the forefathers relies on deploring, to suppress deviance."
BRIHAT SAMHITA: "will be possessed of wealth, grains and storehouses; will delight in frequenting hills and in the performance of religious rites; will be merchants; will be valiant; will take animal food and will be female haters."
TIBETAN: *Chu*. Lord of the Eight Bonds. A Poet.
Ta Chen, the Great Horse. Very enthusiastic. A sensualist. An entrepreneur. Respects power and has a religious mind. Likes flowers and perfume. Much ability. Rich with numerous servants.

XIU

Xing 'Star'
aka: 'Hawk' 'Earth'
Uneven Tropical Zodiac: 20°–26° Leo (12–18 August)
Asterism: Alpha Hydrae (Alphard)
Sky Quadrant: Vermillion Bird of the South
Planet: Sun
Animal: Horse
Artley: The Horse represents speed and perseverance. Sometimes tyrannical. Revolutionary. Comfortable in the company of their own kind. Difficulty relating to opposite sex. Athletic and sociable. Club oriented. Very conscious of social standing. Needs to feel successful. Good conversationalists. Deep seated prejudices. It also symbolizes the passage from one life to another and was associated with the Sea Gods. Military greatness. Inauspicious. Building is favorable. Neutral, governs highway robbery, bridges, piracy, and kidnapping. Good for construction.
Element: Varied
Matanga Sutra: Offering of sesame. Those born here are respectable.

GEOMANCY

Tannery: Via

PGM/GREEK

Horse, 'A Musical Sound'

DEITY: Persephone
(alternatively Charon or Thanatos)

PROTO-SINAITIC/HIEROGLYPH

Heth, Het 'COURTYARD'

WORDS

Tradition, Serpent Haired, Movement of the Soul, Ember to be Transferred and Cultivated, Chain of Transmission, DNA, The Cauldron, Gothic Sensibilities, Controlled Burn, The Court/Courtyard, Familial, Seat of Power, The Reaper, Raised by Wolves, Capital Punishment, The Ancestors, Calling Forth from Below, Strong-Arm, Reproduction/Creativity.

Though most associate this station with the royal star Regulus (Leo), the xiu use a different primary designation; that of Alphard or the heart of the serpent Hydra. As discussed in the previous lunar station, both Hydra and Leo (even more so for the Arabs) are large constellations worthy of multiple divisions into separate parts. As we have seen, the serpent-lion mouth has its own connotation. Moving forward along the proposed double body of the two, we have arrived at its double-chambered heart. Here, the emphasis is less on appetite and the devouring nature, and more on internal stirrings. These are the deep seated motivations of the two predatory animals in question. In this way it is perhaps more apt to conceive of this station as having two hearts; for it is often the vampiric beings of folklore who were thought of in this way. This is appropriate, as we deal here with blood flow over many ages, or that of the ongoing ancestral rivers which flow through time and space. The intertwining serpents of DNA are found here, as well as that stereotypical vampiric hunger for the life force and its perpetuation. Another important aspect of this urge relates to sexuality, for it is the reproductive act itself which continues these lines as well as refreshes them.

It is not the Leonine quality alone which gives this station strong solar connotations. The heart is the center of the body and the director of blood life-force. Regulus is known for its strong regal nature. It is this central, regulatory quality which lends itself to notions of rulership. Note the proposed geomantic figure, which is called *Via* in Latin, or *Al-Tariq* in Arabic. As the single line it partakes of an axial nature. This is the place where life and death decisions are made; perhaps, sometimes very literally to kill or reproduce.

The nakshatra speaks heavily of the dead, but in particular those ancestors of a more prominent stature. These are the beings who laid the foundations on which all future generations walk. After death, these souls become guides for those in the living world as they transition into the beyond. Consequently, this station focuses heavily on the veneration of ancestors. It is this recognition of continued presence that defines it so well. The interpenetration of death into the world of the living is a fundamental reality. It is the past that dictates the future so that it may become the past. The mystery of this unfoldment is highlighted here as it develops and is related to that of the second station (the karmic webs of the afterlife).

PLANETARY PLACEMENTS

The Presence of the ☾

The Moon here is fond of familial environments, as there is much warmth to be found in that which is familiar. Often there is a strong respect for what has come before and the traditional structures related to it. There are drives to study history, ancestral heritages, as well as the past more broadly. Though much of this will be in the context of human beings, there is something of a relationship with all that has passed away. This includes animal and plant life as well as an inclination towards studying the invisible dimension of reality. Like the previous station, these stars of the far south represent the inner depths of the Earth and the chthonic mysteries therein. The Pitris, or the Vedic deities associated with this nakshatra, are less deities in the typical sense as they are akin to shepherds through the other world. In their more frightening aspects, they may resemble something of the grim reaper if the transition becomes challenging or violent. Either way, the Moon here may be drawn towards giving guidance in times of rapid transition and loss; something of a hospice nurse and end-of-life reckoner.

The Presence of ☿

Mercury here speaks of tradition as well as the planet's more psychopompic manifestations. It is these established systems and ways of being found in traditional modalities that allow communication to move smoothly. Mercury here thinks along the lines of universal languages. What are ways that people have communicated in the deep past? This is a planet interested in body movements and musical signs as much as a more predictable study of so-called dead/archaic languages as well as the tongues of one's ancestors. This is an expressive Mercury, as far as they bring life to these inheritances, passing them along to the ensuing generations.

The Presence of ♀

This is a passionate Venus. There may be an oscillation of intensity between the two hearts previously spoken of. It is through this movement that she conquers as well as falls. This placement can be conceived as a paradox between traditional modalities and so-called extreme or alternative ways of living. The paradox lies at the core of this station as one which maintains strong reverence for how things have been done while simultaneously reformulating these same values. She is of the deep Earth here; deep enough and old enough to exist in a state wherein these distinctions were never made. We find Venus in her form of Magna Mater or Cybele, flanked by lions and processing musicians in a display of otherworldly force. Likewise, Inanna and her descent into the underworld is another potent image for Venus in this place, as the station represents the realm of shades and the afterlife.

The Presence of the ☉

The Sun brings out the inherently solar qualities of the lunar station, as he finds himself as the third heart among two. Here he creates brilliance which illuminates the dark interiors of the world. He may adhere to codes and past ways of going about things. The Sun here in particular brings up what may be thought of as traditional masculine qualities. As this nakshatra is related to the ancestral fathers (though, not limited to by any means), there may be a tendency towards certain forms of patriarchal structure. Depending on the placement, it may also signal a rebellion against such structures. The image of the Sun transiting the underworld or the world of the dead is prominent here as his light leads forward those who are lost so that they may find their way. The urge to procreate for the continuation of particular groupings may be found. It is the cyclicity we associate with the Sun, the hand that takes the torch and continues onward. Like Mars there may also be a strong sexual nature to this placement, as libidinal forces pass easily through the sign.

The Presence of ♂

This is a strong placement for Mars as this station shares many of his most prominent qualities. Emphasis on family structures shows an inclination towards protection; though this is most often shared with those who are considered to be part of the family as opposed to those outside of it. Not unlike the Sun, this placement emphasizes qualities we may think of as traditionally masculine as well as sexualities perceived as such. In this way Mars must also be careful not to cut away or bring negativity towards those who would exist outside of these same familial structures. As a researcher and investigator he digs deeply into matters of ancestry and all things hidden. He is driven by and passionate about the maintenance of order in whatever manifestation he finds himself belonging to.

The Presence of ♃

Here, Jupiter is similarly fond of traditional structures especially in a spiritual context. He maintains a strong interest in those spiritual practices that incorporate the ancestors and the dead as opposed to others that might eschew them. This is not a 'new age' oriented Jupiter, as old and established forms are highly regarded. By this same token, as with many of these placements, he is not one who is inherently stuck within previous modalities and ways of being. The more important thing is that these older ways are incorporated within the contemporary moment if he is to succeed. Jupiter feels fatherly here, and has the potential to stand tall yet remain a benevolent patriarch or ruler. In his more benefic manifestations, he is a good husband and spouse. In his more malefic ones, he may become overly traditional to the point of fundamentalism.

The Presence of ♄

The emphasis on the dead, ancestors, and traditional past orientations works well with the planet Saturn. On the other side of this, he who is ever-cold finds discomfort in the warmth typical of this region. It is this same warmth that binds structures together as opposed to Saturn's predilection for rational analysis and taking things apart. This station tends to air more on the side of passion and deep emotional connection, working closer to the animal levels of being. Saturn may adopt these structures but not necessarily in a manner conducive to familial bonding. This is a strong placement for academic studies of the past in terms of archeology, history, and similar sciences. Distance allows for an examination of the older and or lost dimensions of the world. In this way, blood and guts intimacy may be foregone while still remaining nearby.

11.

Treasure of the Pyramid I / Marriage from One Side

Precessed Tropical Coordinates:
7° 27' Virgo–20° 47' Virgo

MANZIL

Al Jaratan AKA *Al Zubrah* 'THE MANE OF THE LION'
TROPICAL ZODIAC: 8° 34' Leo—21° 25' Leo
ASTERISM: Delta Leonis (Zosma)
IBN ARABI: ي (Ya)
The First Heaven, the Sphere of Saturn, the Sky of the Visited House and Lotus of the Extreme Limit, the Abode of Ibrahim (Abraham), The Lord
PICATRIX: Image of a man riding a lion. Talisman for pride and receiving good things. Spirit name is Necol. Fashion out of gold. For the rescuing of captives, to besiege cities and villages, the ordering of trade and profit, to make buildings firm, and an increase in allies' profits.
LIBER LUNÆ: Face of Mercury. For loss, destruction, and binding.
AGRIPPA: Spirit name is Neciel. For voyages and profits.
AL BUNI: ل (Kaf)
Healing, creation of talismans. Treat disease and medicate chronic illness. Buying, selling, visiting kings. Traveling, sojourning. Great works, new clothing. People born here are beloved by the

people but shall have a trickish streak. Can become influential or a center of attention. Comfort and luxury. Issues coming from romantic relationships. Pomegranate peel.

IBN AL HATIM: Spirit name is Aqlul Iqlabul. For seeing desires and appearing in a satisfying manner.

AL ASHRAF: Frankincense bark and pepper.

SOLOMONIC RING (CUNNING MAN): Dragon's blood incense. Spirit names are Qerminat, Baralama, Canempria, and Coriet. For the purposes of making a dragon appear in the air.

NAKSHATRA

Purva Phalguni 'THE FIRST POST OF THE BED' 'PLATFORM'

ASTERISM: Delta Leonis (Zosma), Theta Leonis
TEMPERAMENT: Fierce, Human
CASTE: Brahmin
DIRECTION: North
MOTIVATION: *Kama*
ANIMAL: Female Rat
SOUNDS: Mo, Ta, Tee, Too
TREE: *Butea Monosperma*

The tree's flowers have a bright red color, resembling the rays of the rising Sun. These flowers are very useful on boils and skin ailments. The coal of this tree removes bad-odors. Its gum is useful for bleeding and diarrhea. The seeds of the flower are useful to treat worms.

VIMSHOTTARI: Venus
DEITY: Bhaga, God of Beauty and Wealth
SHAKTI: Power of procreation.
TAITTIRIYA BRAHMANA: "The affectionate man

approaching the Fruit-Giver needs a wife, for his manliness" Deity is Aryama (reversed with next nakshatra).

BRIHAT SAMHITA: "will delight in dance, in young women, in music, in painting, in sculpture and in trade; will be dealers in cotton, salt, honey, and oil and will be forever in the enjoyment of the vigor of youth."

TIBETAN: *Dre.* The Little Horse. Lake Born. The Lotus. Soft and eloquent of speech. Goodness. Likes travel, unstable. Official or prosperous servant. Danger with fire.

XIU

Zhang 'EXTENDED NET'

UNEVEN TROPICAL ZODIAC: 26° Leo–13° Virgo (19 August–5 September)

ASTERISM: Mu Hydrae, Lambda Hydrae, Upsilon Hydrae

SKY QUADRANT: Vermillion Bird of the South

PLANET: Moon

ANIMAL: Deer

ARTLEY: The Deer is much like the buck/stag, except yin. Astrologically auspicious. Building today brings high officials. Funerals and work on the land attract money and riches. Marriages bring unending happiness and harmony. Considered lucky and indicates gifts and wealth.

ELEMENT: Varied

MATANGA SUTRA: Offerings of fruit. Those born here are short lived.

PGM/GREEK

She-Goat, 'A sounding wind.'
Deity: Dionysus
(alternatively, Aphrodite)

PROTO-SINAITIC/HIEROGLYPH

Ziqq, Dayp, 'Brow' 'Manacle'

WORDS

Braid of the Bride, Magnetism, Sexual Power, Ease, The Fruit Tree, Prosperity, The Stage/The Platform of Offerings, Affection, Marble Pyramid, It Takes a Village, Beloved, Comfort, Stability, Sensuality, Cornerstone, Briskness, Determined to Rise and Fall, Activation, Watching Every Direction, Solidarity, Growth Through Mutual Construction.

We continue to move alongside the constellation Leo, now finding ourselves situated among the stars upon his back. It is not by accident that the Arabic image related to this station depicts a person riding upon just that. The primary indicator star is Zosma, most often seen as the back of the lion but also sometimes associated with his loins or genitals. This imagery speaks to the highly sexual nature of the station at a superficial level. We find this region and the next highlighting the mysteries of creativity more broadly.

Like the 5th House of a horoscope, these stations reveal the interconnectedness of generative activity. There is of course the sexual act and its procreative function. Yet we may also expand the notion of eros into fertile imaginations and the like. Consequently, it is agreed upon in every instantiation that this station will bode well for all things bountiful. That said, it must be remembered that potent fertility does not always equal manifestation. As this station is inextricably linked to the one that follows, partnership and romance is heavily emphasized here, as many of these boons may only be born through relationship.

The nakshatra system divides this station and the next into purva and uttara signatures; or that of the first and second, or early and later. The nakshatras which use this division (there are six in total) possess a sort of double mystery. In this station, we find those of marriage, sex, love, and relationship. Fundamentally, it is the act of coming together for the sake of creation which stirs these two stations. What is the difference between the two? As with the others divided into first and later, the one which begins tends to have a rawer form of whatever energy signature marks it. Here we find feelings of love at first sight, the glance, and those 'honeymoon' sensations. It is this 'butterflies in the stomach' feeling which propels sexuality.

The constellation itself was often seen as a marriage bed, or place of procreation. This is in contrast to the death bed or crematory cot found in stations 26 and 27 that lay directly across the zodiac. In this context, the act of marriage cannot be reduced to our ordinary notions. It is the *Hieros Gamos*, or the sacred marriage, which defines this place, just as the sacred death signifies its opposite.

PLANETARY PLACEMENTS

The Presence of the ☾

The Moon in this sign is fundamentally creative. She is capable of harnessing generative powers for various endeavors, the least of which being art, music, poetry, and the like. She is perhaps flirtier here than in the station to come. As a sign of young love (or, love in its earlier stages) the Moon finds a romantic sensibility here as well as a relational one. She is fond of pleasure and those qualities of life which elicit it. If dignified she may grow beyond the possibilities of self-fulfillment into one capable of nurturing growth for others as well. She reminds us about the qualities of life that make it worth living; never simply excess or overindulgence but joy in daily existence.

The Presence of ☿

This is the ultimate poetic placement for the planet Mercury as they may harvest the ripest of fruits to continually fuel inspiration. It is not a brooding or melancholic Mercury as much as a romantic one; something more like a love song, and a tone of being both immensely intelligent and rich in vocabulary. As the fertility of this station demands, their words bring growth and their disposition optimism. Though Mercury is romantic here, it is not of an overly idealistic nature. This is a placement of well-balanced criticality, efficiency, and even business acumen.

The Presence of ♀

There is much to be said for the likeness between her and this lunar station. The planet of aesthetics, trends, and artistry finds a natural home here as the station's significations are only bolstered by Venus. This is a cornucopia placement of sorts. Like the Moon, she may also be perpetually enamored in the youthful phases of love. More so than the Moon, this is a Venus capable of commanding strong sexual magnetism. Like a flower or a fruit tree at its peak, she is undoubtedly attractive. As with other placements here, we must not confine the libidinal energy of this station to somatic manifestations, though this is typically the most noticeable.

THE PRESENCE OF THE ☉

The solary nature of this region bodes well for the Sun's emphasis on growth and attention. Like other strong solar places, this station has a spotlight effect coupled with his own radiance which both warms and attracts. He is exceptionally expressive here, finding strong affinity for performative arts in particular. Here he is interested in growth; shining in business, leadership, and other practices focused on increasing wealth in a variety of ways. This is not solely financial, but also through the avenues of culture and the like. Here he may be a teacher as well as one wise in the ways of nurturing creativity.

THE PRESENCE OF ♂

Mars embraces those creative forms that require vigor, movement, and intensity in this sign. Like Venus, he represents strong sexual energies in this station and the next. The nakshatra name, Phalguni, is a reference to the generative organ, the phallus in its primeval form as a sign of creativity. As this asterism signals the genitals of the constellation Leo, Mars in this position acts as the inseminator par excellence. Once more, we must not limit this to libidinal drives in a purely somatic sense, but remain open to vast creative potentials in this same light. Here the martial act is the penetration of the earth by the plow and the planting of seeds. He shows us fresh perspectives and is interested in innovation.

THE PRESENCE OF ♃

Jupiter is well fed in this station. There are strong wealth signifiers here, as well as great potentials in business and commerce. By and large the Sun fares better in this position as a teacher and guide; his fires capable of burning excess in a way unfamiliar to Jupiter. Like the other benefic, this is a placement of cornucopia. If this station resembles a fruit tree, Jupiter's presence is one of massive growth and possibility. He is a farmer, and his produce is rich in large squash and melons. This Jupiter may be quite fond of gardening and those earthy forms of wisdom becoming more and more lost in the modern world.

THE PRESENCE OF ♄

The planet of limitations efficiently uses resources here. If the benefits bring bountiful cornucopias then the malefics bring regiment and sustainability. Hedonism remains an ever-present factor with this station and the next, though, Saturn and Mars are curiously capable of transmuting these creative potentials into more structured endeavors. Though the bounty may not yield quantity in like manner, there is much to be said for qualitative influence. In this way, Saturn may become an excellent writer, critic, and modeler in this station, as his great powers of limitation are brought to bare among the substances of creative potential.

12.

Treasure of the Pyramid II / Marriage from Another Side

Precessed Tropical Coordinates:
20° 47' Virgo–4° 07' Libra

MANZIL

Al Sarfa 'The Changing of Time' 'The Changer'
Tropical Zodiac: 21° 25' Leo–4° 17' Virgo
Asterism: Beta Leonis (Denebola)
Ibn Arabi: ض (Dah)
The Second Heaven, the Sphere of Jupiter, the Abode of Musa (Moses), The Knowing
Picatrix: Image of a man and a dragon fighting one another. Talisman for the separation of lovers. Spirit name is Abdizu. Fashion out of black lead and suffumigate with asafoetida and lion hair. For the increase of harvests, destruction of riches and of ships, and for the improvement of allies, officials, captives, and servants.
Liber Lunæ: Face of the Moon. Love, society, and goodness.
Agrippa: Spirit name is Abdizuel. Prosperity in harvests.
Al Buni: ل (Lam)
Make implements of war, bear weapons, and ride horses. Do not craft things, treat illness, or engage in spiritual workings. Those born here will have a harsh

nature and be quick to anger. Will be disliked and
face much gossip. Strong personality. Nutmeg.

IBN AL HATIM: For enmity and destruction. Spirit
name is Adbhisha.

AL ASHRAF: Nutmeg.

SOLOMONIC RING (CUNNING MAN): Dragon's
blood incense. Spirit names are Qerminat, Baralama,
Canempria, and Coriet. For the purposes of making
a dragon appear in the air.

NAKSHATRA

Uttara Phalguni 'SECOND PART OF THE BED'
'HAMMOCK'

ASTERISM: Beta Leonis (Denebola)
TEMPERAMENT: Fixed, Human
CASTE: Warrior
DIRECTION: East
MOTIVATION: Moksha
ANIMAL: Male Cow/Bull
SOUNDS: Tay, Too, Pa, Pe
TREE: *Ficus Microcarpa* (Indian Laurel)
This tree is similar to the Peepal with similar medicinal
characteristics. The bark decoction of this tree can
treat burn wounds. The people who belong to this
constellation may suffer from back-pain, neuro-
ailments, bleeding, etc.

VIMSHOTTARI: Sun
DEITY: Aryama (Deity of the Morning Sun, Partnership)
SHAKTI: Power to give prosperity.
TAITTIRIYA BRAHMANA: "Achieving the beautiful
woman needs strength and wealth to be wish-fulfill-
ing" Deity is Bhaga (reverse from previous nakshatra).

BRIHAT SAMHITA: "will be mild, cleanly, modest, heretical, generous and learned; will be dealers in grains; will be wealthy, virtuous and in the company of princes."

TIBETAN: *Wo*. Grandmother. Lady of the Sun. Sensualist. Joyful and happy. Trustworthy, Intelligent, Mental Health. Lively character, Voluptuousness. Popularity. Poor appetite.

XIU

Yi 'WINGS'

UNEVEN TROPICAL ZODIAC: 14° Virgo–3° Libra (6–27 September)

ASTERISM: Alpha Crateris (Alkes), Nu Hydrae, Delta Crateris, Theta Crateris

SKY QUADRANT: Vermillion Bird of the South

PLANET: Mars

ANIMAL: Serpent

ARTLEY: Serpent is much like the dragon but more restrained and refined. Admires subtlety. Elegance of line. Will ride others to the top of the social ladder. Knowledge rather than fact. Truthful, but not averse to double-dealing. Fond of scandal. Aptitude for research, detective work, or academia. Powerful sensuality. The Emperor would give speeches during this time.

ELEMENT: Fire

MATANGA SUTRA: Offering of shark. Those born here abide by precepts.

PGM/GREEK

Asp, 'A WIND-CREATING SOUND.'
DEITY: Hymenaeus
(alternatively, Themis)

PROTO-SINAITIC/HIEROGLYPH

Zayn, Zanab 'COWHIDE AND TAIL'

WORDS

Sensual, Lower Regions, Valley of Personality, Priapus and His Retinue, End of the Stage, The Great Performance/Curtain Drop, Hidden Decorum, Rippling, Wisdom Found in the Vineyard, Library of Leaves, Expansion, Lest We Forget, Holding Dearly, The End of Something Lovely, 'I Heard it Through the Grape Vine'.

We have arrived at the end of constellation Leo. There is a culmination of sorts here. The Arab constellation of the lion or *Al Asad* figured much more prominently than the smaller Greek one. With that it was also much larger in scale. As we have described, the process that has unfolded is one of desire moving through the lion's body. First we begin with the mouth/eyes and raw appetite at the ninth station, moving next into the two hearts of inner passion at the tenth station, and then into the first inklings of love and sexuality at the lion's groin in the previous one. Here we have arrived at the second place of marriage, wherein full consummation occurs. Desire here becomes refined. The Arabic image of a man fighting a dragon is quite apt, as the stellar connection to Hydra persists into the ending asterisms of the lion and the serpent's tail. Past the initial stages of libidinal urges found in the previous station, we arrive at the point of reckoning with them. This may even involve battling them, and at times their cultivation and rarefaction.

The process of the lion and the serpent is one of creative unfolding at large. Like the stages of an alchemical process, raw matter is treated and consequently refined into complete works of art. Once more, creativity is not entirely different from marriage, relational, or sexual processes more broadly. It is a back-and-forth motion, the writhing of a serpent, sexual union, and the like, which marks these stations in their creative capacity. Whether with another human being or the many forms and minds of this world, here these confluences find full consummation. It is a marriage from both sides and the perspective born of it. Though we do not find the same intensity of energy as the previous lunar station, we do become increasingly adept at its shaping and molding into practical manifestations of the desire-energy.

If we observe this process as one of building, here we begin constructing the second half of our pyramid, making for a strong and everlasting configuration. Notions of familial structures emerge here once more as these are the lived organizations which perpetuate human life through creativity. It must be remembered that procreation and the creative impulse is what sustains all life at the most fundamental level. Though this station and the previous one are often gendered into male/female dynamics, more often it is useful to frame them through the notion of coupling or coming together. It is these familial pyramids that civilization is built upon. Consequently this station may be thought of as the eye atop the pyramid, or the complete knowledge of creative currents and how to harness them for human purposes.

PLANETARY PLACEMENTS

The Presence of the ☾

Like the previous station this is an extremely creative placement for the Moon. Here she is both generative as well as interested in the long-term sustainability of creative pursuits. As discussed above, this station is in many respects a culmination of sorts, and therefore gives her strong abilities to see endeavors come to full fruition. It is said that the marriage of Shiva and Parvati occurred here in this nakshatra. Though the Moon does not have the same access to raw generative energy as the previous one, the wedding negotiation has created a new third point or synthesis between the two. She will often find optimal results through partnership of some kind as opposed to doing things in a singular manner. Less romantic and flirtatious than the previous station, here we find an interest in longer term romantic and creative stability.

The Presence of ☿

The commercial nature of this placement is strong. There may be an interest in the selling of goods which are available in plenty. Here Mercury is the store owner and shopkeeper of markets dealing in exotic flares and the like. They may also be quite knowledgeable about what it is in which they are selling. This station focuses more on the acquisition of knowledge and information than the previous one. Consequently their emphasis on the arts tends more towards the niche, intellectual, and literary. If the previous stations produced more dancers with its somatic, energetic movement practices, here we find Mercury as writer and musician; or those creative endeavors which rely on more technical systems. They may be quite the intellectual in this sign; literary aficionado and the like.

THE PRESENCE OF ♀

The richness of this station lends itself well to Venusian principles. Though this is indeed a generative place, it is also one of harvest, and it is implicit in both this station and the last that the build up of these energies will eventually die down. Here she possesses more restraint in her utilization of creative force. It is that much more acute and less scattered. Venus works well with others in this sign, capable of negotiation, business dealings, and even political machinations. Perhaps more than the artist on the front line, here she is an art director or stage manager overseeing the whole of the production.

THE PRESENCE OF THE ☉

The Sun has completed his duties of generation and foreshadows the fall to come. This is the movement of the literal Sun, at least in the northern hemisphere, as the crops are ready to be harvested and processed. This region describes both generation as well as consumption, giving it a strong dual-like quality, capable of restraint in ways less familiar to the previous leonine stars. He is the mature spouse or partner here, capable of guiding processes and directing units towards beneficial ends. The nakshatra is associated with the deity Aryaman, who is solary in nature. He represents the strength of long-lasting partnership as well as fatherhood more broadly. In this way, we may see the Sun here as one of maturity and benevolence.

THE PRESENCE OF ♂

Like the Sun, Mars holds certain connotations of masculinity and fatherhood here. Once more this need not be gendered nor pigeonholed, but rather a role capable of being filled by those of said disposition. Unlike the maturation of the Sun, he may act more as a temptor of the order in this position, if not for the very ends of artistic subversion and the like. As this station holds strong ophidian referents, Mars acts as the venom and the constriction capable of forging long term bonds as well as eroding those already on shaky grounds. Consequently he may be the temptation and also the motivation to move further and to improve.

THE PRESENCE OF ♃

Continuing with the image of the fruit tree, Jupiter comprehends the mysteries of cultivation and harvest as he works towards transforming the bountiful growth. He is similarly capable of harnessing the powers of generation as well as those in decline. Once more, this is not a never-ending abundance that continues to grow unencumbered. There is a distinct knowledge of pleasure and the lack of it, as Jupiter understands the nature of growth for the purposes of surplus and sustainability.

THE PRESENCE OF ♄

This placement often signifies a critical mind, capable of strong intellectual activity, discernment, as well as the sometimes overly practical sensibility. Born from the materiality of this station alongside the criticality of Saturn, this is a placement of long term bonds and creative endeavors of a lifetime. He sees many of his agricultural characteristics come to life here as leader of the farm. As we have seen with the malefics in this station pairing, they tend to bode well as their limiting functions work alongside abundance and generation. Growth for the sake of growth is not always of benefit, even though we seem to wish for it regardless. Longer-term pursuits demand the added discipline; the medicine that malefics can oftentimes bring. Both Saturn and Mars function well in this position as cullers of excess in a place of great fertility. If abided by, the end result may be great works of immense balance and harmony, the rewards of intentional refinement as opposed to those of mindless hedonism.

13.

Whistling Hand / Time-of-Day

Precessed Tropical Coordinates:
4° 07' Libra–17° 27' Libra

MANZIL

Al Awwa 'THE BARKING DOG' 'THE BARKER'
TROPICAL ZODIAC: 4° 17' Virgo–17° 08' Virgo
ASTERISM: Beta Virginis (Zavijava)
IBN ARABI: ل (Lam)
THE THIRD HEAVEN, THE SPHERE OF MARS, THE
 ABODE OF HARUN (AARON), THE VICTORIOUS
LIBER LUNÆ: Face of Saturn. Love and joining
 together.

AGRIPPA: Spirit name is Jazeriel. Good for benevolence, gain, voyages, harvests.

PICATRIX: Image of a man with an erection desiring a woman. Talisman for curing impotence and bringing men and women together. Spirit name is Azerut. Man is fashioned from red wax and woman from white wax. Suffumigate with amber and lignum aloes and wrap in white silk washed with rosewater. For increase in trade and profit, increase in harvests, for good travels, for the completion of buildings, freedom of captives and binding of nobles.

AL BUNI: م (Meem)

Inflame passions and bring men and women together sexually. Embark on studies and learning. Do not craft precious stones. Do not fight enemies or dispute. Those born here are fortunate, find wealth, and are fond of learning. Strong desires. Helpful people with a pleasing demeanor. Frankincense.

IBN AL HATIM: Spirit name is Asarub. For sexual excitation.

AL ASHRAF: Saffron and pepper.

NAKSHATRA

Hasta 'THE HAND'
ASTERISM: Delta Corvi (Algorab), Gamma Corvi (Gienah), Epsilon Corvi (Minkar)
TEMPERAMENT: Quick, Divine
CASTE: Merchant
DIRECTION: South
MOTIVATION: *Moksha*
ANIMAL: Female Buffalo
SOUNDS: Pu, Sha, Naa, Tha
TREE: *Jasminum Auriculatum* (Jasmin)

Jasmine plants are grown in compounds, gardens and
parks. Jasmine leaves are used for jaw-pain, mouth-
boils and anemia. Jatyadi Oil, made from its flowers,
is used on wounds that are having trouble healing.

VIMSHOTTARI: Moon

DEITY: Savitur, God of the Sun and Awakener

SHAKTI: Power to place what we are seeking in our
hands.

TAITTIRIYA BRAHMANA: "The hand of the quickener
needs inspiration to attain objectives"

BRIHAT SAMHITA: "will be thieves, dealers in elephants,
charioteers, chief ministers, painters, merchants and
dealers in pod-grains; learned in the *Śāstras* and of
bright appearance."

TIBETAN: *Mezhi.* Messenger. Knowledge. When the
Moon is benefic: Courageous, learned, enthusiastic,
and endowed with an entrepreneurial spirit. Wealth
in the second half of life. When the Moon is malefic:
Pitiless, shameless, and cruel.

XIU

Zhen 'CHARIOT'

UNEVEN TROPICAL ZODIAC: 4°–23° Libra (28
September–16 October)

ASTERISM: Delta Corvi (Algorab), Gamma Corvi
(Gienah), Epsilon Corvi (Minkar)

SKY QUADRANT: Vermillion Red Bird of the South

PLANET: Mercury

ANIMAL: Worm

ARTLEY: This is the silkworm. All yang things are considered genial to the silkworm. It is a sign of industry
and its product one of refinement, delicacy, and
virtue. These worms are sometimes eaten in dried

form and are considered a delicacy. It is considered to be an extremely auspicious day. The Chariot which transports tributes from foreign land to the Emperor. Travel of all kinds and vehicles. Fortunate returns on business. Accumulation of wealth.

ELEMENT: Water

MATANGA SUTRA: Offering of panic grass. Those born here are thieves.

GEOMANCY

TANNERY: Caput Draconis

AL MAWṢILĪ: Via

PGM/GREEK

Ibex, 'A COERCIVE SOUND.'
DEITY: Helios (Sol)
(alternatively, Apollo or Hermes)

PROTO-SINAITIC/HIEROGLYPH

Kaf, Kap, 'HAND' 'PALM'

WORDS

Crack-Open, Whistling and Whittling, Through-Time, Ingestion, The Full Moon, Industrious, Trickery, Grasping/To Grasp, Skill, Awareness, Silver Tongued, Presentation, Intertextual, Cleanliness, Humming, Trimming Down, Little Bits, Pattern Recognition, Dovetailing, Semblances, Persuasion, Gift of Gab, The Cross-Roads.

The Arabic magical imagery associated with this station is somewhat infamous for its overt sexual qualities. Due to the previous station's phallic imagery, it is sensible to propose that the stars of Leo are the root of this talismanic imagery. In addition to this, the previous two stations deal with exactly the subject of sexual union. It is the tropical and sidereal division that has broken up the original unity of these meanings and magical uses. The process of translation from the nakshatras to the manzils, as well as the eventual adoption of the stations into the Latin West, has continued to scatter these images into deeper and deeper obscurity. It is not our intention to invalidate the magical processes of either method, only to more clearly establish these same chains of transmission.

Though this lunar station does possess outright sexual qualities in the manner of the previous two, there is much to be said for the notion of exchange and communication. It is fitting that we can track the sexual imagery from one station to the other only to inquire in this place so suited to the crossroads. As the symbol of the hand is integral, we find the unfathomable quantity of handshakes across generations here as deals are made, greetings are warmed, as well as novel conflicts begun. This image may be taken far beyond the physical hands and the things we do with them. Here we find all of the intricacies of communication, commerce, transportation, and Mercurial byways; connections of every sort, symbolized through touch. In this way, we see this station as one that tracks various transmissions over time, hand to hand, mouth to mouth, and everything in between, as well as the endless game of telephone, which alters these communications.

Here we find the corvid attendants of Apollo as well as the solar chariot which pulls the Sun across the sky. By and large the stars related to this station may be found amidst those of the Crow, who in our Western constellation system, is seen riding upon the back of Hydra, along with the grail of Crater from which he drinks. We may observe the habits of crows to learn about this station. The xiu speaks of the worm as the operative animal. This is the silkworm in particular. There is a relationship with fine movements here, even outright delicate ones. Both the hand, the worm, and the crow represent fine motor functions of meticulous detail. Consequently this place is one of refinement, which it shares with the station that follows. This is a common theme for many of the asterisms with proximity to Virgo. As stars of cunning, transaction, commerce, cultivation, and sophistication, all art forms are relevant. More to the point of dexterity, we find here the detailed mechanisms in accomplishing great works. Unlike other stations, which emphasize artistic inspiration more than execution, here we find technical know-how of an exacting nature. In all reality, it is the entirety of the process from inspiration to execution.

PLANETARY PLACEMENTS

The Presence of the ☾

The Moon here is crafty. She resembles the crow, a prominent symbol for this station. Her qualities are those of heightened intelligence, communication abilities, and dexterous movements of all kinds. Many forget that the Moon holds mercantile associations. Another quality often neglected in regards to the Moon is her penchant for travel (though, not in this book!). The symbol of the hand emphasizes exchange; not exclusively in a financial context yet it must not be overlooked. The symbol of the chariot is also prominent. Therefore the Moon is excellent here at matters that deal with commerce, movement, and exchange more broadly. Though at times there are associations with thieves (as the hand can also steal), it is important to emphasize a morally neutral quality. Whether these dealings will be honest is of a different nature, and may be examined elsewhere. This station also has a connection with oracles, prophecy, and divination. The nakshatra deity is one of awareness and illumination. She may be quite intelligent and witty in her ways.

The Presence of ☿

As this lunar station is perhaps the most mercurial among the lunar zodiac, this placement is of an exalted quality. They are adept in commercial transactions and movements of money. Along with business skills there is a natural talent for hand movements of the finest details. As both this station and Mercury symbolize the hands we find intricate works of detail here. Whether written, sewn or otherwise, this is a placement for all things particular. There is also an element of prophecy and divination here as well. Mercury as an information gatherer slips through tiny keyholes and the like. This capacity may range from sleuth to scientist yet the brilliance of specificity and exacting quality is almost unmatched. If taken towards the so-called darkside, their skill in thievery will be just as cunning. Mercury is silver-tongued here. Immensely persuasive and skilled in word play, they will use language as a powerful tool for whatever their end.

The Presence of ♀

Like Jupiter, there are strong wealth signifiers with this position. Benefics in this station may indeed tend towards the luxurious, as the solar-signifiers point to things which shine and call attention. As an artisan, she works in fine handiwork and items of great beauty and expense. Here she is perhaps more the owner and connoisseur as opposed to the maker, although this is not exclusively so. In relationships she tends toward variety, having both friendships and lovers from different walks of life, and the like. By and large, Venus is pragmatic, and follows the pathways of what gets the job done.

The Presence of the ☉

This station holds strong solar symbolism as the chariot of Helios is found here. The image of the crow is also solary in nature as they are attendants to the god Apollo. It is also the nakshatra deity Savitur that likens the Sun to this station, as he is related to the process of illumination and coming to understanding. Here we see the image of the hand once more, as the notion of 'grasping' something goes beyond the physical act. Therefore the Sun is extremely intelligent in this position. It is not purely in the sense of rational intelligence, as this station is also intimately linked to visionary experiences of all kinds. This position mirrors something of the Oracle of Delphi. The Sun comes into instantaneous clarity. As a sign of great spirit he sees much brilliance here.

The Presence of ♂

There is a magical quality to this placement wherein Mars becomes a master illusionist, performer, and worker of strangeness. The planet of passion often moves towards aesthetic ends. The wide set of technical skills found in this station allow him to craft and forge with skill and precision. He must be wary of these skills, especially the power of persuasion, in his wheelings and dealings. Without knowing it he may find himself taking advantage or perhaps holding elitist tendencies.

The Presence of ♃

Jupiter makes for a financial guru, counselor, or coach. He is skilled in the art of connecting intellectual concepts, networking, and commerce, as well as those practices which involve communication and speech. He may be quite the big talker here; known for his distinct voice and abilities to bring people together. This is a strong business and political placement for Jupiter, as well as one which emphasizes great wealth potentials while maintaining honest practices.

The Presence of ♄

Though this station has a penchant for quick movements and ways of going about things, Saturn's slower pace brings methodical examinations useful for long-term sustainability. At the level of skill sets, this is a placement that highlights mastery of the highest order; not necessarily leading to mountainous wealth but assuredly immense quality. As he is not necessarily partial to the solar-order, he forges pathways of darkness and journeys into hidden realms. This is a Saturn of magic and the occult, but also clandestine operations and suspicious political machinations. If this is the station of the handshake, Saturn in this position reveals the deals that might not see the light of day; for better or for worse.

14.

A Faceting Gem / The Measure of Heaven

Precessed Tropical Coordinates:
17° 27' Libra–0° 47' Scorpio

MANZIL

Al Simak 'The Unarmed'
Tropical Zodiac: 17° 08' Virgo–0° Libra
Asterism: Alpha Virginis (Spica)
Ibn Arabi: ن (Noon)
The Fourth Heaven, the Sphere of the Sun, the Abode of Idris (Enoch, Hermes), The Light
Liber Lunæ: Face of Jupiter/Mars. For love, but also adversity/evil.
Agrippa: Spirit name is Ergediel. Brings love for the

martyred, cures illness, good for sailors but not for land journeys.

PICATRIX: Image of a dog with its tail in its mouth. Talisman for the separation of men and women. Spirit name is Erdegal. Fashion out of red wax and suffumigate with the hair of a dog and the hair of a cat. For love of husband and wife, to heal the sick, to destroy harvests and lust, and for the benefit of kings.

AL BUNI: ن (Noon)

Mixing poisons and destructive things. Unsuitable for benefic works, buying, selling, or bartering. Those born here are unfortunate tale bearers, lying, and unpopular. Find wealth later in life. Appreciation of art and craft. Frankincense, indigo, and fennel.

IBN AL HATIM: For enmity. Spirit name is Annah.

AL ASHRAF: Frankincense and indigo seed.

SOLOMONIC RING (CUNNING MAN): Fresh milk. Spirit names are Origo, Beandinet, Calilut, and Fimiritis. For the purposes of making a castle appear.

NAKSHATRA

Chitra 'THE BRIGHT ONE' 'JEWEL'
ASTERISM: Alpha Virginis (Spica)
TEMPERAMENT: Soft, Daemonic
CASTE: Farmer
DIRECTION: West
MOTIVATION: *Kama*
ANIMAL: Female Tiger
SOUNDS: Pay, Po, Raa, Ree
TREE: *Aegle Marmelos* (Indian Bael)
The fruit of this tree is sweet-hot, bitter, digestive, and stimulative. It is used as a medicine for indigestion, diarrhea, and acidity. Its root, bark, and leaves are

used in Typhus/Typhoid (Enteric fever). The oil extracted from its seeds is used as a remedy. The sticky substance on the seed is used to join broken things. It is also used in drawing, painting, and coloring. Its mixture with lime powder is used as cement. This tree is a favorite of Lord Shiva and its God of worship is Lord Vishwakarma. It is believed that this tree must have been associated with the Chitra constellation because of its great ability and power.

VIMSHOTTARI: Mars
DEITY: Tvashta, Celestial Architect and Tools of Creation
SHAKTI: Power to accumulate merit in life.
TAITTIRIYA BRAHMANA: "Brilliant sensual creativity needs ingenuity for true beauty"
BRIHAT SAMHITA: "will be dealers in jewels, precious stones, fine cloths, writers and singers, manufacturers of perfumes, good mathematicians, weavers, surgeons, oculists and dealers in *Rājadhānya*."
TIBETAN: *Nakpa*. Black Bird. Good natured. Fair of face. Likes luxury and ornaments. Careful, indecisive, mind rather heavy, sordid.

XIU

Jiao 'HORN'
AKA: 'END' 'SHEEP' 'THE BLACK' 'COLORFUL PAINTING'
UNEVEN TROPICAL ZODIAC: 23° Libra 54'–4° Scorpio 34' (17–29 Oct)
ASTERISM: Alpha Virginis (Spica)
SKY QUADRANT: Azure Dragon of the East
PLANET: Jupiter
ANIMAL: Scaly Dragon

ARTLEY: The Dragon is also called a crocodile, or earth dragon. Exotic, flamboyant, extroverted. Elegant and trendy. At the forefront of fashion. Fertile imagination. Dreaming and often impractical. Mercurial. Strong and decisive. Resolute but undependable. Great interest in the supernatural and occult. Narcissistic. Ideally suited to stage and acting. Public life. Astrologically auspicious. Glory and prosperity to all who build on this day. People of letters are able to approach the Emperor. Marriage produces large numbers of children. Funerals and tombs should be avoided, though, bringing only grief. Associated with rains and floods. Buying land and construction. Great for marriage. Daemon that can transfix/hypnotize serpents with his gaze.
ELEMENT: Wood
MATANGA SUTRA: Offering of flowers. Those born here are skilled in music and adornments.

GEOMANCY

TANNERY: Conjunctio

AL MAWṢILĪ: Carcer

PGM/GREEK

He-Goat, 'A COERCIVE EMANATION FROM PERFECTION.'
DEITY: Hephaestus

PROTO-SINAITIC/HIEROGLYPH

Waw, Vaw 'Tent Peg' 'Hook'

WORDS

Bound to the Wheel, The Craft, The Forge, Artisanal, Mineral Contents and Extractions, Blueprints, Chiaroscuro, Cornerstone, Radiance, Assemblage, Apotheosis, Faceting. The Planning Board, Celestial Iron, 'It's All a Show,' Weapon's Gallery, Hand Made, The Railroad Spike, Chronicled, Refining Action, Magnificent, Stage Speak, Brilliance.

The radiance associated with the nakshatra Chitra comes from the presence of that ever shining star Spica in the hand of Virgo. Its prominence has led to its use in the positioning and measurement of the zodiac. The Chinese lunar zodiac actually begins with this star/lunar station. The Proto-Sinaitic letter refers to this station's position as a kind of tent peg or nail; something which it shares with its stellar twin Arcturus of the station that follows. Together the two stars form the stake implanted in the Earth which emanates from the celestial dimension into the soil itself. From this point of fixity, all else may be measured. In particular this is the establishment of agriculture and the domain of settled living. It is the regime of measurement and timing with which all so-called civilization is born; from calendar cycles, to food production, to building construction and all manner of orderly structure.

The image of the Virgin's hand of wheat also gives this star associations with refinement. In order for the wheat to become edible it must undergo a process of transformation. The plant is ground down into powder, mixed with water and the growth of bacteria, only to be exposed to fire in the creation of the complete edible foodstuff: bread. Archaic forms of food processing are perhaps the best example as we have maintained many of them to this very day. These same technological skills later allowed for the refining of metals and other materials. Consequently, this is a sign of production through all manner of breaking down and building back up. It is through these methods that inner essences can begin to express themselves, just as the faceting of a gemstone allows for greater brilliance.

PLANETARY PLACEMENTS

THE PRESENCE OF THE ☾

The Moon here is constantly in touch with processes of refinement. She is quite capable of working towards the 'essence' of a thing. Here the Moon understands how to extract and utilize particular parts for whatever end is desired. More often than not this lunar station is related to artistic pursuits; yet less often in loose and expressive ways and more so in ways that deal with calculation, measure, and precision. Like Venus, she is a designer and planner of beautiful works. Her skills may be many, as this is a placement of talent, particularly related to artistic pursuits. As Spica is considered to be jewel-like, this is a Moon of adornment. Even as we witness her real life night time travel, she would seem to be glimmering with gems as Spica rests near to her silvery light. Consequently, this is a placement of sophisticated tastes and luxurious items. She appreciates fine works of craft and all manner of delicate skill.

The Presence of ☿

Mercury in this lunar station finds power in words and speech, with a particular emphasis on the beauty of language and the heights of communication. Here they are well skilled in writing and speech. This station holds an ideal balance for Mercurial tendencies as it is simultaneously analytical and creative. More than most, this is a placement for Mercury as a poet in the traditional sense. Here they use values of time, measure, and structure. Similarly we may find them as a musician also using measure, mathematics, and scientific observation more broadly towards aesthetic ends.

The Presence of ♀

This is a strong placement for the planet of artistic refinement as it shares much with the lunar station at hand. The beauties attained here are of a high level of sophistication and skill, as aesthetics reach marvelous heights. She may hold a presence of a similar manner: beauty, elegance, and composure; all ingredients necessary for precision in an aesthetic sense. There is an inclination towards material wealth and finer things here. This is a high fashion Venus if ever there was one. She may be a great designer with the keenest of eyes. There is virtually no art form that this placement is not able to excel at when functioning at her prime. Like Jupiter, this is a most auspicious place for a benefic to reside.

The Presence of the ☉

The star Spica has often signaled the beginnings of the harvest season as the Sun moves into fall and the leaves begin to yellow. Grain is plucked or cut from the ground.

This act of severing begins the process of transformation into something edible or usable. This lunar station, and Spica more broadly, function in this manner. Here he acts much like an artist. Receiving from the imagination, he transforms the message through some medium or tool into that which is of use. This must not always be taken literally, or with an overly utilitarian mindset. Beauty and art are also of utility.

THE PRESENCE OF ♂

The deity associated with this nakshatra is Tvasta, a god of planning and architecture but also one who is involved in the crafting of weaponry. There is an affinity here born from this same refining process. Consequently here we find all of those technologies powered through martial effort: engines, weapons, and all manner of heavy industrial processes. This is a Mars who relies heavily on the powers of scientific observation and the like. If not explicitly so, he may be involved in the creative process through technical means. There is a striving towards perfection with this placement that is never fully realized.

THE PRESENCE OF ♃

Here Jupiter carries himself in beautiful and resonant ways. There might be a strong emphasis or desire for fine things and the acquisition of material wealth. The planet of abundance has an appreciation for luxury and quality here. He is well fed in this sign and knows what he must do to perpetuate this abundance. Jupiter speaks to all manner of elite and refined crowds. All in all, this is a positive placement for abundance and opportunity.

The Presence of ♄

In this station, we find Saturn as an agriculturalist and master of ceremonies. This is a placement for accomplishing great works which might take a lifetime, as it is a sign of masterpieces and ultimate sophistication. He is a composer of intricate systems, blueprints, and buildings that will stand for many lifetimes. Saturn in this position takes something of the mind of a great pyramid. Strong in his foundations and deeply in touch with Earthen cycles, he is an architect of existence, planner of civilizations, and ever-wise in culture. The nakshatra deity Tvashtha is sometimes thought of as an architect, or, at the very least, embodying architectural energies. Saturn takes on demiurgic qualities as a planner of cities in this sign. Civil architecture and the like go well with this lunar station, as the individual vision of the artist or designer goes beyond themselves into their broader society. The outer planets express this quality more so than the inner ones.

15.

The Long Breath/A Feather, Windswept, Metal-Sharpened

Precessed Tropical Coordinates:
0° 47' Scorpio–14° 07' Scorpio

MANZIL

Al Ghafr 'Hair of the Lion's Tail' 'The Covering'
Tropical Zodiac: 0° Libra–12° 51' Libra
Asterism: Iota Virginis (Syrma)
Ibn Arabi: ر (Ra)
The Fifth Heaven, the Sphere of Venus, the Abode of Yusuf (Joseph), The Form Giver
Picatrix: Image of a seated man holding scrolls. Talisman for the acquisition of friendship and good things. Spirit name is Achalich. Fashion with ink and parchment and suffumigate with frankincense and nutmeg. For digging wells, to seek underground treasure, separate husband and wife, impede travelers, to scatter enemies from your area.
Liber Lunæ: Face of Mars. For adversity and evil.
Agrippa: Spirit name is Ataliel. Digging and extracting treasure, discord.
Al Buni: س (Sin)
Begets love, amicability, and ease. Benevolence from kings. Suitable for cures and antidotes for deadly poisons. Prepare precious stones, spiritual healing,

making talismans. Those born here are unfortunate and treacherous. Benefits from teachers. Frankincense.
IBN AL HATIM: Ending enmity. Spirit name is Aqalidh.
AL ASHRAF: Frankincense
SOLOMONIC RING (CUNNING MAN): Intestines. Spirit names are Gribery, Daliaremerat, Fracaday, and Georim. For the purposes of having one's money return after it is spent.

NAKSHATRA

Swati 'THE SWORD' 'BLADE OF GRASS' 'CORAL'
ASTERISM: Alpha Bootis (Arcturus)
TEMPERAMENT: Mutable, Divine
CASTE: Butcher
DIRECTION: North
MOTIVATION: *Artha*
ANIMAL: Male Buffalo
SOUNDS: Ru, Ray, Ra, Ta
TREE: *Terminalia Arjuna* (Arjun)
This is a big evergreen tree with wide branches and a vast shed. It is fond of the banks of rivers and streams. It is also grown in gardens, parks, and roadsides. Its wood is used for making agricultural tools, building material, small boats, rafts, Ply-wood and water-tubs. The bark of this tree is used for rearing tussar silk-worms. The bark is also used as a medicine for heart disease and for the joining of fractured bones. The extract of its fresh leaves is useful for ear pain.
VIMSHOTTARI: Rahu
DEITY: Vayu (God of Wind and Breath), Saraswati, Hanuman
SHAKTI: Power to scatter like the wind.

TAITTIRIYA BRAHMANA: "The far-blowing wind needs to drift, for imperfection"

BRIHAT SAMHITA: "will delight in keeping birds, deer, horses; will be grain merchants; dealers in beans; of weak friendship; weak, of abstemious habits and skilled tradesmen."

TIBETAN: *Sari*. Goddess of the Wind. High Celestial Vision. Charitable and generous. Wise child, filial duty, scholar. Soft-spoken, in control of himself. Fair minded and modest. Honest trader. Suffers from thirst.

XIU

Kang 'NECK'

AKA: 'SHADOW'

UNEVEN TROPICAL ZODIAC: 4° 34' Scorpio–15° 05' Scorpio (29 October–8 November)

ASTERISM: Iota Virginis (Syrma), Kappa Virginis, Lambda Virginis

SKY QUADRANT: Azure Dragon of the East

PLANET: Mercury

ANIMAL: Sky Dragon

ARTLEY: This is a winged dragon. It presides over the vaults of Heaven. It is said to purge one of their sins. The scaly dragon is also capable of this. Guards and supports the mansions of the Gods and prevents them from falling. Astrologically inauspicious. Building on this day causes the eldest son not to succeed. Doing things the next ten days will be disastrous. Funerals and marriages spell disaster. Patron deity of alchemy. Mansion of illness, considered Unlucky. The release of prisoners and animals.

ELEMENT: Water/Metal

MATANGA SUTRA: Offerings of barley mixed with butter. Those born here are good at calculations.

GEOMANCY

TANNERY: Puer

AL MAWṢILĪ: Carcer

PGM/GREEK

Baboon, 'A COERCIVE EMANATION FROM PERFECTION.'
DEITY: Aeolus

PROTO-SINAITIC/HIEROGLYPH

Peh, Pasu, 'CORNER' 'TO TURN'

WORDS

Bird's Eye View, Wind, Heights, The Decision to Change Directions, Mountain Peaks, *Al A'raf*, A Staircase of Glass, Perching Above, Form, Independence, Invert, High Mindedness, A Bird Who Nests in Heaven and Hunts in Hell, Break With Tradition, Cornerstone, Panopticon, Tall Countenance, Elevations, Alchemy and Transformation.

This nakshatra is the abode of the wind/breath deity. Commonly symbolized by a plant bending over through the force of air, it represents both the tests we face and the strength built through facing them; primarily as unique individuals. For the stalk of the plant grows stronger in not bending to the power of the air. Arcturus' far north position above the ecliptic gives many of these associations. Distance, leaving for a faraway place, movement, but more often than not it is where we individuate and leave the crowd behind. Perhaps choosing something for the depths of our souls as opposed to what is desired of us.

Svati, as sword, Arcturus, Guardian of the Bear, act as Cherubim to the Edenic Garden, barring those who have forsaken unity. Arcturus reminds us of the price we must pay to stand on our own. Without the crowd, our body is susceptible to the elements. We stand vulnerable. Similar to the nakshatra Mrigashira, the Head of Orion—another representative of the wild—Arcturus guards the sacred wilderness of the north; the undying ones and their resplendent mysteries. To step foot in this distant land is to forgo the horizon and the chattering voices that linger there. The presence of the headless body mirrors Svati's sword in the act of separation. As we are speaking of breath/air, we must continuously engage so that our body and mind do not divide. Akin to the plough of the north, it must never cease to turn lest the cosmos fall into ruin. Not only is this toil necessary, but enemies are forever afoot (there is a wolf who is thought to gnaw on the plough). To stand and persist can be grueling. Yet the reward for that endurance is ever so precious.

PLANETARY PLACEMENTS

The Presence of the ☾

With such a strong connotation of distance, the Moon's presence here allows for great leaps and bounds in many fields of discovery whether they be creative, scientific, or otherwise. She is adventurous and a natural trailblazer. She may manifest quite literally as someone who travels far away or leaves behind their homeland with (usually) great distance. What is meant by this is that 'distance' from where one began may also connote creative, intellectual, and spiritual distance. The common theme here is a far-reaching movement away from one's origins into a new dimension of existence. As the abode of the wind deity, this lunar station mirrors this element in its ability to sweep afar, scatter, and glide from place to place. The symbol of the blade of grass and of the sword mirrors the Arabic associations with scholars and scrolls of written material. The Moon here, in all of her abilities to intelligently move between dimensions resembling air flow, is naturally gifted in creative pursuits; in particular those which involve the narrative element seen by this allusion (to the pen and its *feathery* quill...). To possess the 'elevated' vision of this station she better grasps larger arcs of story and therefore time in general. This bird's eye view makes her a visionary of great wonder; yet, this vast breadth does naturally come with its own set of challenges. Being of such an airy nature, she may find trouble with things traditionally thought of as 'lunary.' For example comfort, familiarity, groundedness, and consistency.

The Presence of ☿

Mercury's placement in this lunar station often finds much similarity with that of the Moon, yet the emphasis is more heavily placed on intellectual and even rational elements. The ability to enact abstract calculations through a variety of dimensional and planar paradigms is strong here. Similar to a Jupiter placement within this station, they may be in the business of preserving information at a heightened intellectual standard or abode. The star Arcturus, forever the great mountain top dweller and wisdom keeper, witnesses the Mercurial heights in the act of intellectual grandeur. Striving towards 'objectivity' and seemingly immutable facts, is a pursuit quite familiar to this placement. The danger, as with much of those found in this station, is that something is perceived as so rarified, so elevated, that it is no longer subject to 'grounded' examinations and scrutiny.

The Presence of ♀

Love and relation atop the mountain has limited options for growth and change. Similar to the Moon, Venus struggles to cultivate through warmth and moisture that which she knows so well. Instead, and perhaps typically to her benefit, relationships and the pursuit of love take on far-reaching consequences here; both literally and metaphorically. Also, like the Moon, her relationships, romantic or otherwise, may be with those in faraway places and foreign lands. If this is less literal, sometimes she will be inclined towards values, aesthetics, and all-around artistic sensibilities of an 'alien' nature; vision gliding on gusts of wind into far-off dimensions and new territories. The planet Venus may be hindered in her ability to connect amidst deep martial urges to cut new ground and drive obsessions forward. Through the airy nature of this lunar station, Venus' ability to connect and cultivate through consistent and grounded effort becomes subsumed under a desire to explore and move in more radical and independent ways.

The Presence of the ☉

With so much focus on the elevated and windswept regions of Arcturus, it is important to return here to this station's connection to the stars of Virgo found in both the Arabic and the Chinese systems. Per the seasonal round, the Sun begins its Fall here in the Northern Hemisphere as the plants move towards harvest and the yellowing begins. Iota Virginis, or Syrma as it is called, is seen as the trailing garment of the Virgin's body as well as the verdant neck of the Emerald Dragon that is Virgo. As the most 'earthly' manifestation of the heights of Arcturus described, we still may observe the air moving through textile; yet, in this instance, it is one of wave-form along the clothing line and that of daily practice. Distinct from the heights yet still of them, this emphasis falls more on the whisper of the air amidst our daily chores and duties. It is something of a beckoning towards the other world and its callings. so foreign to our perhaps constrained sensibilities. The Sun here may feel this very call from among the doldrums. Unlike others who simply cannot hear it or even those who would choose to ignore it, the presence of the Sun brings illumination to those callings far away (once more, in all of the ways we may speak of distance). He has an innate connection to the sound of this calling as well as having the capacity to answer it. The strongly independent nature of this station combined with the Sun's illumination is capable of eliciting alchemical transmutations from the most mundane, such as the stereotypical Virgoan labor of laying the laundry out to dry, into the most heightened and visionary experiences in art and life.

THE PRESENCE OF ♂

Martial drives do quite well in this station. We see him here in his presence as the eagle. To have Mars in this lunar station may be thought of in this light, embodying many of the qualities of this creature as an apex hunter. For one, we have the far-seeing and penetrating sight capable of accurate perception over great distances. We see the power of flight, of course, capable of soaring to the greatest heights with ease as well as descending to the terrestrial dimension with similar ease and deadly force. Mars in this placement is perhaps better than any other at traversing the great distances as well as the more mundane manifestations found in this station. The eagle's dexterity and abilities in handling minute details over vast spans are a perfect example of this powerful position.

THE PRESENCE OF ♃

Taking on a similar presence to Mercury and Mars, Jupiter in this lunar station soars as if an eagle, yet for the imperative of knowledge and information. Wisdom articulated from the heights may still have a profound impact on that which is 'below.' As we have seen time and time again, these polarities and directional sensibilities are inextricably linked and cannot be reduced to hierarchical simplicities. Though Jupiter may indeed take the form of the storm god on high dictating laws from the elevated and inscrutable regions, there is always the potential for grounded knowledge with awareness and priority. The tendency for soaring abstraction and heightened revelation remains strong with this placement. The desire to travel, both physically and perhaps metaphysically to distant lands also remains strong here. Yet the question persists in him when he achieves such leaps and bounds; to what end? The intimate kernel of wisdom may be lost, purpose always residing 'out there.' Perhaps the greatest lesson or mystery for him may be what lay right before his eyes or right below his feet.

THE PRESENCE OF ♄

The planet of the concrete in such an airy dimension finds himself a tad precarious, though this isn't per se a negative thing. Many of the pitfalls of the other placements do not occur as easily with Saturn, as the quality of the mountain itself (distinct from those who simply dwell upon it) is apparent within him. Similar to Mercury, he may pursue 'objectivity' in inscrutable facts and information. That same capacity for far-reaching abstract thought remains present. At the same time, it is Saturn's weight in contrast to the airy planets such as Mercury and Jupiter that may find greater ease in grounding the windswept revelations of this station into hard-earned achievements and systematic structures.

16.

The Replicating Branch/Rain-Light

Precessed Tropical Coordinates:
14° 07' Scorpio–27° 27' Scorpio

MANZIL

Al Zubana 'The Claws of the Scorpion'
Tropical Zodiac: 12° 51' Libra–25° 42' Libra
Asterism: Alpha Librae (Zubenelgenubi), Beta Librae (Zubeneschamali)
Ibn Arabi: ط (Ta)
The Sixth Heaven, the Sphere of Mercury, the Abode of 'Isa (Jesus), The Numberer
Picatrix: Image of man seated on a throne carrying a scale. Talisman for profits in selling merchandise. Spirit name is Azeruch. Fashion in a plate of silver and suffumigate with nice odors. For destruction of merchandise, discord between husband and wife, destruction of women, liberate captives.
Liber Lunæ: Face of the Sun. Desolation, binding.
Agrippa: Spirit name is Azeruel. For hindrances.
Al Buni: ف (Fa)
Opposite natures. Good and bad. Suffer from dog bite or bodily injury. Whoever is born here will be fortunate in what they do. Successful in business but not always legal. Chamomile.

IBN AL HATIM: For selling and buying, profits. Spirit name is Asarut.
AL ASHRAF: Chamomile and wormwood.
SOLOMONIC RING (CUNNING MAN): Intestines. Spirit names are Gribery, Daliaremerat, Fracaday, and Georim. For the purposes of having one's money return after it is spent.

NAKSHATRA

Vishaka 'THE FORKED SHAPE' 'ARCHWAY' 'POTTER'S WHEEL'
ASTERISM: Alpha Librae (Zubenelgenubi), Beta Librae (Zubeneschamali)
TEMPERAMENT: Mixed (Soft and Sharp), Daemonic
CASTE: Outcast
DIRECTION: East
MOTIVATION: Dharma
ANIMAL: Male Tiger
SOUNDS: Te, Tu, Tay, To
TREE: *Maytenus Emarginata* (Kankera)
Shrub or small tree with pale brown bark. Leaves are thick, coriaceous.
VIMSHOTTARI: Jupiter
DEITY: Indragni (Rain and Fire), Radha (Consort of Krishna)
SHAKTI: Power to achieve multiple fruits in life.
TAITTIRIYA BRAHMANA: "When light and rain couple, seeds can be harvested"
BRIHAT SAMHITA: "will grow trees yielding red flowers and red fruits; be dealers in gingelly seeds, beans, cotton, black gram and chickpeas and worshippers of Indra and Agni."

TIBETAN: *Saga*. She Who Has Power. Lower Celestial Vision. Jealous, mean, indiscreet. quarrelsome but prudent. Lively temperament. Ability and good sense, business person. Religious fear in spite of everything.

XIU

Di 'ROOT/BASE'
AKA: 'LEOPARD'S HEAD'
UNEVEN TROPICAL ZODIAC: 15° 05' Scorpio–3° Sagitarius (8–24 November)
ASTERISM: Alpha Librae (Zubenelgenubi), Beta Librae (Zubeneschamali)
SKY QUADRANT: Azure Dragon of the East
PLANET: Saturn
ANIMAL: Marten/Badger
ARTLEY: One of the Five Seers, along with weasels, hedgehogs, small deer, and snakes. These animals have to be treated with reverence and respect. If they are not well-treated, unpleasantness follows. If anyone is made ill by one of these it is difficult to find a sorcerer to exorcise them because the work is very specialized. A sorcerer for one may not be able to deal with the other. They were also depended upon to keep diseases off of farmland. Considered unlucky and brings storms and illness. Calamity through improper ritual. Deity has the power of flight and secrets of magical recipes.
ELEMENT: Earth
MATANGA SUTRA: Offerings of flowers. Born here will become a king's minister.

GEOMANCY

Tannery: Puer

Al Mawṣilī: Cauda & Caput Draconis

PGM/GREEK

Cat, 'a coercive sound.'
Deity: Dinus (Ares) (alternatively, Dike)

PROTO-SINAITIC/HIEROGLYPH

Ayin, 'Eye'

WORDS

Collaboration, Crossroads, Gathering, A Forest of Replicating Branches, Attraction–Repulsion, Shaper of Clay, Examination, Downward Funnel, One Hand in the Market and One Hand at Home, Retrieval, Evaluation, Touch, Storm Dynamics, Call and Response, Sending Away and Sending Back, Titillation, Emblematic, Cross Quarter.

Previously known as the claws of Scorpio, the relevant stars have now become the scales of Libra. Whether they are still looked at as claws, hands, or otherwise, there is enough similarity between these images to emphasize the act of weighing between two things. In this way, two of the most frequent associations with this station are those of justice and monetary exchange. We can observe how these two ideas relate to one another. Together, they form the backbone of political movements related to the stars of this place. Right action is determined through relationality and all of the things associated with it. Without the energy flow back and forth through these points of crossing, there is no generation or creation. Such is the nature of this station as the forked road, always splitting and coming back together for the sake of growth.

Like the 13th station, we find a strong emphasis on finance and commercial exchange. The primary difference between them is akin to the difference between the money handling of a salesperson and a financial speculator. The salesperson must have some investment in what they are selling, ideally even an emotional one as it inspires their drive to persist. They must persuade people of their cause and appeal to these same sensibilities. Money in the context of this station is more like that of the financial speculator. As a numbers game, or one of various odds and stats, connections are made more on the basis of data and abstract notions.

The nakshatra is multifaceted in character as well as the imagery associated with it. Here we find the forking branch, showing the inherently relational nature of the sign. The deity related to this nakshatra is a form of Agni (his primary station is the third, Pleiades) related to Indra, the deity of the storm (his primary station is the eighteenth, Antares). There is a fertilizing quality to this place as fire mixes with water; disparate elements colliding, allowing for new growth. It is the bonding together of opposites that gives this station its power. Radha, the consort and lover of Krishna, is also related to this nakshatra in a similar manner. There is much to say about the devoted lover and the challenges between her and the god. This nakshatra's relationship with the one which follows is also interesting as it is named in explicit reference to Radha, or the act of following her, Anu-Radha. Both may be expressions of love and relationality, yet often in different manners. Vishakha, this current station, is often devoted to unorthodox forms of love. This may be purely in the context of spirit and disincarnate form entirely. This may be the nun devoted to God in erotic mystical union as much as an artist fully in love with their craft. Anuradha, on the other hand, tends to emphasize more explicitly sexual and embodied forms of love.

PLANETARY PLACEMENTS

The Presence of the ☾

The Moon here functions well in partnership towards whatever ends they may be wishing to achieve. This sign is surely one of the more partner oriented along the lunar zodiac, many of its symbols being so explicitly relational. At the same time, this relationality must not be confused for an innate sense of intimacy. Though she may very well possess qualities of kindness, the relationality spoken of in this sign may also be with things beyond the regular human scope. She may fall in love with or become deeply devoted to something that is not a romantic partner. In this way, her capacity as such may go far beyond what another person is capable of reciprocating. It is important for the Moon here to find practices, often spiritual ones, wherein they may give themselves fully, and receive what is deserving of their entire devotion. The stars in question are also often spoken of in the context of political and justice oriented alignments. So much so, that she may find greater intimacy with those struggles that represent freedom and liberty in the world.

THE PRESENCE OF ☿

As far as this station is commercially interested, this may be a strong wealth and business placement. There is a natural sensibility with financial exchange here, an ability to analyze data and numbers as well as the ways in which patterns connect to one another. Mercury has strong technical abilities here as they find what goes together to make things work. This is the financier and investor par excellence, as emotion may be taken from the situation to analyze optimal results. It is frequently forgotten that the scales of Libra are one of the few mechanical devices of the zodiac. Therefore, a detached outlook becomes possible with planets in this sign, as mechanical objectivity is brought to the forefront.

THE PRESENCE OF ♀

As this is a place known for its quality of pairing it is no surprise that Venus finds a foothold here. This may be an intensely attractive placement in certain respects. She may have very little trouble finding romantic partners. Yet there are often great challenges in mismatched sentiments and the like. She may be greatly devoted to one who does not share in this same manner. As an artist and creative there are few capable of giving what she has to give in terms of passion towards her pursuit.

The Presence of the ☉

Expression becomes a means of connection in this sign; the way a branch forks outward as if a hand extended. Seasonally speaking, this is the point at which the Sun begins its deepest descent into the lower worlds, almost as if grasped and forced beneath the scorpion's body by its great claws. The relational or partner orientation of this sign emerges in the context of the Sun's singular orientation here. No longer on his own, he must acknowledge the dark 'Other,' ceding his light to that which is beyond his own. In this way, he becomes focused on whatever other it may be in intense forms of relationality. As it goes with this station, there is always the danger of hyper-fixation or devotional obsession which emerges from it. His shining of the light on the beloved may lead to his forgetting of his own, therefore as with all things here, the Sun must have his means of expression beyond the limitations of human frailty.

The Presence of ♂

Mars connects at the deepest layers of our psyche in this sign, sometimes through art, sometimes through sexuality, yet the process of connection is always marked by intense passion. He may be well versed through study and intuition on power dynamics as they play out in the lives of individuals. He is strong to this effect, as one who recognizes these subtle flows of energy; where they meet, cross, and continue past one another. Once the path of devotion has been realized, there may be no swaying him away from it. This is a Mars prone to obsession and fixation of the singular type. Darker and alternative forms of sexuality are found here in subcultures and erotic play which value binding, domination, and even raw aggression. Themes of 'dark eros' reign here.

THE PRESENCE OF ♃

This placement brings out Jupiter's more fertile elements as the nakshatra and its deity Indragni are well aligned with him; especially as a storm deity who brings rain. As a spiritual seeker or guide, he is fiercely devoted, perhaps even to the point of self-negation in this sign. This is a Jupiter who reconciles opposites, yet not without a bit of fight. To this end, his justice orientation is one of bringing back together those lovers who have been scorned. His stated purpose may very well be for the sake of love, yet, in practice, it may not feel this way to those around him.

THE PRESENCE OF ♄

There is a strange alchemical effect with Saturn in this position. One important symbol for the nakshatra is that of the potter's wheel. The transformation of raw clay into practical implements is one of his techniques here. As one who lays down limitations, his ability to mold matter comes through in this station. He is bound to the wheel here, that of his craft, and must continue pressing onward regardless of his circumstances. In the context of devotion to something, someone, and the like, there are few positions of Saturn capable of holding more long-term loyalty than this one.

17.

Wreath of Flowers / A Hare Upon the Moon's Face

Precessed Tropical Coordinates:
27° 27' Scorpio–10° 47' Sagittarius

MANZIL

Al Iklil 'The Crown of the Scorpion'
Tropical Zodiac: 25° 42' Libra–8° 34' Scorpio
Asterism: Beta Scorpii (Acrab), Delta Scorpii (Dschubba)
Belongs to the retinue of Sunday, Angel Ruqiel, and Jinn King Al Madhab
Ibn Arabi: د (Dal)
The Seventh Heaven, the Sphere of the Moon, the Abode of Adam, The Evident
Picatrix: Image of a monkey with its arms held up. Talisman for the protection of property and ones home. Spirit name is Adrieb. Fashion out of an iron seal and suffumigated with the hair of a monkey and the hair of a female mouse and wrap it in monkey skin. To make buildings stable, for sieges, to cause deceptions, for long lasting friendships. For love to last.
Liber Lunæ: Face of Venus. Tribulation, discord.
Agrippa: Spirit name is Adriel. Improvements in fortune, love endurance.
Al Buni: ف (Fa)

Urges malice and corruption. Both unnefarious things
and nefarious things are done. Do not travel or marry.
Do not do most things. Those born here are miserable and disliked. May be skilled in manipulation.
Pepper, saffron, and aloeswood.

IBN AL HATIM: Spirit names are Aryath and Adhyniab.
For expelling thieves.

AL ASHRAF: Pepper, saffron, and aromatic wood.

SOLOMONIC RING (CUNNING MAN): Hairs of
a woman. Spirit names are Facygrat, Davmilbe,
Parinilbe, and Cliody. For the purposes of gaining
love from women.

NAKSHATRA

Anuradha 'FOLLOWING RADHA' 'LOTUS'
ASTERISM: Beta Scorpii (Acrab), Delta Scorpii
(Dschubba)
TEMPERAMENT: Soft, Divine
CASTE: Worker
DIRECTION: South
MOTIVATION: *Dharma*
ANIMAL: Female Rabbit
SOUNDS: Na, Nee, Nu, Nay
TREE: *Mimusops Elengi* (Spanish Cherry)
A medium-sized evergreen tree found in tropical forests.
English common names include Spanish cherry,
medlar, and bullet wood. Its timber is valuable, the
fruit is edible, and it is used in traditional medicine.
As the trees give thick shade and its flowers emit
fragrance, it is a prized collection for gardens. The
bark, flowers, fruits, and seeds of Bakula are astringent, cooling, anthelmintic, tonic, and febrifuge.
It is mainly used for dental ailments like bleeding

gums, pyorrhea, dental caries, and loose teeth. Extracts of its flowers are used against heart diseases, leucorrhoea, and menorrhagia. The snuff made from the dried and powdered flowers is used in a disease in which a strong fever, headache, and pain in the neck, shoulders, and other parts of the body occurs. Ripened fruits are a cure for burning urination. The ripe fruit pounded and mixed with water is given to promote delivery in childbirth. A decoction of bark is used to wash the wounds.

VIMSHOTTARI: Saturn
DEITY: Mitra, God of Cooperation and Contracts
SHAKTI: Power to worship.
TAITTIRIYA BRAHMANA: "The reward of expressing love needs arousal for climax"
BRIHAT SAMHITA: "will be valiant; heads of parties; fond of the company of Sādhus, keep vehicles and grow every species of crop."
TIBETAN: *Lhatsam.* The Hand. The Friendly God, The Prosperous. Honored by the great risk taker. Fond of travel. High position in a foreign country. Magnificent head of hair, red eyelashes. Often dissatisfied and cannot tolerate hunger.

XIU

Fang 'ROOM'
AKA: 'HEAVEN'
UNEVEN TROPICAL ZODIAC: 3° Sagittarius–9 50' Sagittarius (24 November–1 December)
ASTERISM: Delta Scorpii (Dschubba), Beta Scorpii (Acrab), Pi Scorpii
SKY QUADRANT: Azure Dragon of the East
PLANET: Sun

ANIMAL: Rabbit

ARTLEY: The rabbit is a servant of an entity related to the remedy of the elixir of life in a mortar A symbol of longevity. Strongly social. Reserved and withdrawn away from people, but independent within groups. Humble, submissive, will avoid confrontation. Happiest with friends. Loves a good conversation, reading and literary pursuits. Remarkably brave when faced with danger. Excellent judge of character. Able to see deeply into people. Often gifted healers, both emotionally and physically. Astrologically brings wealth, prosperity, and family burials. Happiness, longevity and honor. Connected to the opening of closed things. Burnt Sacrifices.

ELEMENT: Varied

MATANGA SUTRA: Offerings of wine and meat. Those born here are skilled in management and sales.

GEOMANCY

TANNERY: Amissio

AL MAWṢILĪ: Cauda & Caput Draconis

PGM/GREEK

Lion, 'A WIND-CREATING SOUND.'
DEITY: Urania (alternatively, Philotes or Eros)

PROTO-SINAITIC/HIEROGLYPH

Ga, Ghain 'Side' 'Boundary' or 'Grape Processing'

WORDS

A Jester Veiled in Regalia, Perfume of the Space, Shamelessness, Intoxication, Confluence, Thickening Mind, Gathering of Ways to See, The Drunken King, Blooming Flowers, Glance Across the Room, Something Extraordinary in the Ordinary, Ecstasy, Coming Together for a Common Cause, Abundance.

As described in the previous nakshatra, both Vishakha and the current station of Anuradha are relational places more broadly; in particular for that which we call love. We now find ourselves in greater embodiment, coming together in a manner which was not as tangible before. The nakshatra's name, 'following Radha,' outlines a process not unlike the purva/uttara distinction found in other stations. We see love as a force which descends from the stars only to inevitably occupy discrete bodies. In the context of romance, this station represents the reaching of the sexual act itself. Here we are less wrapped up in the abstract devotional qualities of the previous. This is not to speak of a lack of it, only that they take on more concrete form. Of course, relationality is not limited to romance. We see the workings of friendships, business partnerships and the like here as well. In business we find the handshake which seals the deal; or perhaps the contract which binds the matter wherein the interested party may refer to it as a token of the relationship.

In this way, the nakshatra deity is appropriate as it is Mitra; a god of friendship, relationships, and contracts. This station is a crossroads. Like other parts of the solar and lunar zodiacal circles, certain regions represent boundaries between particular areas. There are solar associations here. Though we think of Libra as the beginning of this downward movement, having now reached the head of the great scorpion/serpent we have now officially entered the underworld from a solar perspective. The Chinese image of the room is also apt as this station figures as a kind of waiting place, a moment of pause between the lower and the upper worlds.

This same deity is thought to figure within the so-called Mithraic Tauroctony described in the third station of the Pleiades. If the third place is that of the great bull Taurus, here we are in the dimension of Mithras, or the hero who slays it. It is the relationship between him and the bull which outlines the traditional stars of spring and autumn equinoxes. Though precession has shifted these stars from those seasonal positions, they hold the memory of precession itself as a force capable of shifting the so-called 'fixed stars.' Between these two poles is the ongoing negotiation of the contract that is the cosmos, which must also include its erotic qualities. To say that one side is aligned to life and the other is not, is purely a hemispheric bias. Though this is the waiting room for the Sun's descent in the northern hemisphere, this is not so for those in the south.

PLANETARY PLACEMENTS

The Presence of the ☾

Both the Moon and Mercury share strong significations with this station through the Chinese animal of the rabbit. As per the crossroads nature of this place, there is rapid decision-making and movement from back and forth which is characteristic for her. More than other placements it would seem that these individuals are put before a variety of opportunities at any given time. She may have an impulsive nature, yet it is also not far from an acute sensitivity towards inspiration and artistry. The Moon may be exceptionally creative; adept at moving through life's various shapes and forms through novel solutions and the like. There may also be a strong business inclination as this station deals with transactions and contracts of all kinds. Per the crossroads nature of this Moon, sexuality plays an important role, oftentimes as a manner of erotic exchange as an extension of creative expression. Along with the Phalguni nakshatras, this placement is at the top of the list for emphasizing eros as a dominant principle.

The Presence of ☿

Once more, we may see Mercury as the rabbit of this sign, darting from place to place, as well as rapidly growing in its means of movements and modes of communication. This is a placement of exploratory intelligence, capable of finding inspiration in strange and unassuming places. Out of all of the stations, this is one of the more artistic placements for Mercury, as speech becomes song-like and poetic. This is a voice with a softer disposition, and one which has the ability to warm those of colder hearts. They prefer things of a sweeter manner here. If anything, we see Mercury's significations as 'friend' emerge; another appellation of the deity Mitra.

The Presence of ♀

Venus aligns well with this station as they share many of the same qualities. She tends towards friendship, support, and caretaker here, holding a strong concern for equality and likeness. Similarly but also of a different wavelength are the intense erotic qualities of Venus in this sign. It is challenging to see an expression of Venus here which is not distinctly sexual in manifestation. More than perhaps any other placement in the lunar zodiac this is a high sex-driven Venus. Ecstatic dances, movement, and trance may be found here. One of the lesser-discussed aspects of this station are its qualities of intoxication. We often forget that it still belongs to the constellation Scorpio, long associated with substances that alter consciousness. Her role here is one of facilitator and partaker of these ways. Pleasures which drive one to a sense of unity are surely present in this station.

The Presence of the ☉

This is a social position for the Sun as he leads groups of alternative ways in this sign. There is something of the original ethos of the hippie movement with this placement. Freedom and equality of a political nature may be found here. He holds the so-called 'golden rule;' treat others how you wish to be treated. Similarly, if nobody is being hurt then people should be allowed to express themselves as they wish to. Like Venus there may be a bonding through social intoxication. This may be through the use of substances, but it is also just as likely with art, music, and convivial gathering. As the Sun is in a position of leadership, he may find himself representing or guiding those of a similar disposition.

The Presence of ♂

This is an adventurous placement for Mars, especially in regards to sexuality. He may have many sexual partners as well as being interested in lifestyles which value sexuality as a strong priority. The Arabic image of the monkey for this station is fitting, as there is an intensity of energy capable of very real physical power and strength. Oftentimes the monkey is an image of unrestrained urges of a base nature. Yet the monkey's resemblance to human beings is a reminder of how close we are and susceptible to these forces at any given moment. As this station remains close to them, in particular around sexuality, Mars enflames desire with great passion. If attention is given to this and taken care of, like Venus he may be a great facilitator and partaker of ecstatic experience, all the more in safer ways. This same inclination naturally leads to creative interests as a means of expression for this energy. Therefore he may be quite the vibrant performer, musician, and the like.

The Presence of ♃

The deity Mitra is thought of as 'the friend,' representing one who assists and offers their hand. Though the darker sides of this may look something like a deal with the devil, Jupiter brings out the more positive quality of 'the deal.' He may be a skilled negotiator, or perhaps directly involved with laws and agreements that deal with contractual obligations. This is also one of the more creative Jupiter placements as well as philosophical. Like the lotus flower, another image of this station, he nurtures growth here through well balanced character and a strong collaborative streak.

The Presence of ♄

The nakshatra deity Mitra shares some resemblances with Saturn here as lord of contracts. Similar to his exaltation in the sign of Libra, we find Saturn acting as a judge in this position. The judge requires objective points of view and thoughtful deliberation. Unlike other placements which emphasize the raw sexual qualities of this station, Saturn here is something of a fair dispositor. Though he is largely of an asexual nature, he finds arousal in keeping things balanced between the worlds and helping to deliver authentic justice. Like Saturn in other signs of a more intoxicating quality, he may bring skepticism and renunciation around these matters as well.

18.
The Soaring Heart / Red-Ghost in the Machine

Precessed Tropical Coordinates:
10° 47' Sagittarius–24° 07' Sagittarius

MANZIL

Al Qalb 'The Heart'
Tropical Zodiac: 8° 34' Scorpio–21° 25' Scorpio
Asterism: Alpha Scorpii (Antares)

IBN ARABI: ت (Tah)
THE SPHERE OF ETHER, METEORS AND FIRE, THE SEIZER
PICATRIX: Image of a snake with its tail above its head. Talisman for the removal of fever and stomach pains. Spirit name is Egribel. Fashion out of wax and suffumigate with the horn of a stag. For vengeance, for conspiracy against kings, to build firm buildings, and to free captives.
LIBER LUNÆ: Face of Mercury. For good, binding of tongues.
AGRIPPA: Spirit name is Agibiel. Discord, sedition, conspiracy against authorities.
AL BUNI: ص (Saad)
Fortunate and watery. Rectifies corruption. Suitable for buying weapons, war equipment, and livestock. Felling trees, farming, plowing, digging up buried things, curing animals, taking purgatives, bloodletting and cupping. To be born here is to be unfortunate and have a trickish streak. They are bold and act quickly. Prideful. Strong and battle and typically victorious.
MYROBALAN LEAF.
IBN AL HATIM: Spirit names are Ahbiyal and Aghiyal. For protection from pain and snakes.
AL ASHRAF: White myrobalan, betel nut leaf.
SOLOMONIC RING (CUNNING MAN): Hairs of a woman. Spirit names are Facygrat, Davmilbe, Parinilbe, and Cliody. For the purposes of gaining love from women.

NAKSHATRA

Jyestha 'THE ELDEST' 'EARRING OR UMBRELLA'
ASTERISM: Alpha Scorpii (Antares)

TEMPERAMENT: Sharp, Daemonic
CASTE: Farmer
DIRECTION: West
MOTIVATION: *Artha*
ANIMAL: Male Rabbit
SOUNDS: No, Ya, Ye, Yo
TREE: *Bombax Ceiba* (Red Silk Cotton)
This tree is found everywhere in India. It blossoms during summer without leaves. It is thorny with attractive shapes of branches. Different parts of this tree are used as medicine. Its thorns are useful in pimples. The wood is soft and therefore it is used in match box, packing and plywood industries.
VIMSHOTTARI: Mercury
DEITY: Indra (King of the Gods), Jyestha (Alakshmi, Antithesis of Lakshmi)
SHAKTI: Power to rise, conquer, and gain courage in battle.
TAITTIRIYA BRAHMANA: "The power wielder's ambition needs attack, for counter-attacks."
BRIHAT SAMHITA: "will be valiant, of good descent, wealthy, famous; disposed to cheat others of their property, fond of traveling, rulers of provinces or commanders of armies."
TIBETAN: *Nron*. Bracelet. Divine Might. Charitable and content with himself. Easily loses temper and flies into rage. Hard words. Few friends, poverty. Struggles with words.

XIU

Xin 'HEART'
UNEVEN TROPICAL ZODIAC: n/a
ASTERISM: Alpha Scorpii (Antares)

SKY QUADRANT: Azure Dragon of the East
PLANET: Moon
ANIMAL: Fox
ARTLEY: The fox is endowed with highly supernatural qualities. They are said to be near the yin forces of the underworld. It passes between life and death. Enables the dead to return to life. Also carries out the behests of the dead, often relating to vengeance. The dead can also ride on a fox's back to the underworld. Takes human form only at night, usually in the form of a pretty girl in order to do mischief. Generally wicked in this guise, but sometimes good. Disarms suspicions. Longevity and craftiness. Aids in the recovery of lost documents. Following a fox's footsteps over ice guarantees safe passage. One of the five feared animals, either beneficent or maleficent, depending upon circumstances. Considered unlucky and tied into the selling of property. Symbol of the Emperor. Swift movements. Deity sits in the clouds and can create soldiers.
ELEMENT: Varied
MATANGA SUTRA: Offerings of non-glutinous rice. Those born here are foolish with short lives.

PGM/GREEK

Leopard, 'A SOUNDING WIND.'
DEITY: Moirai (alternatively, Zeus)

PROTO-SINAITIC/HIEROGLYPH

Mem, 'WATER'   〰〰〰

WORDS

Blood in the Machine, Power, Meteoric, Clashes and Contrasts, The Centipede, Heart of the Dragon, Sparse, Colorful, Infiltration, A Shield of Iron, Ambitious Efforts, War Machine, Passion, Excellence, Bloodshed, Career Climber, The Flag Planter, Electricity, World-Dissector, Certainty of Words, Standing Atop the Globe, Battlecry, Secret Society.

The eighteenth station is dominated by the large red star we call Antares. This star is the heart of the Western constellation Scorpio. It is often considered war-like in character, sharing the quality of its associated sign. Bright red stars also get this connotation as they are thought to be fiery and intense. The heart persists as the most immediately recognizable image of this station; not only of the Scorpion but also of the great Eastern Dragon of the Chinese.

Jyestha nakshatra is likened to be 'the most senior' or 'the eldest.' Of the same name is a fierce female goddess sometimes considered the opposite of Lakshmi. The deity associated with this nakshatra is Indra, the storm god considered to be the king. Similar to the other two stations of the royal stars, four (Aldeberan) and ten (Regulus), it may signify those who wield worldly (and sometimes otherworldly) power. Each of the royal stars manifests this in its own unique way. True to the martial quality of this star, it often signifies the necessary struggle to achieve one's desired ends. If it is of this station or the star Antares, these ends may be quite lofty and explicitly power-driven. As the story of Indra teaches us, to achieve this level of power often takes underhanded means, intrigue, and conflict.

Consequently, this station and the one which follows are both associated with strong magic, witchcraft, and sorcery. As the world's original means of clandestine action, these tactics may also be thought of in a contemporary context as those financial, social, or technological means that one might alter the circumstances in their favor. Another primary image is that of the amulet. There is a common thread through the nakshatras described as *tikshna* or sharp, wherein they are associated with power struggles, intrigue, as well as forms of magic that deal with overcoming others. Beyond the particular actions that one takes within the context of this station, it may be glossed as ambitious and favoring those who make efforts to climb. If Regulus functions within the law-abiding paradigm, Antares represents the challenges to established and traditional orders.

PLANETARY PLACEMENTS

The Presence of the ☾

The Moon in this lunar station may be possessed by strong ambitions and drives towards authority and power. Unlike other stations, here she often has the qualities necessary to accomplish them. It is not that the Moon or any placement in this station wishes to dominate per se. Yet her standard and desire for excellence here is often taken for granted. Similarly, her charisma may propel her forward in marvelous ways. In other words, this is a natural position of authority that may exist in a variety of capacities. It is this innate sense which drives ambition forward; for better or worse. She may not feel comfortable with her lot in life, and therefore venture into new places to attempt to get what she desires. There is confidence here. There is a sense of travel and exploration driven by one's passion. More than any oversimplification of a 'will to power,' the Moon here is restless, and it is this friction which propels the intensity of accomplishment.

The Presence of ☿

Another strong mercantile placement as Mercury means business in this sign. They may speak with authority, strength, and command, sometimes even a domineering sense. It is through strong appeals to emotional language that this becomes possible. True to the station's martial character, Mercurial pursuits are driven by passion first and foremost. It is also worth noting that there is a quality of machinic intelligence found here. Similar to the sixth station, there are massive reservoirs of power capable of being drawn from. Put towards Mercurial ends of craft, technology, and intellectual ability, they may be quite the powerhouse if channeled correctly.

The Presence of ♀

Venus takes on the role of art director, advertiser, and those who exert power through aesthetic or even erotic means. This is a passionate Venus, and like other fiery Venus', she commands attention and respect. The original figure of Jyestha is one lacking materiality in her opposition to Lakshmi's wealth. In truth it is the absence itself which drives ambitions forward; not only to achieve but also to create. Though this may exist in a drive towards purely material ends, it is not limited as such. Venus wishes to fill that void with creations both beautiful and eye-grabbing.

The Presence of the ☉

Leadership qualities are put to the forefront as the Sun is in a strong position of authority here. As described by this sign, there is an almost innate sense of confidence and command; a generally regal attitude. He may come across as self-righteous and pompous. Similar to Mars, this emerges from exaggerated masculine energies. By and large it is that natural drivenness which has him striving towards positions at the center or the top. Unlike Mars, this may also manifest in ways less driven towards material or overtly power-hungry pursuits and towards those excellence in knowledge and character. He may be practical and grounded in these ways just as much as he may be metaphysical and spiritual.

The Presence of ♂

This is a bold place for Mars as the intensity and drive related to this sign are heightened to great proportions. From the standpoint of the lunar stations, this is perhaps the most ambitious placement for the planet of warfare. It almost goes without saying that he must have outlets and goal orientations here. Lacking principle, this Mars may come to the conclusion that the ends justify the means. It is less a placement of volatility and the dangers therein and more the troubles of doing whatever it takes to obtain one's desires.

The Presence of ♃

As Indra, storm god and king of the gods, is lord of this nakshatra, it is indeed a strong placement for the planet Jupiter who holds these same qualities. In this manifestation the planet of law and parentage is capable of exercising harsher measures, playing the game in full when it comes to the acquisition of wealth, business endeavors, and political machinations. While some Jupiter placements may emphasize the planet's orientation towards wisdom, this is a practical and strong placement that is more than capable of achieving his ambitions with intelligence and vigor.

The Presence of ♄

Though the pace here may be a little too quick for our slowest of planets, there are possibilities of long-term achievements born through tireless efforts and work. The reward of which elevates Saturn into the aerial dimensions wherein he observes from above and extends his knowledge outward. In this way, it is also a placement that lends itself to a little more levity than the typical Saturn, as this station's tendency towards upward movement levels out some of his heavier aspects. This same weight that Saturn is thought to bring may work the other way as well, wherein the intensely passionate drives may be tempered so as not to become overly egotistical or self-obsessed in the capacity of Mars or the Sun. If found in a more challenging placement, he may also highlight a contrast between one's intense desires for achievement with the reality of what one is truly capable of.

19.

Origin/Red-Root of the Cosmos

Precessed Tropical Coordinates:
24° 07' Sagittarius–7° 27' Capricorn

MANZIL

Al Shaula 'THE RAISED TAIL OF THE SCORPION' OR 'THE STING'
TROPICAL ZODIAC: 21° 25' Scorpio–4° 17' Sagittarius
ASTERISM: Lambda Scorpii (Shaula), Upsilon Scorpii (Lesath)
Belongs to the retinue of TUESDAY, ANGEL SEMSAMIEL, AND JINN KING *Al Ahmar*
IBN ARABI: ز (Zay)
AIR, THE LIVING ONE
PICATRIX: Image of a woman holding her hands in front of her face. Talisman for hastening menses. Spirit name is Annucel. Fashion out of brass and suffumigate with liquid storax. For sieging, for destruction of wealth, to expel people from a place, free captives, increase harvests, kill captives, destroy ships.
LIBER LUNÆ: Face of the Moon. Fornication, lust, discord.
AGRIPPA: Spirit name is Amutiel. Sieges, driving people away.
AL BUNI: ق (Qaf)

Good and bad. Tying and unbinding. Making and
breaking agreements. Ambivalent nature. Unsuitable for talismans or spiritual healing. Seclusion
is preferred. Those born here to be blameworthy,
slanderous. Rebellious. Insatiable curiosity, restlessness. Pomegranate skin and mastic.

IBN AL HATIM: For the flowing of menses. Spirit
names are Adhniyal and Abriyal.

AL ASHRAF: Pomegranate skin and mastic.

SOLOMONIC RING (CUNNING MAN): Hairs of
a woman. Spirit names are Facygrat, Davmilbe,
Parinilbe, and Cliody. For the purposes of gaining
love from women.

NAKSHATRA

Mula 'ROOT' 'ELEPHANT'S GOAD'
ASTERISM: Epsilon Scorpii, Lambda Scorpii (Shaula),
Upsilon Scorpii (Lesath)
TEMPERAMENT: Sharp, Daemonic
CASTE: Butcher
DIRECTION: North
MOTIVATION: *Kama*
ANIMAL: Male Dog
SOUNDS: Yay, Yo, Ba, Be
TREE: *Cassia Fistula* (Golden Shower)

It is known as the golden shower tree. The species is
native to the Indian Subcontinent and adjacent
regions of Southeast Asia. It ranges from southern
Pakistan eastward throughout India to Myanmar
and Thailand and south to Sri Lanka. It is the
national tree of Thailand, and its flower is Thailand's
national flower. It is also the state flower of Kerala
in India and of immense importance amongst the

Malayali population. It is a popular ornamental plant and is used in herbal medicine. Cassia fistula is widely grown as an ornamental plant in tropical and subtropical areas. It blooms in late spring. In Ayurvedic medicine, the golden shower tree is known *asaragvadha*, meaning "disease killer". The fruit pulp is considered a purgative, and self-medication or any use without medical supervision is strongly advised against in Ayurvedic texts.

VIMSHOTTARI: Ketu
DEITY: Niriti (Goddess of Destruction), Kali
SHAKTI: Power to break things apart.
TAITTIRIYA BRAHMANA: "Destroying the roots of untruth needs mutual crushing, for mutual annihilations"
BRIHAT SAMHITA: "will be druggists, heads of men, dealers in flowers, roots, fruits and seeds; will be rich and will delight in garden work."
TIBETAN: *Nub.* Root. Vitality. Pride, a firm mind, wealth. Likes luxury, comfort, and stability. Disciplined. Good temperament but sometimes coarse.

XIU

Wei 'TAIL'
UNEVEN TROPICAL ZODIAC: n/a
ASTERISM: Epsilon Scorpii, Lambda Scorpii (Shaula), Upsilon Scorpii (Lesath)
SKY QUADRANT: Azure Dragon of the East
PLANET: Mars
ANIMAL: Tiger
ARTLEY: The tiger is the embodiment of animal magnetism. Fiercely competitive. Likes a good fight. Born leader with natural authority. A great stimulator

of others. Strong on appearances for the sake of impression. Brave, rash and impetuous. Very strong competitive streak. Mercenary in business, good in personnel management and in uniformed careers. Warm, sincere, and even ardent in love. Unfortunate for building and marriages. Denotes the finding of treasure and promotion to high offices.
ELEMENT: Fire
MATANGA SUTRA: Offerings of fruit. Those born here have many offspring and are well respected.

GEOMANCY

TANNERY: Tristicia ◆ ◆
                         ◆ ◆
                         ◆ ◆
                           ◆

PGM/GREEK:

Fieldmouse, 'A MUSICAL SOUND.'
DEITY: Hekate
(alternatively, Gaia or Ananke)

PROTO-SINAITIC/HIEROGLYPH

Lamed, 'TO GOAD'

WORDS

Stimulation, Depth, Amassing, Hammer Dropping, Rhizomatic, A Vampire's Kiss, Elegant Simplicity,

Observation of Fire, Where Head Meets Body, Where Spirit Meets Soul, Clustering Together and Binding Together, Red Clay, Animal and Plant Communication, Ground Warfare, Broken Down and Re-Fashioned, Roadkill, Disassembled, The Emptiness That We Have Longed For.

There seems to be a consistent theme across the various understandings of this lunar station . For the Chinese it was the tail of the great Eastern Dragon. The nakshatra sees this station as a root. The Arabic holds it as the tail of the Scorpion; in particular the action of stinging and the delivery of poison. There is an astronomical phenomenon which ties these cultural similarities together. This is the great black hole at the center of the Milky Way. Designated Sagittarius A star, this super massive black hole is the true origin of the cosmos as we know it. This includes every visible star in the night sky, all of which is contained in the Milky Way and all emerging from this same anti-space. It is not solely poetic language or exaggeration to call this place 'the root,' as it is very much the hidden origin of existence.

As mentioned in the previous station, there are strong connotations of poison and destruction found along the later stars of Scorpius. The nakshatra deity is Niritti, close to Kali in character and image; the Dark Mother who destroys all falsities, as not even time itself can escape her grasp. Consequently we are not speaking of destruction purely for its own sake. This is, if anything, a degenerated version of this region's functioning. To return to the root or origin of something is to reveal so many false accretions. The surgical act is indeed dangerous and destructive, yet it is oftentimes no less necessary for the sake of healing. In regards to poisoning, there is a strange persistent paradox found here: 'One will find the medicine in the poison.'

As described in station six and seven, we have now arrived at the other side of the Milky Way's path as it crosses that of the luminaries. While the opposite side of this crossroads sees the furthest distance from center representing the realm of hunters who venture out into the wilderness, here we find proximity to those ancient forms of life who go forever deeper into the Earth. Like Rahu (North Node) who goes outward into the depths of space and Ketu (South Node) who burrows further into terrestrial abysses, there is a strong similarity between this axis and the Milky Way dynamic spoken of. If station six is the storm deity who cries out and destroys outward forms, then here we find his mother, wife, or compliment, the abyss from whence it all came and the abode of those who destroy inward forms. This is the MesoAmerican entrance to *Xibalba* or 'the land of awe,' that great underworld and realm of the dead in Maya thought. Upon death, souls were thought to enter the underworld realms through this same region of the sky and begin their journey along the Milky Way into the afterlife. This is but one more example of how these crossings are inextricably linked; the land of the dead found on either end, as well as the land of the living. We must not forget that as the true origins of the cosmos, it is not solely a place of death but also the quintessential place of birth; the infinite womb of potential from which all things have arisen and shall return.

PLANETARY PLACEMENTS

THE PRESENCE OF THE ☾

This is a Moon with traditional awareness as we would expect in regards to a station which refers heavily to the roots of things. Very much like the tenth station and its emphasis on the ancestors, here the Moon emphasizes reality structures which have endured through vast stretches of time; almost literally that which has stood the test of time's crushing power. She may be drawn to plants and their various uses. Medicines and potions derived from plant substances are a common theme here as well. The Moon in this station has the ability to milk the venom of serpents or that of a scorpion's tail. It is these same substances that often end up inside of our common pharmaceuticals. This is a station of pharmacists and those who make their livelihood from 'root' substances. Chemistry and alchemy may also be found here as this station speaks heavily of transformation of substances at their most essential levels. In order for long term sustainability this is how it must be done.

THE PRESENCE OF ☿

This is often a placement of quiet intelligence, as many of Mercury's sensibilities are linked to deeper ways of knowing, intuition, and archaic connection. Quiet should not be thought of in the conventional sense, as their voice may still be of high volume and even somewhat sharp (as this is the scorpion's stinger no less!). Rather, it is an understated or subtle form of intellect which prizes qualities nowadays thought of as 'irrational' or 'subconscious.' At a metaphysical level, Mercury is capable of grasping mystical and abstract concepts with ease here. In this sign they may even be a scholar of religious and philosophical studies, as their ability to articulate such works is highly rarefied. Similar to the Moon there may also be magical and scientific knowledge of plants and the ability to transform them to various ends.

The Presence of Venus ♀

The planet of relationships forms deep connections here. There is something of a return back to the ways that humans and animals have related to one another in the deepest stretches of time. Pre-civilization ways of harmonizing at the visceral level are found here. She embodies an unmatched sense of community wisdom and long term survival. Venus wears the furs of wild animals and speaks far beyond anthropocentric dimensions into those of deep forests and caverns. This is a placement of accountability and responsibility as much as it is of the Dark Mother and her retinue.

The Presence of the ☉

He often shines in structured circumstances that call for levels of depth, research, and investigation. The Sun here is thoroughly chthonic in character, taking on the qualities of movement through the underworld. As this station is sometimes thought of as headless, the Sun must learn new ways of seeing as he glances through the otherworld from the bottom up. He has the capacity to be thoroughly grass roots in his approach. More than any other placement for him this station is the so-called Black Sun; a kind of anti-star akin to a black hole. As this is perhaps the 'lowest' point that he may find himself, this is a challenging position for all things which the Sun may normally crave. In fact, this station has more in common with eclipses than the luminaries themselves, lending their positions here to similarly unorthodox or outright opposite manners. He may change the cosmos in the most profound manner here yet rarely is it obvious or given proper recognition. Here he must ponder the death of the king as opposed to his rise.

The Presence of ♂

Mars holds immense strength here. As this station naturally plumbs the depths, Mars seeks out the deepest and sometimes the most ancient lifeways here as a means of satisfying his hunger for the most arcane. There is a reckoning with the past, perhaps even a conflict with places and people of origin as Mars often signals in the stations of ancestry. Due to the strange nature of this station, it may not be the recent past but that which touches on the very beginnings of humanity as we know it. As this is the sign of the serpent's bite and the scorpion's tail, Mars is capable of delivering brutality here unmatched in the rest of the zodiac (besides perhaps the first decan of Scorpio). Though this is very much possible, it is more likely that this destructive power is aimed at the falsehoods and those forces which would seek to dominate and confuse. When functioning well, this is a Mars of complete clarity down to the very root of existence itself.

The Presence of ♃

Jupiter similarly finds his way in traditional modalities and the like. He may be drawn to spiritual practices of an ancient or archaic quality. This is not a Jupiter of the New Age or of the next spiritual fad. Here he is a priest of dead languages and forgotten religious rites. Like Mercury, there is a strong metaphysical and philosophical inclination to this position. Unlike Mercury, he may go beyond intellectual understandings into lived practice and embodiment. Here is akin to John the Baptist, preacher and poet of the wilderness who moves through the world wearing animal skins and feeding on the plants below his feet. This may be a Jupiter thoroughly disinterested in material forms of wealth; or, perhaps, of a deep enough wisdom capable of integrating material existence into lived spiritual practice.

The Presence of ♄

Like most planets in this sign, there is a strong orientation towards the ancestors, the dead, and archaic ways of knowing here. Once more, this is typically not the recent past, especially in regards to Saturn, as he is interested in exploring the absolute depths and origins of consciousness here. Animal, plant, human, and spirit life blend here as Saturn is quite at home in this station with its emphasis on the darkest aspects of life in whatever capacity he may structure their study; psychology, spirituality, and the like. As this is the station of the destructive force of time and what remains afterward, this is without a doubt a thoroughly Saturnine place. Here is in full power as harvester of souls and dealer of fate. In this same manner, this is a station where Saturn as masculine fits far less than she of the Dark Mother. As the womb of all necessity, Ananke in her truest form, here she swallows time whole reaching back to the furthest realms of creation.

20.

Jamal (Divine Beauty) / The Water Sieve

Precessed Tropical Coordinates:
7° 27' Capricorn–20° 47' Capricorn

MANZIL

Al Naa'im 'The Ostriches,' 'The Gathering'
Tropical Zodiac: 4° 17' Sagittarius–17° 8' Sagittarius
Asterism: Zeta Sagitarii (Ascella), Sigma Sagittarii (Nunki)
Ibn Arabi: س (Sin)
Water, The Life Giver
Picatrix: Image of a centaur holding a bow. Talisman for hunting. Spirit name is Queyhuc. Fashion out of tin and suffumigate with the hair of a wolf. For taming wild beasts, for people to gather where you wish, to bring good people together.
Liber Lunæ: Face of Saturn. Arousal, love, friendship.
Agrippa: Spirit name is Kyriel. Taming wild animals, destroying wealth, luring people to a certain place.
Al Buni: ر (Ra)
Urges goodness, love, and favor. Good for most things. Suitable for crafting, precious stones. Embark on new studies and matters of wisdom and religion. Make talismans, build buildings, and plant crops or trees. To be born here is to be happy with comfort. Good

with legal matters.
FRANKINCENSE AND MUGWORT.
AL ASHRAF: Frankincense and wormwood.
SOLOMONIC RING (CUNNING MAN): Hairs of a woman. Spirit names are Facygrat, Davmilbe, Parinilbe, and Cliody. For the purposes of gaining love from women.

NAKSHATRA

Purva Ashhadha 'EARLY VICTORY' 'WINNOWING BASKET' 'FAN' 'TUSK'
ASTERISM: Epsilon Sagittarii (Kaus Australis), Gamma Sagittarii (Alnasl), Delta Sagittarii (Kaus Media)
TEMPERAMENT: Fierce, Human
CASTE: Brahmin
DIRECTION: East
MOTIVATION: *Moksha*
ANIMAL: Male Monkey
SOUNDS: Bu, Dha, Bha
TREE: *Calamus Rotang* (Common Rattan)
Is used in the making of furniture, baskets, walking-sticks, umbrellas, tables and general wickerwork, and is found in Southwest Asia. The basal section of the plant grows vertically for 10 meters or so, after which the slender, tough stem of a few centimeters in diameter, grows horizontally for 200 meters or more. It is extremely flexible and uniform in thickness, and frequently has sheaths and petioles armed with backward-facing spines which enable it to scramble over other plants. It has pinnate, alternate leaves, 60–80 cm long, armed with two rows of spines on the upper face. The plants are dioecious, and irs flowers are clustered in attractive inflorescences, enclosed

by spiny spathes. The edible fruits are top-shaped, covered in shiny, reddish-brown imbricate scales, and exude an astringent red resin known medicinally and commercially as 'Dragon's blood.' Calamus is a genus of some 300 species found in the tropics of Africa and Asia. They are mostly slender-stemmed leaf-climbers, where the pinnae at the outer end of the leaf have been modified into stout, backward-pointing spines.

VIMSHOTTARI: Venus
DEITY: Apas, God of Water
SHAKTI: Power of invigoration.
TAITTIRIYA BRAHMANA: "Beginning an invincible action needs vital power for concordance"
BRIHAT SAMHITA: "will be of gentle manners; fond of sea-voyage, truthful, cleanly and wealthy; will delight in earth work; will be boatmen; will be dealers in fruits and flowers of water."
TIBETAN: *Chuto*. Higher Water, Measure of Water. Tall, Proud, Perspicuous, Ambitious. Faithful Friend, Loves His Mother. Loving Spouse. Traveler, Likes Women, and Powerful Friends.

XIU

Ji 'WINNOWING BASKET'
AKA: 'HEAD OF THE WATER' 'HIGHER FOOTPRINT'
UNEVEN TROPICAL ZODIAC: n/a
ASTERISM: Epsilon Sagittarii (Kaus Australis), Gamma Sagittarii (Alnasl), Delta Sagittarii (Kaus Media)
SKY QUADRANT: Azure Dragon of the East
PLANET: Mercury
ANIMAL: Leopard
ARTLEY: The Leopard is one of the four power animals,

along with elephants, tigers, and lions. Bravery and martial ferocity. Associated with the military. Assuredness, forthrightness. Considered lucky. Considered a good time to inter the dead. Most likely a fertility deity.
ELEMENT: Water
MATANGA SUTRA: Offering is fruit of the banyan tree. Those born here are fond of meditation.

GEOMANCY

AL MAWṢILĪ & TANNERY: Populus

PGM/GREEK

Deer, 'NEIGHING.'
DEITY: Ceto (alternatively, Hera)

PROTO-SINAITIC/HIEROGLYPH

Tann, Shin, 'BOW'

WORDS

The River Gathering, Bleak/Blank, Vast, Subsume, Unreactive, Fertile Darkness, The Sieve, Stricture, Cultivator, A Beautiful Lure, Confidence and Bravery, Irrigation in Kind, Certainty, The Pious, Discerner, The Grand Mind, Liquid Movement, Aesthetic Senses, Rain Cloud, The Courtroom of Animals.

The arched shape of the bow and the elephant tusk, prominent symbols for this station, are critical in comprehending it. It is this curving shape that harkens to the bends of a river, or those natural flows of water and the means by which they carve through the land. Similar to the previous station, we remain close to the river of the Milky Way. Like stations six and seven on the opposite side, each entrance/exit to the great celestial river emphasizes a place of death and one of birth. Though each station simultaneously holds both, here we find the birth emphasis to that of station nineteen's destructive power. Water associations abound, and it is these liquid flows and their life-bringing qualities which give this place its auspicious nature.

The elephant tusk symbolizes regality and rulership as well as wealth. It is the pristine quality of ivory and its resemblance to cooling water that mirrors the nature of this station. This is seen quite directly in the Arabic asterism as the animals come to gather to drink from the Milky Way. This is a clean source if ever there was one. The renewal which occurs in the previous station, perhaps even the digging of the well to reach freshwater, then flows freely here. Proximity to water has driven commerce and the growth of civilizations for many millennia. On a smaller scale, it allows for people to settle down and cultivate lives with one another. On a larger scale, it is river and oceanic travel that has allowed cultures to grow beyond those same settlements. Consequently, this station is thought to have a civilizing quality about it. Here we see an emphasis on law, art, and culture through proximity to the deepest sources of growth.

Another prominent symbol is the winnowing basket, an agricultural tool wherein edible grain may be separated from the rest. The energy of this station is one of flow, and in order for this to occur, the cycle must continue;

the old is swept away so that the fresh may emerge. This is perhaps the hidden but altogether necessary element of this station as it also speaks to death as 'natural order.' Like stations six and seven we cannot escape the life-death dynamic along the Milky Way. We find a different aspect to this curved nature, as the bow of the archer Sagittarius represents the death-dealing action of the hunter. The gathering place of animals is where the hunter is most likely to succeed in their task. Here we find the balance between life and death as it pertains to these same qualities of civilization. As the bow takes life, and the elephant tusk is life taken for the sake of wealth, we see here that the two are inextricably linked to one another. The fruits of culture and all of its richness, the fineries and luxuries, the pleasures we so enjoy, must still be hunted for. In addition, they often come at the expense of others.

PLANETARY PLACEMENTS

The Presence of the ☾

There is an emphasis here on natural cycles, marked by Sun rises and settings, seasons, and the like. The Moon in this position may hold a faith and reliance on them as a means of organized living. There is often a natural acceptance of the flow of things; as life is a coming and going in its various parts. Consequently, her perspective may be one of enjoying life's offerings as she has them. There is a deeply felt sense of appreciation for how they have emerged; from the root level all the way to the present moment; a broad sense born of witnessing the breadth and width of the river in all of its flows. This may be quite the creative placement as well, as water is thought to be generative and cultivating of life-expression. The same richness held as a perspective on life may be reflected in these expressions as works of creativity here embody the very traditional sense of the beautiful as a reflection of the natural world's curves.

THE PRESENCE OF ☿

Mercury often functions with a damming effect for these same flows. They think in the sense of improving movements and harnessing currents. This may be a scientific place for Mercury as much as it may be one of art, law, and other cultivated practices requiring a discipline of flow. They are expressive here and life-giving. Speech and communication is soft spoken and even poetic.

THE PRESENCE OF ♀

This is a Venus who decorates with natural materials, plant substances, and the like. She may be quite fond of animals and their presence. She desires to take care and hold space with those non-human beings who are an expression of nature's beauty and diversity. Her principles may be those of vegetarianism, peace, and nonviolence. Consequently, she brings together those like minded individuals who wish to alter society through the shaming of brutality and an emphasis on expanded consciousness. In so much as this is a creative station, art born from this place is capable of finding the essential beauty of things; similar to the winnowing basket and its power. Like station 24 there is an emphasis on movement and flow wherein her expression emerges in dance and somatic practices.

The Presence of the ☉

Here the Sun represents the orderly nature of things. He is a political leader, not of force and obedience, but of pomp and high culture. As an artist, he is a landscape painter of great vastness. As a musician he cultivates soundscapes which mirror those of the world outside; in forest, sea, desert, and jungle. This is a Sun of exploration and creative curiosity. He is interested in the cultural achievements of various people, and how they may be preserved. Here we find the Sun in a position of life giving, as his light is no longer harsh.

The Presence of ♂

Unlike the following sign where Mars as dominator becomes apparent, here he is less interested in conquering and more in exploration and creativity. Like Venus he battles on the side of life, bringing courage and work ethic capable of change through various levels of culture. This is a Mars which brings direction to the arts as a medium of change itself; acknowledging here that the movement of images and beauty shapes the world more so than warfare. This is one of his more generous positions, as well as one of expression and artistic orientation.

The Presence of ♃

Jupiter in this station fairs surprisingly well, as the life-giving qualities of water and fertility are familiar to him. This is an extremely creative Jupiter, as well as one of generosity and wisdom. He is a rain bringer here, even a great fertility dragon of sorts, as his riverine body moves through the landscape bringing verdancy and the like. He is a great teacher, and deeply in touch with natural cycles and the ways they ebb and flow. He shows fealty towards familiars, keeping things enclosed and of themselves. In this way, he is a Jupiter of the land and sky, of particular places, and not as much of the global sphere.

The Presence of ♄

This is an excellent place for Saturn as a planet already aligned with longer natural cycles and the non-human world. There is an appreciation for the world beyond the city. This includes plant and animal life as well as wild spaces little touched by human intervention. He may tend the forest of whatever it is that he holds deep respect for. Here we see Saturn as the winemaker and agriculturalist once more. It is his deep wisdom of process which aids in the creation of things highly prized and well cultivated.

21.
Jalal (Divine Majesty) / Silence

Precessed Tropical Coordinates:
20° 47' Capricorn–4° 07' Aquarius

MANZIL

Al Balda 'The Empty Place' or 'The City, 'The District'
Tropical Zodiac: 17° 8' Sagittarius–0° Capricorn
Belongs to the retinue of Tuesday, Angel Semsamiel, and Jinn King *Al Ahmar*

ASTERISM: Pii Sagittarii (Albaldah)
IBN ARABI: ص (Saad)
EARTH, THE DEATH GIVER
PICATRIX: Image of a man with two faces. Talisman for destruction. Spirit name is Bectue. Suffumigate with sulfur and carabe (asphaltum, dried tar). For strengthening of buildings, increase harvest, profit, and separate husband and wife.
LIBER LUNÆ: Face of Jupiter. For silence, cooperation.
AGRIPPA: Spirit name is Bethnael. Good for harvests and buildings. Causes divorce.
AL BUNI: ش (Sheen)
Enmity, hatred, separation. Beware crafting talismans or gemstones. Do not do most things. Those born here will be tricksters. Desire to help others. Spikenard and aloeswood.
IBN AL HATIM: For misfortune and emptiness. Spirit name is Kawyakifah.
AL ASHRAF: Musk and saffron.
SOLOMONIC RING (CUNNING MAN): Parts of a cow's horn and pasture grass. For the purposes of multiplying cattle and growing herds. For growth and prosperity.

NAKSHATRA

Uttara Ashadha 'THE LATER VICTORY' 'BED PLANKS OR TUSK'
ASTERISM: Sigma Sagittarii (Nunki), Zeta Sagittarii (Ascella)
TEMPERAMENT: Fixed, Human
CASTE: Warrior
DIRECTION: South
MOTIVATION: *Moksha*

ANIMAL: Male Mongoose
SOUNDS: Be, Bo, Ja, Je
TREE: *Artocarpus Heterophyllus* (Jack Fruit)
This tree is found in hot regions. It is an evergreen, huge & fruitful tree. The fruits hang on the main stem or bigger branches. Pickles and vegetables are made from unripe, raw fruits. The ripe fruit is very tasty and healthy-nourishing. Its wood is used in furniture, musical instruments, and wood-carving. Small fibers from beating green wood produce a saffron/orange color. This color is used by Buddhist Monks to color their sacred clothes. The gum extracted from this tree is also useful.
VIMSHOTTARI: Sun
DEITY: Visvedevas (Universal Gods or All Perceivers), Ganesha
SHAKTI: Power to achieve unchallengeable victory.
TAITTIRIYA BRAHMANA: "Perceivers of everything need to engage in conquest to achieve supremacy"
BRIHAT SAMHITA: "will be chief ministers or wrestlers; will keep elephants and horses, will be religious; will be men of principles; soldiers; happy and of bright appearance."
TIBETAN: *Chume*. Perfect. Accomplished. Well built and muscular. Long nose. Discreet, well mannered, virtuous, grateful and loved by parents. Popular, has many friends. Style and good manners.

XIU

Dou 'DIPPER/LADLE'
AKA: 'LOWER FOOT PRINT' ' FEET OF THE WATER' 'PORCUPINE'
UNEVEN TROPICAL ZODIAC: 11° Capricorn–3°

Aquarius (1–22 January)
ASTERISM: Sigma Sagittarii (Nunki), Zeta Sagittarii (Ascella), Mu Sagittarii
SKY QUARTER: Black Turtle of the North
PLANET: Jupiter
ANIMAL: Unicorn/Griffon
ARTLEY: The unicorn's body is multi-colored. Walks on water as well as on land. It never eats or drinks dirty things. It has a highly musical voice. Solitary. Like the Phoenix, it never harms other creatures. The prince of all beasts. It is one of the four intelligent animals. Said to be able to appear and disappear at will. Its appearance brings blessings to all who see it. Symbolizes perfect fidelity, longevity, fecundity, industrious descendants, wise administration. The monastic life. Gentleness to every living thing. It is able to detect the appearance of wise kings and sages. Prefers the company of scholars. Considered lucky and good for endings and finishing projects.
ELEMENT: Wood
MATANGA SUTRA: Offering of peach flowers. Those born here are wealthy.

GEOMANCY

TANNERY: Cauda Draconis

AL MAWṢILĪ: Puer & Puella

PGM/GREEK

Multi-Form, 'BELLOWING.'
DEITY: Physis
(alternatively, Athena or Nike)

PROTO-SINAITIC/HIEROGLYPH

Tab 'GOOD'

WORDS

Composite, Thinning Air Upon the Summit, Mastery, Accumulated Knowledge, Silence, The Mountain Climber, Bulldozer, The Monk in a Monastery, Climax, Traditional Wisdom, The Watchtower, Closing In, Strangling the Vocal Cords, Elephantine, One Who Has Fashioned Themselves a Weapon, Light on Light and Darkness on Darkness, Epitome, 'It is Lonely at the Top.'

This lunar station represents the final movement into the dimension of the pole. One way it is represented is through the winter solstice in the northern hemisphere. In the tropical solar zodiac this is seen by the Sun's movement into the Saturn-ruled sign of Capricorn. As the Neo-Platonist Porphyry described it, this 'Gate of the Gods' is the dwelling place of the immortals. Along with Cancer, these two signs form an axis of death and resurrection marked by the Sun's movement in the northern hemisphere. Cancer, or the 'Gate of Humanity,' is where new souls are born into this world while Capricorn is the point of exit. At one time this axis coincided with that of the Milky Way road, which, as we have seen for other stations in this text (six through seven and nineteen through twenty), has served a similar function of bringing souls in and out of manifestation. The stars of our current region are something of a build up to the tropical point of solstice. The station consists of stars from Sagittarius, that great hunter who leads in an instructive manner for the times ahead.

It is interesting to note the composite nature of both Sagittarius and Capricorn, as many of the station's images share this quality. The PGM refers to it as 'multi-form,' the Chinese animal is the Unicorn, the nakshatra deity are the 'Visvedevas' or 'all of the gods,' and the Arabic image is one of a city. Al Balda, or the Arabic name for the station as well as the star, is seen as Janus-faced. Our double-bodied water-goat or horse-bodied archer is not dissimilar. The jewel of consciousness which awaits in the following station asks us to collapse our vision into a circular gaze. We must not forget that the serpent in the garden is entwined around this same pole. The serpent's tongue begs the same question as the face which looks both ways. For if we come upon it without preparation we may easily fall prey to its venom-lubricated kiss. The Arabic imagery is quite specific in this way, recognizing this very point as an impasse or a fork in the road. One direction leads to destruction while the other leads to complete individuation.

The difference in opinion in regards to the effect of this station mirrors the notion of double bodies or two faces. The xiu and the nakshatra largely see this station as auspicious while the Arabic manzil thoroughly emphasizes its destructive quality. Though the differences in interpretation are quite valid, there does seem to be a connection in the notion of the warrior. The nakshatra in particular emphasizes battle, while the Arabic station sees the results as such. Warfare is marked by the general assumption that there is a winning and losing side. By and large, this is a station of the action which overcomes all else. It is the final blow which annihilates one's enemies or oneself; the vehicle of transportation through an honorable death. This is auspicious if one has conquered their enemies or secured a position in the afterlife. It is not auspicious if you are on the receiving end. Either way, it embodies a kind of heroism implied with this station that must be enacted to reap its best results.

PLANETARY PLACEMENTS

The Presence of the ☾

The Moon in this station has the disposition of a warrior or one who feels the urge to conquer. If ever there was a station for the 'million dollar man' or 'übermensch' phenomenon it would be this one, as the power of the winter solstice compels her to climb great heights. Here she is interested in rarified positions, sometimes more or less a part of the world, but always elevated in some manner. Though this impulse may very well exist within the context of climbing corporate, business, and creative structures, it may also come about through spiritual endeavor. In this station the Moon may be quite mystical. As this is a place of arriving in the north, she is gifted with the blessing/curse of seeing 'from above.' In this station consciousness has reached the height of individuality. Her way of existence is particular and stands out among the rest. At the same time, this may not be readily apparent, as the gifts of this station emerge through various forms of struggle.

The Presence of ☿

Mercury here brings strong inclinations towards inventive and combinatory acts much to the likeness of the Chinese unicorn associated with this sign. The multiple-nature of this station allows for complex understandings. Here is the power of an engineer or great scientist. Intellect is strong, as Mercury balances systematic behavior alongside a boldness to break new ground. Theirs is a voice which commands the masses, speaking with authority and strength. As this is a sign of warriors there may also be an inclination towards martial arts and those physical skills emphasizing battle.

The Presence of ♀

The planet of love forges powerful bonds here, worthy of long lasting relationships and potentials. We see her as a warrior of great principle. If Mars stands upon the bodies of those he has conquered, Venus reaches her peak through alliances, negotiations, and displays of luminosity. Here she is the artist who sees beyond the trends and temporary aesthetic hazards of any given time. She taps into long lasting and forward thinking ideas which resonate to people in mundane circumstances, balancing accessibility and skill. Otherwise, she is a powerhouse in most pursuits she strives to achieve.

The Presence of the ☉

The Sun is a great achiever in this sign. As the Sun reaches his last breaths here, he is witness to the birth canal and inevitable ascension. Though this exists only within the tropical-solar paradigm, it is still instructive in the functioning of the Sun in this position. If well cultivated, he may similarly ascend to great achievements, powerful positions of leadership, and victory in battle. Unlike Mars, he represents less the ruler who has reached his position through battle and more the ruler who has achieved his way through excellent examples. This is a position of ambition as well as heroism and character building. When these qualities align, the Sun becomes a noble leader of the masses. He must have room to climb and grow. If not, he may find himself pontificating to the so-called 'empty city' of Al Balda. Here he is every person and no person; a well-suited leader in his understanding of the masses, yet it must be won through effort and noble deeds.

The Presence of ♂

This is perhaps the most powerful position for Mars in the entire lunar zodiac. As this is the lunar station for achieving complete victory, he holds the power to ensure this in almost any field of action. If well placed and prominent within the chart, this position is a sign of absolute greatness; something even capable of shaping the world at societal levels of lengthy endurance. The ascent to the pole seen in this lunar station is fueled by a seemingly inexhaustible drive and willingness to sacrifice towards a particular end rarely achieved by the average person. This is a Mars who storms the heavens through and through. He may even become famous for his achievements here, as he conquers the world in whatever capacity he sets his mind to.

The Presence of ♃

Jupiter must rely on alternative means to stay afloat and grow. Here he needs routine, evidence, discipline, and most often traditional modalities so that he may do his best work. Jupiterian luck will not come naturally here, but if worked on in a more concrete manner the results may bode well for great wealth and achievement. This station sees him as the stern father figure, more than perhaps any other.

The Presence of ♄

Saturn gives steady and productive gains as he embodies the strategist. Though he does not have the direct-acting power of Mars, Saturn is capable of addressing the enduring concerns of battle without becoming bogged down by temporary losses. He is in touch with sacrifice here, seeing it as a necessary element of long term stability. He is a Saturn quite comfortable with isolation and idiosyncrasy. He is the aged warrior who lives upon the mountain having accumulated a lifetime of wisdom. Having met every persona the world has to offer, he retreats into seclusion to forge great works and explore the heights of mind and spirit.

22.

A Thread to Heaven / Darkness at the Pole

Precessed Tropical Coordinates:
0° 37' Aquarius–5° 35' Aquarius.

*Coordinates are between the next and previous mansion and determined by ¼ of the end of *Uttara Ashadha* (21) and ⅕ of the beginning of *Shravana* (23).

MANZIL

Sa'd Al Dabi 'THE PROPITIOUS ONE OF THE SACRIFICER' 'THE LUCK (FORTUNE) OF THE SLAUGHTERERS'
TROPICAL ZODIAC: 0° Capricorn–12° 51' Capricorn
ASTERISM: Alpha Capricorni (Giedi), Beta Capricorni (Dabih)
IBN ARABI: ﻆ (Za)
MINERALS, METALS, THE PRECIOUS
PICATRIX: Image of a man with winged feet. Talisman for binding tongues. Spirit name is Geyel. Fashion out of an iron ring and suffumigate with mercury. For curing illness, causing discord, for captives and servants to escape.
LIBER LUNÆ: Face of Mars. Desolation, discord.
AGRIPPA: Spirit name is Geliel. Release of servants and captives.
AL BUNI: ﺕ (Ta)

Nothing done in it will work out well. People regret buying or selling unless they are nitpicky. Kings become enraged. Suitable for digging things up and farming. Secrets are dug up and also hidden. Those born in it will be attractive, blessed, and covetous toward material things. Deep knowledge of subjects. Great teachers. Safflower.

IBN AL HATIM: Spirit name is Ufit Arafit. For separating kings from their viziers.

AL ASHRAF: Safflower

SOLOMONIC RING (CUNNING MAN): Parts of a cow's horn and pasture grass. For the purposes of multiplying cattle and growing herds. For growth and prosperity.

NAKSHATRA

Abhijit 'VICTORY'
ASTERISM: Alpha Lyra (Vega)
DIRECTION: North
MOTIVATION: *Dharma*
VIMSHOTTARI: Sun
DEITY: Vidhata or Brahma, Creator God, Writer of Destiny
TAITTIRIYA BRAHMANA: Power to give special victory, even in a losing battle. The war against the Asuras was finally won here.

XIU

Niu 'OX'
AKA: 'HUMAN BEING' 'GATHERER OF ANIMALS' 'BIRD'

UNEVEN TROPICAL ZODIAC: 3°–10° Aquarius (23–29 January)
ASTERISM: Beta Capricorni (Dabih), Alpha Capricorni (Algedi)
SKY QUADRANT: Black Turtle of the North
PLANET: Venus
ANIMAL: Ox
ARTLEY: The Ox is considered steadfast and methodical. Practical, at times, even to the point of dullness. Reliable and sensible. Fears taking the initiative because suspicious of anything untried and unproven. Conservative. Often passed over out of reserve. Affectionate with those close to them. Loyal but sometimes possessive. Prosperous in business through logical thought, practicality, and endurance. Gains through steady persistence. Inauspicious astrologically. Do not leave doors open. Deity of roads, paths, and barriers.
ELEMENT: Metal
MATANGA SUTRA: No offerings necessary. Those born here have renown.

PGM/GREEK:

Virgin, 'BARKING.'
(ATLAS OR URANUS)

PROTO-SINAITIC/HIEROGLYPH

Tau 'MARK'

WORDS

It is understood that Krishna, being much like Abhijit in type himself, was aware of the power of initiating battle during this nakshatra's time and therefore removed it from the wheel of time so that his enemies may not use it against him. As a nakshatra of Brahma, father and great progenitor of the gods, he is far away and detached from the rest of the nakshatras. As the *Dhruva* or Pole, it is unconquerable because it exists on its own plane entirely.

Every cultural iteration of the lunar stations has its relevant stars laying fairly near to the ecliptic (path of the Sun). There are certain exceptions including the stars Arcturus, Aquila, Alphard, and others which are further north and south compared to the rest. Yet, with Abhijit, or the star Vega, it is so far North that it was at one time our Pole Star (and in 14,000 years, it will be again); almost doubling the distance between the ecliptic and other far off stars. Unlike the Vedic nakshatra Abhijit, the Chinese system like the Arabic keeps this lunar station closer to the ecliptic. For the Chinese, the frontal stars of what we know as the Capricorn goat are the main indicators of this station. There is a well known Chinese folk tale, perhaps the most well known, that tells the story of the Oxherd and the Weaving Girl. The story goes something like this:

A young cowherd encounters beautiful bathing fairy maidens at the river, having descended from heaven as if birds from the sky. In dialogue with his companion, the ox, he is led to steal their clothing as they bathe. The youngest of these fairy maidens is chosen to retrieve the clothing but is witnessed naked by the cowherd; inadvertently resulting in an agreed marriage proposal due to being witnessed. They lead a happy life together until the fairy woman's mother asks for her return from the terrestrial realm, back to the sky from which she came. Upon his wife's disappearance, he is told by the ox to slaughter his friend and don his skin so that he may travel to the sky realms to once more be with his beloved wife. The fairy mother then casts a gap between them to keep them apart, yet, every so often a bridge of magpies forms together so that they may meet once and reunite in love; but only for that limited time.

In Chinese culture the figures in this story take on particular astral forms. The Ox is the frontal star of our Western constellation Capricorn, The Cowherd is the star Altair, and the weaving fairy maiden is the star Vega. The dynamic between these three figures speaks deeply to the perplexing vertical dimension of this station. Similar stories of bird maidens descending to bathe and falling into relation with humans exist all over Eurasia; most likely forming one of the deepest narrative layers of early and pre-Indo-European beliefs. As the reader might have surmised, this story also shares much with the mythology of Krishna; famously stealing the clothing of his adoring Gopis.

Due to the avian nature of these stars, one may also include that of Deneb (Cygnus) in this same milieu, as the three bird constellations, Cygnus, Aquila, and Lyra were often thought to form a distinct grouping in that region of the night sky. Cygnus, often thought of as a swan, also mirrors many of these same stories as the bird maiden who frequently descends in swan form. What is this other world signaled by the 'descent of the birds'? There are strong inklings here of falling down (or is it up?) and underworld journeying figures like Orpheus seen through the constellation of the Lyre. This otherworld is not like ours in all of our mortalities. Its timelessness shines black as the night sky. Here we find the jewel in Lucifer's crown, the key to the realm of the immortals. Just as Vega was once a pole star, we see this part of the sky as being inhabited by fallen angels who seek to return to their former axial position. Concretized in matter spirit has forgotten the heights to which it had once soared.

These downward (or, once again, upward?) movements into our dimension are facilitated by the Pole Stars and their uniquely 'interior quality.' Due to their axial nature, they exist somewhere towards the center of everything. This quality is the primary reason they are deemed 'unconquerable,' as access to this central dimension becomes barred to those who have not undergone initiation or proper trial. This station, 'The Lucky of the Slaughterers' and its relationship to oxen more broadly speaks to the highly reverential and sacrificial nature of this place. As the cowherd must slaughter the ox (his confidant) and don his skin for the sake of reaching this domain, we see that a kind of death is necessary to move along the pole.

PLANETARY PLACEMENTS

The Presence of the ☾

Due to the emphasis on stars of the far north, many of the planetary delineations resemble the nakshatra Svati in their quality of elevation and 'looking from above.' This same sense, though described as a kind of aerial view, is felt much more deeply as an internal stability likened to the Vedic term *dhruva* meaning 'fixed.' It is no coincidence that this lunar station is related to the ox and its solidity. As a pole, this is the tower in which the three bird constellations circle. Not unlike the following nakshatra of Shravana, there is a connection here to paths and walking as the Pole is also likened to a road. On this road is written the destinies of all and to walk upon it is to become closer to the hidden awareness of our unity. These are our commonly held origins in consciousness.

At a mundane level, this is represented in the figure of the ox who holds a more 'conservative' connotation. This does not necessarily equal political conservatism, as much as emphasizes older human modalities of family and closeness to the land. The natural world remains important as it brings proximity to 'the center.' Once more, planets here are sensed in subtle ways, as it is precisely the root of perception which this lunar station harkens to.

The nakshatras Uttara Ashadha, Abhijit, Shravana, and Dhanista have much to do with consciousness and perception at their most fundamental levels. This may be addressed in the form of mysticism and esotericism. On the other hand, in its more mundane manifestation, the roots of consciousness discussed here, the 'unity in darkness' sought by the most advanced mystical achiever, may be found in the most everyday of activities and relationships. The story of the Cowherd is testament to this. And in this way we see so much of what is taken for granted in modern life: verdancy, the presence of animals, acts of cultivation, and of course intimacy. These things are in some sense the closest we may achieve to the root of consciousness itself. Therefore the presence of the Moon or a planet here may feel deceptively simple. Almost as if hiding in plain sight. That which is most ontologically essential may feel utterly distant as well as suffocatingly close. This is the nature of The Pole as an axis and as a center.

23.

Subtle Listening / A Walk Through Eternity

Precessed Tropical Coordinates:
4° 07' Aquarius–17° 27' Aquarius

MANZIL

Sa'd Bula 'The Auspicious of the Swallower'
Tropical Zodiac: 12° 51' Capricorn–25° 42' Capricorn
Belongs to the retinue of Wednesday, Angel Michael, and Jinn King Barqan
Asterism: Epsilon Aquarii (Albali)
Ibn Arabi: ث (Tha)
Plants, The Nourisher
Picatrix: Image of a cat with the head of a dog. Talisman for destruction. Spirit name is Zequebin. Fashion out of iron and suffumigate with the hair of a dog. For healing illness, joining friends, and for captives to flee.
Liber Lunæ: Face of the Sun. For goodness.
Agrippa: Spirit name is Requiel. For divorce, and health of the sick.
Al Buni: ث (Tha)
Suitable for buying livestock, speaking with shaykhs and the elderly. Sewing crops, crossing rivers, and flowers. Digging wells and manual labor. Hosting and preparing banquets. Those born here will be

upright and blessed. Will be charitable and enjoy travel. Chamomile.

IBN AL HATIM: Spirit name is Sani Sanahin. For imposing ruin and disease.

ABL ASHRAF: Chamomile and cumin.

SOLOMONIC RING (CUNNING MAN): Parts of a cow's horn and pasture grass. For the purposes of multiplying cattle and growing herds. For growth and prosperity.

NAKSHATRA

Shravana 'THE EAR' 'THREE FOOTPRINTS'
ASTERISM: Alpha Aquilae (Altair)
TEMPERAMENT: Mutable, Divine
CASTE: Outcast
DIRECTION: North
MOTIVATION: *Artha*
ANIMAL: Female Monkey
SOUNDS: Ju, Jay, Jo, Gha
TREE: *Calotroopis Gigantea* (Giant Calotrope)
This tree is found everywhere in India. It grows in forests, sandy soil, barren land and around ruined houses. It is considered to be a useless tree but sometimes as a medicinal plant. Its leaves, roots, bark are used in coughs, asthma, and lack of appetite.
VIMSHOTTARI: Moon
SHAKTI: Power of connection.
DEITY: Vishnu (The Preserver), Saraswati
TAITTIRIYA BRAHMANA: "The limping walker needs to fix a goal, to walk the path"
BRIHAT SAMHITA: "will be cunning, of active habits, efficient workmen, bold, virtuous, god-fearing and truthful."

TIBETAN: *Drozhin.* God of the wind or Sun. Pleasant voice, She Who Satisfies. Famous and popular, learned and careful. Liked by the opposite sex. Appreciates perfume. Enthusiasm. A perfect gentleman. Generous and rich, giving.

XIU

Nu 'GIRL'
AKA: 'HORSE' 'GHOST OF THE HORSE'
UNEVEN TROPICAL ZODIAC: 10°–20° Aquarius (30 January–9 February)
ASTERISM: Epsilon Aquarii (Albali), Mu Aquarii (Albulan)
SKY QUADRANT: Black Turtle of the North
PLANET: Saturn
ANIMAL: Bat
ARTLEY: The bat deals with the avoidance of obstacles, clear vision (possibly clairvoyance), good luck, auspicious undertakings, happiness and longevity, can cause jealousy due to increases. Inauspicious in astrology. Marriage is inauspicious on these days and siblings will fight amongst themselves. Deity of Music. Considered unlucky. Disputes, quarrels, disturbing peace.
ELEMENT: Earth
MATANGA SUTRA: Offerings of bird meat. Those born here are much honored and favored by the king.

PGM/GREEK

Torch, 'MOANING.'
DEITY: Apollo

PROTO-SINAITIC/HIEROGLYPH

Peh, Puh, 'MOUTH'

WORDS

Sound Transmissions, Guidance, Structures Become Smoke, Observation, Curative, Pristine, Musical, Pathwalking, Learning of One's Surroundings, Transportation, Attention/Intention, Life Extension, The Well Worn Road, The Voice from On-High, Mystical Insights, Wisdom Seeker, Celestial Rupture, Locomotion.

After having risen up into the dimension of the Pole with its inevitable descent, the following two stations deal with the movement of sound and the directing of consciousness at fundamental levels. Having reached the center of awareness in the previous station we are dropped by the birds into vast realms of vibration and abstraction. Here begins a region of celestial darkness spanning the Saturn-ruled signs of Capricorn and Aquarius into Jupiterian Pisces. This part of the sky has often been conceived of as a celestial ocean. Consequently these stars and lunar stations deal with energies in non-terrestrial and non-solid ways. Currents of air and liquid are more common here. The deepest reaches of space become less and less familiar by our conventions; all the same as the depths of the ocean. To navigate and comprehend these places we must broaden our senses and attune them to invisible dimensions.

As both of these stations are composed of the stars in the constellation of Aquarius, we may surmise how the imagery of the water bearer lends itself to these same themes. Perhaps one of the oldest associations with this constellation is that of the agricultural field. The Babylonians conceived of this portion of the sky as that of their deity Enki, a skilled magician and agriculturalist privy to the mysteries of fresh water. In many cultures, some of the first technologies emerged from the harnessing of fresh water for both drinking and agricultural purposes. The innovations necessary for the irrigation of fields (especially in arid climates) give Aquarius much of its archaic symbolism as well as its more modern associations with technology and science. The Arabic images related to this lunar station frequently maintain this agricultural symbolism as they have corresponded with Saturn and his relationship to farming. Saturn in his oppositional role to the Sun becomes associated with science and abstract calculation for precisely this reason. Given circumstances are not conducive and must be altered. Foreign to the Sun is this emergence from a sense of lack. The Saturnian disposition is one of critical analysis. It has the capacity to alter environments to suit whatever purpose.

Both the Chinese xiu symbol of the bat as well as the nakshatra's consistent reference to sound is quite important here. Even the Proto-Sinaitic hieroglyph of 'the mouth' and the PGM's reference to 'moaning' line up quite nicely with these themes. The nakshatra Shravana is often referred to as the listening star and relates to the transmission of consciousness through the medium of sound. The deity associated with the nakshatra is Vishnu, The Preserver, another reference to consciousnesses as all pervasive. The locomotion implied by both Vishnu and the image of a footprint speaks to the movement of consciousness from one place to another.

Take the Chinese symbol for this station of the bat as one example. Using echolocation this animal emits ultrasounds that bounce off of other beings and objects only to be returned to their acute ears. It is navigation through the use of subtle emissions and retrievals that allows animals like bats to exist in the darkened Saturnine realms. The realm of the Sun is clear and navigable. The Saturnian dimension, on the other hand, requires technological innovation to survive. At the most fundamental level, this lunar station may be summed by the echolocation of the bat. Unlike the following station which deals with the mapping of these same abstract forms, here we become deeply in touch with the movement from form to form and the sense of travel implied with it.

PLANETARY PLACEMENTS

The Presence of the ☾

The Moon in this sign becomes involved with practices of speaking and even more importantly listening. Teaching, preaching, and recitation in general may be found here; especially those sermons of a mystical or spiritual bent. Unlike the station that follows which emphasizes roundabout and creative vibrations, here we see a stronger emphasis on the movement between A and B. This does not preclude expressive acts, yet the Moon here tends toward proclivities of analysis more than ambiguity. As the indicator star is that of the Eagle, or Altair, there is a sense of flight and vantage from above. She may be quite philosophical and hold deep interest in all matters of the inner workings of the cosmos. These understandings may reach a level of depth unattainable by superficial scientific reasoning, as this station maintains a connection with the intuitive levels of reality alongside those of the rational intellect.

The Presence of ☿

The planet of intelligence moves deeply into and through the circuit-structures of the cosmos in this sign. Electrical impulses surging through interconnecting threads are a strong image for this placement. Pathways and neural networks weave together here. They may be fashioned and re-fashioned in unorthodox manners leading to a kind of neurogenesis. This placement may hold a deeply felt sense of understanding complex scientific and experimental theories. Like the Moon, we see a merging of intuitive faculties with those of rational analysis.

The Presence of ♀

Venus in this lunar station signifies a colder sense of connectivity. It is important to note that it is not a lack of connection or disassociation, but one which sees the underlying structures of relations in their more 'objective' qualities. She is simultaneously quite matter-of-fact yet also abstract. The movement factor so important to this place lends itself well to non-static creative practices (which it shares much with the following lunar station). Venus must feel mentally stimulated here. Her experiences of pleasure often come through travel, research, and the extension of passion into study of far-off places and subjects. There are also strong connections to the paranormal and supernatural phenomena here; seen perhaps more often with the darker planets yet no less important.

The Presence of the ☉

The Sun is not at home per se in this dimension. The planet of clarity must adopt the means of his opposer, that of Saturn, to thrive more fully in these realms. Here the Sun becomes particularly aware of other suns (other stars, if you will) wherein the sonorous mouth of stellar light bounces back in echoing motion as the mirror is put before him; as he encounters himself in full brightness. This is a challenging position for a planet which typically relishes his singular experience. He is queried to feel into processes of transmission and reception. In the manner of the bat's echolocation we see this same process play out with solar light. Here he must have a means of receiving back his radiance so that he may be situated properly.

The Presence of ♂

As this lunar station is related to the eagle star of Altair, it is instructive to observe Mars' placement in this station as he resembles a bird of prey hunting in the darkness. Like an owl, he is a natural in his pursuits through all things hidden and obscure. He is not effective in the typical Martial sense here. His bearing on the world is fleeting, as if air momentarily brushing up upon the land, yet his senses are keenly attuned to things otherworldly. As this is a sign of speech and sound transmission his words may emerge harshly and combative. If he has lessons and teachings for the world they are of power, strategy, and even covert movements. Similarly, we find an equal possibility of anxiety towards the hidden world here.

The Presence of ♃

Jupiter finds himself among the cold and Saturnine dimensions of restricted movement. Faith is often not sufficient for navigating these same places. Therefore Jupiter may begin to put his trust in more predictable means such as those of science and so-called fact. Processes must be systematized and replicable, as well as egalitarian for

Jupiter to function well. In regards to notions of parenting and tutelage, he may excel in this sign as he is indeed a planet of sound and vibratory transmission.

The Presence of ♄

The planet of darkness does well here in the domain of abstract calculations and deep mystical speculation. He is indeed at home in these darkened realms with little worry. Out of all of the planets, it is Saturn who is the best equipped to formulate pathways through the stranger dimensions of reality. Like many of the other placements, there are profound means of analysis and inquiry here. Complex metaphysical systems and the like may be learned and taught as this airy dimension of the planet mirrors his affinity for Aquarius. Like Venus, there may also be deeply rooted connections to paranormal and supersensory phenomena. This is a Saturn deeply attentive to and in dialogue with the strangest aspects of reality and their ongoing study.

24.

Reverberating Sound / Beauty Conquers All

Precessed Tropical Coordinates:
17° 27' Aquarius–0° 47' Pisces

MANZIL

Saʿd al Suʿud 'The Auspicious of the Auspicious'
Tropical Zodiac: 25° 42' Capricorn–8° 34' Aquarius
Belongs to the retinue of Friday, Angel Aʾaniel, and Jinn King Zawbaʾah
Asterism: Beta Aquarii (Sadalsuud)
Ibn Arabi: ذ (Dhal)
Animals, The Humblers
Picatrix: Image of a woman breastfeeding her child in her arms. Talisman for the increase of herds. Spirit name is Abrine. Fashion from the horn of a castrated ram. For increase of merchandise and profit, goodwill between husband and wife, for soldiers to report victory, and to not meet officials.
Liber Lunæ: Face of Venus. For goodness.
Agrippa: Spirit name is Abrinael. Good for married couples, victory of soldiers.
Al Buni: خ (Kha)
Suitable for all deeds. Love, affection, and the reconciliation of hearts. Spiritual healing, meet with kings, craft talismans. Works of love. To be born here is

to be blessed and righteous. Inclination towards philosophy and religion. Hermits and secretive. Aloeswood and mastic.

IBN AL HATIM: Spirit name is Afratim Abriyas. For improving and growing herds.

AL ASHRAF: Aromatic wood and mastic.

SOLOMONIC RING (CUNNING MAN): Parts of a cow's horn and pasture grass. For the purposes of multiplying cattle and growing herds. For growth and prosperity.

NAKSHATRA

Dhanishta 'THE RICHEST ONE' 'MOST FAMOUS' 'DRUM'

ASTERISM: Alpha Delphini (Sualocin), Beta Delphini, Gamma Delphini

TEMPERAMENT: Mutable, Daemonic

CASTE: Warrior

DIRECTION: East

MOTIVATION: *Dharma*

ANIMAL: Female Lion

SOUNDS: Ga, Ge, Go, Gay

TREE: *Prosopis Cineraria* (Jand)

This tree is of two sizes, i.e. big and small. It is very useful medicinally for coughing, phlegm, and like ailments. Its leaves, bark, and pods are used in these ailments. It is good fodder for domestic animals in dry areas. The person under the influence of this constellation often thinks too much.

VIMSHOTTARI: Mars

DEITY: Vasudevas, Elemental Forces

SHAKTI: Power to give abundance and fame.

TAITTIRIYA BRAHMANA: "Desirable objects need tangible resources for wealth"

BRIHAT SAMHITA: "will be shameless, of weak friendship, haters of women, generous, rich and free from temptation."

TIBETAN: *Mondre*. He Who Attains. Higher Friend. Intrepid, independent, valiant. High ideals. Liked by his elders. Fond of music. Rich and generous.

XIU

Xu 'EMPTINESS/VOID'
AKA: 'RHINOCEROS'
UNEVEN TROPICAL ZODIAC: 10°–28° Aquarius (10–17 February)
ASTERISM: Beta Aquarii (Sadalsuud), Alpha Equulei (Kitalpha)
SKY QUADRANT: Black Turtle of the North
PLANET: Sun
ANIMAL: Rat
ARTLEY: The rat deals with charm, adaptability, creativity, and inventiveness. Quick-witted, bright and sociable, ostentatious. Irritable. Upwardly mobile. A crafty and opportunistic character who will use friends before eventually losing or dropping them. Erratic in financial matters. Bright and gregarious, with a love of gossip. Nasty when riled. Remarkable command of abstractions. Especially good with detailed and complex calculations. Yin animal. An emblem of timidity and meanness, though also of sharp intelligence. One of the five feared household animals, and was said to be able to bring on insanity. Inauspicious. Brings disturbed sleep and debauchery. An indicator, too, of writers and historians. Deity of

cemeteries. Considered unlucky. Funerals, illnesses, tears. All negative things.
ELEMENT: Varied
MATANGA SUTRA: Offerings of bean gruel. Born here are bellicose.

PGM/GREEK

Lightning, 'A CRY OF JOY'
DEITY: Muses

PROTO-SINAITIC/HIEROGLYPH

He, Hillel, 'PRAISE' 'JUBILATION'

WORDS

Elemental, Particulars/Particles, Attention-Seizer, Echolocation, Universal Threads, Constituent Parts, Music of the Spheres, The Curtain of Oz, Titillation, Spectral Labor, 'Shiny Things,' Coalescing Voices, The Rhythm of the Cosmos, Contrapuntal, Plasmatic, Connecting of the Dots, Dancing With No-End in Sight, Navigating Gravity, Resonating/Sonorous.

It is emptiness and oceanic navigation which marks this lunar station. Once more, this region of the sky is less populated with starlight and constellation imagery. Cultures have observed this and consequently found a likeness to the ocean and its vast darknesses. Yet, concealed in this darkness is the energetic patterning for all visible phenomena. Here we find strange and unseen threads that connect our existences in bizarre and unexpected ways. One of the more important stars associated with this lunar station is Alpha Delphini, also known as Sualocin. As its name attests to, we see a whole bevy of aquatic creatures and their subtle forms of navigation and communication across the liquid dimension. Due to the musical nature of this station, the drum being one of its primary symbols, echolocation is perhaps the best example as it involves the movement of sound waves bouncing off of objects in the determination of space.

Another example may be that of self-generated luminosity used by some creatures of the deepest waters. Like the previous station, here we are similarly confronted by darkness and its necessary innovations for survival. It is this creative process that marks this region as well as generates its unique beauty.

Though this station shares much with the previous one, it is oftentimes thought to be of a more auspicious nature. Both deal with the movement of consciousness from place to place; perhaps best conceived as sound and vibration. If the 23rd station consists of paths then here we find the various destinations and places of origin. The Chinese name for this station is 'emptiness,' while the Arabic imagery is populated by animals, fecundity, and nourishment. It is in some sense the generative darkness from which all form arises. Even more than simply form, this station speaks to form that is attractive.

As the nakshatra is sometimes called 'the most wealthy or famous,' it is this generative and attractive quality which brings so many positive associations. Beauty elicits vibrations and movements of energy. Beauty as desire has the ability to bring things together, to draw them nearer to one another. The nakshatra deity of Vasudev is something akin to what we call elemental forces. These are the constituent threads of the natural world. If the previous station represents the invisible energy of sound/consciousness itself, then here we find the 'objects' or vessels which contain it. It is these containers that elicit attraction and desire, those things we may call beautiful, which best reveal the underlying and invisible energies already spoken of. Consciousness perpetuates itself through these desirous actions, cohering the world through magnetic frequencies. If we have already witnessed the station of locomotion, here the desire which motivates this movement becomes apparent. Between the two the engine of consciousness spreading is established, patterning the whole of creation by spreading forth through desire.

PLANETARY PLACEMENTS

The Presence of the ☾

The Moon in this lunar station is deeply invested in the creation of beauty in the world. As the nakshatra deity is related to the elemental forces of the cosmos, the Moon here acts as a medium of mediums wherein this placement brings an innate ability to fashion attractive forms. She may be extremely aesthetic in her orientation towards life, taking up practices that involve design, curation, and attention to space. Much like the previous station, there is also a strong emphasis on movement here, both of sound but also of discrete physical bodies. She may find expression in dance and rhythmic practices. Movement is critical here for whatever mode of expression the Moon tends towards. Expression is dynamic and captivating as she naturally draws eyes to her, inspiring others to similarly express themselves. This is a placement of deep nurturance and growth, the spreading of art and music as spiritual practice, as well as all things which enliven consciousness to expand outward.

The Presence of ☿

Mercury's wordsmithing is strong here as both analytical and aesthetic writing/speaking are heightened with this placement. If this lunar station emphasizes the fashioning of beautiful vessels, a Mercury placement uses language as the means to achieve this. They may be quite adept at the use of musical instruments and those technologies requiring agile finger movements and expressive sound. As one might expect, they are poetic and elegant in language, their speech and the actual sound of their voice capable of drawing audiences and attention. Commercial endeavors in this sign may focus on aesthetics and practices which bring people pleasure. Similarly, we see here one of the most media-oriented placements for Mercury, as the transmission of arts and culture takes on great importance in this sign.

The Presence of ♀

Venus compliments Saturnine qualities well here, especially those parts of her which emphasize the structuring of form for the sake of adoration. This is the fundamental nature of the 24th lunar station. She shares much with both the curator and the artist here as the relational planet easily interweaves through aesthetic modalities in a multiplicity of ways. Though it might not seem obvious, this is perhaps one of the strongest positions for Venus in the lunar zodiac. Aside from her more visceral associations, her characteristics as a planet are almost completely matched with this sign albeit in an almost abstract manner. Her drive towards the beautiful is unmatched, and she may very well be recognized and applauded for these qualities by those around her.

The Presence of the ☉

Not unlike the previous station, the Sun here finds himself distant from a position of comfort. With that said, he must utilize alternative methods of action in order to thrive. This station does indeed confer a kind of spotlight, though it is not of the Leonine sort. Performativity remains strong here, though by its nature it emerges in more subtle ways to those familiar solar lands. The fostering of art and culture among communities and larger groups is found here, as the Sun becomes a leader yet of a more egalitarian kind.

The Presence of ♂

The planet of war functions well when engaged in the battle dance here. We find technical minutia but also grace in terms of conflict. This is an artsy Mars easily frustrated by the mundane workings of the world. Secretly passionate at times, he is capable of fighting for what he feels is right and beautiful in the world, yet perhaps reticent to shout it out to the world at large. Like the Sun he is performative and well-suited towards the arts and entertainment. If involved as such, he may be drawn to those forms considered 'alternative,' and slightly out of step.

The Presence of ♃

This is a placement with no question or doubt as to the creative potential of humankind. The dolphin is a wonderful instructor in this instance, as a primary animal for this lunar station as well as a being who moves freely and expansively in the dark waters. This placement is a whale song of sorts, and he holds great breadth and deep wisdom in matters of attention grabbing. His words echo from ear to ear and he may be remembered and much beloved for his generosity and philanthropy. Jupiter in this station may attain to great wealth cultivated through art, aesthetics, music, design, collecting, marketing, and even outright celebrity.

The Presence of ♄

This is a strong placement for the dark planet's creative expressions. Here, as the molder of form and shaper of limitations, he may use his abilities for the creation of long-lasting and treasured works of all kinds. This aspect of the beautiful often goes unrecognized. Just as in Jyotish wherein Saturn and Venus are naturally aligned, we must remember that the creation and maintenance of things we find beautiful takes structure, discipline, and containment. Works of the finest craftsmanship and detail may be found here as Saturn's endurance combined with aesthetic sensibilities births the timelessly adored. Here he is a creator who has spent the duration of his life dedicated to the mediums he knows so well. He speaks with the clay before he sculpts, as much as his breath is embedded within the instrument with whom he plays.

25.

Stirring of the Old Gods / Pharmacopœia

Precessed Tropical Coordinates:
0° 47' Pisces–14° 07' Pisces

MANZIL

Saʿd al Ajbiya 'The Auspicious One of Hiding Places or Hidden Things'
Tropical Zodiac: 8° 34' Aquarius–21° 25' Aquarius
Asterism: Gamma Aquarii (Sadachbia), Alpha Aquarii (Sadalmelek)
Ibn Arabi: ف (Fa)
The Angels, The Strong
Picatrix: Image of a man planting trees. Talisman for guarding plant life, crops. Spirit name is Aziel. Fashion out of fig wood and suffumigate with the flowers of trees. For revenge against enemies, sieging, that messengers convey messages, that men and women are bound from having sex, for destruction of crops, to bind whichever part of the human body.
Liber Lunæ: Face of Mercury. For silence, and binding.
Agrippa: Spirit name is Aziel. Binds sexuality, sieging, revenge.
Al Buni: ذ (Dhal)
Stirring of division, separation, and war. Things done here do not reach fruition. Those born here will

be faithless and have many doubts. Frankincense, astragalus (*anzarut*), and pepper.
IBN AL HATIM: Spirit name is Asyal. For the improvement of crops and land.
AL ASHRAF: Frankincense, *anzarut*, and pepper.
SOLOMONIC RING (CUNNING MAN): Horse hoof. Spirit names are Carior, Fortunelich, and Hunambilich. For the purposes of having a swift horse take one wherever they wish. For rapid transportation/movement.

NAKSHATRA

Shatabhishak 'THE HUNDRED HEALERS' 'EMPTY CIRCLES'
ASTERISM: Gamma Aquarii (Sadachbia)
TEMPERAMENT: Mutable, Daemonic
CASTE: Butcher
DIRECTION: South
MOTIVATION: *Dharma*
ANIMAL: Female Horse
SOUNDS: Go, Sa, Se, So
TREE: *Neolamarckia Cadamba* (Burflower)
This is an evergreen tree with huge-sheddy leaves of medium size and round shape. It is found everywhere in India. The fruit of this tree is green-yellow and sweet. Its wood is soft. It is used in furniture, building material, tea container boxes, and packing material. The wood is useful for carving and designing. The gum, wax, and resin are also useful from this tree. The bark and juice of its leaves are used medicinally for cardiac problems, blood pressure, and rheumatism. Its bark and roots are very effective for children with fever

and stomach ache. This tree is very much favored by Lord Krishna.
VIMSHOTTARI: Rahu
DEITY: Varuna, God of the Sea
SHAKTI: Power to heal.
TAITTIRIYA BRAHMANA: "The master of myriad combinations needs all of space for all the Earth"
BRIHAT SAMHITA: "will be fishermen or dealers in fish and hogs; washermen; dealers in wine and birds."
TIBETAN: *Trumtö.* Goddess of the Mountains. Goddess of the Place. Bull's Foot. Learned. Good speaker but mean, jealous, pained and sad. Loss of money due to women.

XIU

Wei 'ROOFTOP/DANGER'
AKA: 'GODDESS OF WATER'
UNEVEN TROPICAL ZODIAC: 30° Aquarius–15° Pisces (18 February–6 March)
ASTERISM: Alpha Aquarii (Sadalmelek), Epsilon Pegasi (Enif)
SKY QUADRANT: Black Turtle of the North
PLANET: Moon
ANIMAL: Swallow
ARTLEY: Inauspicious. Build nothing large on these days. Not good for business or irrigation, either. These will bring unhappiness and trouble with the legal system. Flock of swallows is a good omen and presages the coming of spring and prosperity. Favorable for medications and renovations. Good for construction. Bad for travel.
ELEMENT: Varied

MATANGA SUTRA: Offering of non-glutinous rice. Born here become commanders.

GEOMANCY

TANNERY: Fortuna Minor

PGM/GREEK

Garland, 'HISSING.'
DEITY: Aegeon
(alternatively, Poseidon or Proteus)

PROTO-SINAITIC/HIEROGLYPH

Qubbah, Qoph 'TENT'

WORDS

Coalesce, Rapturous, Beginnings and Endings, Infinite Combinations, Ecstatic Inklings, A Snow Covered Peak, Council, A Hinge, Leaving Behind a Life for Something Other, The Druggist/Pharmacist, Movement of Flocks, Hive-Minded, Experimental, Clouds, Mysteries of the Depths, Counseling the Interior, Banishment, God's Initial Words Upon the Waters.

This station focuses on the last stars of Aquarius. Here we see the manifestation of the many combinations of the previous two stations in an almost overwhelming outpouring of novelty. The Arabic images maintain this notion of perpetual fertility through use of agricultural imagery associated with this manzil. As discussed in the previous two stations, the constellation we know as Aquarius has historically held strong agrarian symbolism. Extending into the modern sphere of understanding, this bears upon the technological impulse associated with this sign. Often this impulse seeks to alter the environment towards particular ends. This theme persists in the station, yet it is far less abstract than the previous two. Here we find a strong emphasis on medicine, healing, and somatic sciences. How does the scientific impulse affect our bodies through the intake of various substances? How might these substances alter our consciousness?

The present station floats in ethereal tones far more than most. The nakshatra is related to the deity Varuna, god of the celestial waters and previous high god of the Vedic pantheon before being supplanted by the storm god Indra. Much of the water imagery persists across various cultures and their conceptions of this stellar region. To this, there is a strong sense of the old ways in which circumstances might be handled. In that so-called 'Golden Age,' before political intrigue brought on by the new gods, perhaps when things felt 'closer to nature.' There is a relationship with plants and animals here, as well as to their healing powers and unique awareness. Lifeways that were once so ubiquitous, such as traditional forms of medicine, are found here with the recognition that they have fallen from a previous stature. Not unlike the ninth station or Ashlesha nakshatra, we find a realm of banishment occupied by beings and personalities who represent these older byways.

PLANETARY PLACEMENTS

The Presence of the ☾

The Moon in this lunar station may be deeply dreamy in character, even otherworldly. These qualities make for surreal creative potential. There is a fascination and ease with the shifting of consciousness into unfamiliar states. She is a natural psychonaut and may be fond of psychedelic substances, the enjoyment of intoxication, as well as those practices which take one outside of the body through ecstatic means. It is this same disposition which has been 'banished' from the modern world, sent to the so-called black markets of society as drug enthusiasts and recreational drug users. These alternative forms of consciousness are considered taboo. It is often the sensual substances where she excels. This is not solely limited to what we would call intoxicating or mind-altering. This may also extend to food, scent, and other more subtle materials which alter us through pleasure. Art, poetry, music, and immaterial forms may also be included here. Many of the older texts speak of perfumers and druggists being born here. Therefore the Moon may be quite talented at cataloging various substances and the effects that they possess.

The Presence of ☿

This is a realm of the natural poet, word-play-creatives, and writers. Mercury here brings unorthodox means of communication best suited towards art and alternative ways of speaking. They may struggle to relate in more 'conventional' manners, with consequent frustrations through the alienation born from this. At the same time, they excel greatly in all artforms which require this by necessity. Here we listen to the *Mantiq al Tayr* or the Language of the Birds as communication with the natural world also takes precedence. Think of dream logic but applied to language, as it is essential that Mercury is not boxed in here and allowed to explore freely.

The Presence of ♀

Unlike Venus placements on the more structural ends of Aquarius, this lunar station brings strong aesthetic sensibilities of a dream-like nature. This is a fertile placement for her in relationships, sexuality, and sensual qualities. As one of the strongest stations for Venus, she thrives here amidst the creative potentials born of the watery and oneiric dimensions of this place. She is capable of moving through the multiple-dimensions of aesthetic experience as well as possessing a Jupiterian sense of luck and faith. This is a nakshatra of the flower, representing the blossoming potential of those planets well aligned to the station's energies.

The Presence of the ☉

The light of the Sun reflects along rainbow arches here as the planet of light begins to glow. He is naturally inclined towards alternative spiritual pursuits and expressions. He may be much aligned with the qualities of this station, yet often this manifests in more behind-the-scenes manners. Just as Varuna was the previous leader of a bygone era, now exiled to the other world as a forgotten ruler, he may partake of this story as his own. There is a strong sense of leadership found here, yet it is often in some alternative fashion or sub-cultural domain. There may be challenges in handling solary pursuits in direct or more conventional ways. At the same time, excelling and shining in worlds less familiar to the everyday may come quite easily. Here he garners cult fame and the like; the stuff of legends and mythical status if not notorious at some level. As we know it is the victors who write the history. He may be so fortunate to achieve great status in addition to being well liked in future ages.

The Presence of ♂

Mars can be quite experimental here as we see his pharmaceutical orientation strongly nourished. The planet of transformation shines as the mixing and alteration of substances through intense and fiery means aligns nicely with this station. Mars is often a patron of alchemy. He may excel at scientific pursuits involving chemistry, cooking, fermentation and the like. This placement has a quality of boiling beakers and bustling laboratories. When well positioned, he may also possess vision which drives these same transformations, lest he risk the dangerous results of going beyond the measurements of the known.

The Presence of ♃

This is a strong placement for the planet of buoyancy and joy, as he finds comfort here. Unlike the previous placements in more Saturnian realms, Jupiter's inclination towards wisdom seeking experience and expansive creativity may grow in abundance, as this is a fertile region for such explorations. Jupiter is the 'cool parent' here, who might prefer to raise his children in a free and open fashion. Similarly, this placement is quite licit and open-minded in disposition, as the boundless celestial waters endlessly beckon exploration. He is a teacher of the strange and the uncertain, as well as all of those philosophies and religions that exist outside of orthodox paradigms. Jupiter may very well champion the underdog as well as those causes which favor the marginal and oppressed.

The Presence of ♄

Curiously enough, Saturn may be inclined towards the other end of the spectrum with this placement showing suspicions of intoxication and substance use. It is those things which take a person from their base state of being that may be called into question. That said, it is not at the expense of creative possibility. He may be quite prolific in imagination here, though his methods are altogether different from the other placements that value ecstatic means and the like. With regimen, sobriety, and regularity, Saturn is capable of molding this cloud-scape of a place into beautiful and enduring forms. There is sometimes a reluctance to cede measure and refrain. Nevertheless it remains necessary for the accomplishment of greater and more productive ends.

26.

Water-Ash / Burning

Precessed Tropical Coordinates:
14° 07' Pisces–27° 27' Pisces

MANZIL

Al Farg Al Muqaddam or *Al Farg Al Awwal* 'THE FIRST SPOUT'
TROPICAL ZODIAC: 21° 25' Aquarius–4° 17' Pisces
ASTERISM: Alpha Pegasi (Markab)
IBN ARABI: ب (Ba)
THE JINN, THE SUBTLE
PICATRIX: Image of a woman with her hair in front of her falling into a vessel. Talisman for the creation of love. Spirit name is Tagriel. Fashion out of white wax and mastic and suffumigate with pleasant odors. For binding people in mutual love, to travel safely, and strengthen buildings.
LIBER LUNÆ: Face of the Moon. For alliance, cooperation.
AGRIPPA: Spirit name is Alheniel. For union and love.
AL BUNI: ض (Dah)
Inflames love and lust and makes people susceptible to affection. Suitable for alchemy, spiritual healing, and talisman making, Poisons cured and beneficial medicines made. Those born here shall have a good life. Will be liked and influential. Able to see others' motives. Frankincense, black seed, and saffron.

IBN AL HATIM: Spirit name is Nafsiyal Taghriyal. For the creation of love and lust from women.

AL ASHRAF: Frankincense, black seed, and saffron.

SOLOMONIC RING (CUNNING MAN): Spirit names are Hegur, Manopall and Mortatalio. For the purposes of turning ants into cents (pennies).

NAKSHATRA

Purva Bhadrapada 'THE FIRST LEGS OF THE FUNERAL COT' 'SWORDS'

ASTERISM: Alpha Pegasi (Markab), Beta Pegasi (Scheat)

TEMPERAMENT: Fierce, Human

CASTE: Brahmin

DIRECTION: West

MOTIVATION: *Artha*

ANIMAL: Male Lion

SOUNDS: Say, So, Da, De

TREE: *Mangifera Indica* (Mango)

The Mango tree is found in hot and semi-hot places, and in hilly regions as well as plains. Mango tree is very useful and everyone loves its fruits. Mango is considered to be one of the best and sweetest fruits in the world. Pickles and powders are made from the unripe fruits. Its wood is used for fuel and building material. During festivals and auspicious occasions, green leaves of mango trees are tied in string and kept at the front door for goodness and protection. During the Yagna ceremony its wood is considered sacred as fuel.

VIMSHOTTARI: Jupiter

DEITY: Ajaikapada (One Footed Goat or Celestial Fire Dragon), Rudra

SHAKTI: Power to elevate spiritual people in life.
TAITTIRIYA BRAHMANA: "The divine serpent coming to the altar's base needs the universal fire to dissuade material existence"
BRIHAT SAMHITA: "will be thieves, shepherds, torturers; wicked, mean and deceitful; will possess no virtues; neglect religious rites and will be successful in fights."
TIBETAN: *Trumto.* Goddess of the Mountains. Goddess of the Place. Bull's Foot. Learned, good speaker but mean. Jealous, pained and sad. Loss of money due to women.

XIU

Shi 'ENCAMPMENT/HOUSE'
AKA: 'UPPER QUAD-ANGLE' 'FROG'
UNEVEN TROPICAL ZODIAC: 15° Pisces–3° Aries (6–24 March)
ASTERISM: Alpha Pegasi (Markab), Beta Pegasi (Scheat)
SKY QUADRANT: Black Turtle of the North
PLANET: Mars
ANIMAL: Pig
ARTLEY: The pig is always working for future security. Fun-loving, family-oriented. What you see is what you get. Loves company and a good time. Caring and industrious. Good manual skills. Will see things through to the conclusion. Can become extremely financially savvy. Can be naive and overly trusting. Career-minded. Volunteer work. Hospitable. A large and varied collection of friends. Live and let live. Astrologically auspicious. Everything increases.

Associated with the ceremonial pyre. Favors and riches are found here.
ELEMENT: Fire
MATANGA SUTRA: Offerings of blood and meat. Those born here will lead thieves.

GEOMANCY

TANNERY: Fortuna Minor

PGM/GREEK

A Herald's Wand, 'GROANING.'
DEITY: Chimera

PROTO-SINAITIC/HIEROGLYPH

Shems, Sims, 'SUN'

WORDS

Fire, Sacrifice, True Love, Working Towards the Future, Entangling, Resistance, Compulsion, Solace of Self, Rejection, Doubling-Down, The Threads That Bind, Shooting Stars, Underlying Powers, Wildfire, The Great Escape, The Candle Strewn Altar, Ever-Subsistent Dragon, Meteor Shower, "Goodness Gracious Great Balls of Fire."

This lunar station begins the constellation sometimes called The Square of Pegasus. The asterism forms what resembles a giant rectangle near the Aquarius constellation. It is the ancient Babylonian constellation known as The Field. Here the water bearer tends his seeds. This same region was also thought to be the stellar representation of the *Absu* or the domain of underground freshwater ruled over by the deity Enki. At a fundamental level, the Square is a place of manifestation. It is this combination of freshwater with the primordial spark of the gods which drives the process forward. Though the following station focuses on the element of water, it is the fire of stars which mixes with it here to bring new life forward in endlessly novel ways.

The Picatrix holds this station to be one of 'true love.' Unlike other places which speak more to sexuality, the emphasis on love takes a far stranger turn as our understanding of the term remains largely superficial. Love is a force of great passion and sacrifice. It is perhaps the only force capable of moving mountains, yet much of it remains completely out of our control. When in the deepest throes with our beloved, destruction is not altogether far away. The power as such resembles a fire that cleanses impurities; anything not of love is reduced to nothing. It is the act of sacrifice, specifically through fire which dominates the nakshatra. As we will see in the station that follows, this is one of the primary themes found in the Square at large. Creation and destruction are intimately linked here as well as all aspects which we would consider dualisms. Practically speaking, in order to achieve anything in these two places, the mystery of sacrifice must be held in the foreground.

It is no accident that these stars, the Great Square, were conceived of as a funeral cot. It is the first stage of this process, or that of the cremation of the flesh which is symbolized by this station. The symbolism of Pegasus is curious in relation to this theme. Born from the blood of the Gorgon's slaying, it is this act of death-sacrifice which allows for the horse's flight. Freshwater springs forth from wherever he steps. Encapsulated in this act lies the mystery of the Square as fertility and abundance are born from the ending of life. The proximity and tension between them become the heat born of this station.

PLANETARY PLACEMENTS

The Presence of the ☾

The Moon here is often brought to acts and times of great sacrifice within her life as this station demands a shedding of conventions for things more ever-lasting. As described above, love is a force that often elicits these kinds of actions, as most are not willing to go forward with large sacrifices without it. The Moon here may be somewhat idealistic. Love as a motivation is often framed in exactly these terms. Yet it is not limited to the love of other people solely. Here we find ideals above, below, and alongside those more conventional, yet strangely rooted in the older ways. Most modern societies do not hold these principles at the forefront any longer. She may seem irrational or perhaps rebellious in this manner. In this respect, there is also a strong mystical inclination. This station is a strong testing ground yet rewards great sacrifice; typically with immaterial knowledge and the like. Doubt may be the greatest of these tests as she reckons with ideals and is perhaps called to move beyond them. There is a death-like process illustrated with this station. It is the dissolving of materiality which often makes her even more inclined towards security around the same. Perhaps the most mundane reaction remains the awareness of non-existence; both the spiritual and material efforts in turn propelled forward by this.

The Presence of ☿

Mercury is capable of exploring the vast and strange expanse here. They may dive in and out of currents and complexes often unknown even to them. Mercury dialogues with mysteries here, and enjoys writing about them and engaging with them more broadly. The planet of exchange sees things almost in black-and-white terms; alive or dead. Paradoxically it may be all nuance or none of it all. They may be romantic in their words and concepts yet not necessarily capable of living out their words in day to day life.

The Presence of ♀

Venus sees her ultimate sacrifices for the sake of love here, as this powerful placement is capable of creating great martyrs, saints, and everything in between. Once more this love is not limited to other persons. Those who would give everything to achieve their end in regard to Venusian matters are found here. She is a great artist, the kind who would put their lives on the line for the sake of achieving immense beauty. In this same instance, there remains a threshold. Through it she may all the same sacrifice her own dreams for the sake of others; giving up love for love. She may also be a fierce protector here, not limited to her own family and kin but to all of humankind.

The Presence of the ☉

Like the other fiery planet Mars, the Sun here is innately connected to the mysteries of this station as a celestial furnace. The fire planets bring forward this element inherent to the station quite strongly. This is a generative Sun, as the swirling of sparks and hot water fuel the engines of creation in rapid succession. Like our other luminary, he may also have a mystical bent as the afterlife transition signaled by this station is made clearer through his light. What lay on the other side of that great leap forward?

The Presence of ♂

The hottest planet burns brightly here. There is a kind of knight-like sensibility, lost on much of the modern world, found at home here. Unlike the Sun, Mars' heat may be the catalyst that solar fire isn't always capable of handling. Here he is the searing ember, the brand which glows and prods through the densest of material to instigate. This is one of the more war-like positions for him, as he is capable of fighting for those values less often found on the disassociated digital battlefield. He may fight for that which he loves, even going as far as self immolation if the cause is worthy. Here he sets his attention toward the mysteries of what follows. Like Venus, we see the work of saints and martyrs with this placement.

The Presence of ♃

This is a strong placement for Jupiter's orientation towards immaterial wisdom. Though Western astrology has largely associated this planet with wealth, Jyotish understands Guru or Brihaspati as inherently less materially oriented, focused more on knowledge and wisdom as opposed to the accumulation of material goods (associated more with Venus). Like the Moon, there is a tendency towards accumulation and its inevitable relinquishing born from a deep sense of non-existence to come. Curiously enough, he may be extremely generous and indeed wealthy. This is a fundamental paradox borne of these two stations wherein material circumstances cause friction with spiritual and philosophical ideals. Unlike other planets, Jupiter may more easily navigate these binaries with his wisdom, finding ways of achieving both. As the master of the sacrificial art, he is ideally placed in this station.

THE PRESENCE OF ♄

Saturn aligns with the immaterial orientations of this lunar station as well as its end-of-life circumstance. Sacrifice of the material for the immaterial is a strength of the dark planet. This station's orientation towards esoteric and occult philosophies also bodes well in combination. Unlike planets such as Jupiter or Moon, his skepticism may curb some of the more generous possibilities of this station. Swings toward doubt and uncertainty may dislodge the faith necessary to see these processes through to the other side. In this way he is quite capable of managing the crematory yet it is less likely that he will be the one to offer himself to it.

27.

Ash-Water/Drowning

Precessed Tropical Coordinates:
27° 27' Pisces–10° 47' Aries

MANZIL

Al Farg Al Mu'ajjar or Al Farg Al Thani 'The Later Spout'
Tropical Zodiac: 4° 17' Pisces–17° 8' Pisces
Belongs to the retinue of Thursday, Angel Sarfiel, and Jinn King Shamhurish
Asterism: Gamma Pegasi (Algenib), Alpha Andromeda (Alpheratz)
Ibn Arabi: م (Meem)
Humanity, The Uniter
Picatrix: Image of a man with wings holding an empty dish and a bone. Talisman for destroying springs. Spirit name is Abliemel. Fashion out of red earth and suffumigate with asafoetida and liquid storax. For the increase of merchandise and profit, unite allies, increase harvests, impede buildings being built, prolong incarceration.
Liber Lunæ: Face of Saturn. Separations, binding.
Agrippa: Spirit name is Alheniel. Gains in harvest and profits.
Al Buni: ظ (Za)
Ill deeds. Refrain from war, disputes, or meeting with enemies. Suitable for bleeding. The prevention of sex between men and women. Visit baths and cut

hair and nails. Those born here will be wicked and traitorous, struggling with commitment. They will grow in time with knowledge. Pepper and cinnamon.

IBN AL HATIM: Spirit name is Amriyal Lamiyal. For corruption of baths and water.

AL ASHRAF: Pepper, cinnamon, and frankincense.

SOLOMONIC RING (CUNNING MAN): Spirit names are Hegur, Manopall and Mortatalio. For the purposes of turning ants into cents (pennies).

NAKSHATRA

Uttara Bhadrapada 'BACK LEGS OF THE FUNERAL COT' 'TWINS'

ASTERISM: Gamma Pegasi (Algenib), Alpha Andromeda (Alpheratz)

TEMPERAMENT: Fixed, Human

CASTE: Warrior

DIRECTION: North

MOTIVATION: *Kama*

ANIMAL: Female Cow/Bull

SOUNDS: Du, Tha, Aa, Jna

TREE: *Azadirachta Indica* (Neem)

Hot atmospheric areas of dry weather and forests have abundant growth of the neem tree. This tree has a natural insecticide. In towns and villages this tree is grown on road-sides, open land, and near houses. It is given a very important status in Ayurvedic treatment. Soap-cakes are made from its extracted oil. It is also effective in treating some diseases. Its dried leaves are kept in foodgrains and woolen-clothes to protect them from harmful insects and ants. It is also used for ailments of animals. Its wood is used for building material and agricultural tools.

VIMSHOTTARI: Saturn

DEITY: Ahirbudhyana (Celestial Water Dragon), Rudra, Lakshmi

SHAKTI: Power to bring rain.

TAITTIRIYA BRAHMANA: "The coiled serpent above the sacrificial altar needs to moisten to extract the essence"

BRIHAT SAMHITA: "will be Brāhmins, performers of sacrificial rights; will be generous, devout, rich and observant of the rules of the holy orders; will be heretics, rulers, dealers in rice."

TIBETAN: *Trume*. Snake Net. Skilled and prolific speaker but deceitful. Charitable, tactful, and good at study. Many children, spiritual, and sensitive.

XIU

Bi 'WALL'

AKA: 'LOWER QUAD-ANGLE' 'FROG'

UNEVEN TROPICAL ZODIAC: 4°–13° Aries (25 March–3 April)

ASTERISMS: Gamma Pegasi (Algenib), Alpha Andromeda (Alpheratz)

SKY QUADRANT: Black Turtle of the North

PLANET: Mercury

ANIMAL: Porcupine

ARTLEY: One of the five calamity animals, (as well as one of the Five Seers) along with foxes, weasels, snakes, and rats. Paying homage and respect to these animals brings good fortune. It is said to lie in the way of people and stepping on it causes an attack from the animal. Building brings good fortune. Marriages bring peace and joy. Businesses started on

this day bring wealth and happiness. Associated with archives, treasuries, scholarship, and fine arts.
ELEMENT: Water
MATANGA SUTRA: Offerings of meat. Born here are skilled at mixing perfumes.

GEOMANCY

TANNERY: Fortuna Minor

PGM/GREEK

Child, 'A POPPING SOUND.'
DEITY: Phorcys
(alternatively, Oceanus or Gorgon)

PROTO-SINAITIC/HIEROGLYPH

Sirar, Saphah 'MOON'

WORDS

The Water Filled Saucer, Indigo Dying, Alabaster, Blood Woman, Our Mirror, The Well at the Edge of the Village, Bleach, Drowning and Resuscitation, Soaking-In, The Deepest Blue Become Black, Diamonds/Coal, Communal Baths, Abstraction, (Inside), Absolute, The Aching Sense of No-thing, Abyssal, The Oceanic Depths and Their Mysteries.

Much like the lunar station before it, we are dealing with a realm of transformation. As the second portion of the funeral cot known as The Square of Pegasus, movement through this region of space has a death-like quality to it. This is anything but overt, as transformations born from here occur under blankets of fertile darkness, wherein life and death are inextricably bound in swirling mass. Materiality must be shed before change can occur. The immensity of weight found here cannot be held up through conventional means. Without recourse to the spiritual dimension, the ashen remains of the previous station cannot become diamonds. In this way we are once more introduced to a paradox of materiality. How does one thrive and actualize potential while maintaining spiritual principles?

Connections to wells and underground sources of freshwater are made clear in the Arabic talismanic imagery. Its primary use for the corruption of springs and various waters. Though both the two Square of Pegasus stations are related to water in constellational terms, the nakshatra deity here is explicitly a water serpent (as opposed to the fiery manifestation of the previous one). This serpent is Anandashesha, or the many-headed snake on which the deity Vishnu rides. He represents the base matter of consciousness when all else has been annihilated. The previous station is annihilation by fire and here by water. The serpent, or better yet dragon, which dwells in these two stations, represents what is left over after the world has been burned and flooded in its entirety. Returning to the funeral cot, what is left when our bodies have passed back into the Earth through the processes of decomposition? As our bodies bring nourishment to the soil so is the fertility of this sign born.

There is a strong sexual element to this station, first signaled by the star Alpheratz also known as Alpha Andromeda. For though this star is one of the four primary in the Square of Pegasus it also partakes of the Greek constellation Andromeda or The Woman in Chains. She is the beautiful daughter meant to be sacrificed. Before her looming death at the hellmouth of the monster Cetus, she is saved by the hero Perseus. It is this element of attraction, capable of bringing both the monster and the hero, which becomes a strong theme here. She accepts annihilation as the inevitable conclusion in either instance. This becomes the signal of rebirth, or the ecstatic acceptance of being devoured by the great mysteries of the sea. Unlike the previous station which destroys through fire moving outward, the function here becomes destruction through pulling inward. Something of the downward motion of water.

PLANETARY PLACEMENTS

THE PRESENCE OF THE ☽

The Moon here has a natural gravitas about her which brings depth unlike many stations, though the actualization of this potential may come through much trial. Many of her greatest qualities emerge from a sense of magnetism that people have towards her, as this placement brings abundant moisture. Akin to a kind of palette wetting, desire is stoked and grown in this rich environment. There may be much wealth and beauty in her life here, yet, much like the previous station, there is an inherent challenge in obtaining her desires. This is a station of sacrifice and it must be approached in this way if hidden treasures are to be revealed. Unlike other ophidian stations that deal more with material goods and the pursuit of them, here the

Moon is more explicitly sexual as well as philosophical/spiritual. This brings to mind once more the pervading themes of the Square of Pegasus stations; a spiritualizing quality brought to the material. Here she makes knowledge precious; the pearl at the bottom of the sea. It is the polishing and revelation of this wisdom which makes her shine as if a diamond from the coal.

The Presence of ☿

Mercury may become a bit water-logged in this station as their normal swift-footed nature is hindered by the weight of this station. Yet, if they embrace these heavier modalities, they may be capable of deeper examinations on any given matter. Like Mercury in the previous station, there is less of an emphasis on particulars in any given set of data. The region described by this place lay at the bottom of large bodies of water, wherein precise movements must give way to broader strokes of all kinds. This is the same for communication and commerce. At the same time, they may be gifted writers and speakers known for non orthodox writing, spoken, and intellectual habits; especially in the creative fields. There may also be a natural magnetism to the voice here, yet it is one which often entices the listener into greater depths, and not altogether clear as to what is being communicated.

The Presence of ♀

This is a placement of strong sexuality, revealing one of the more powerful stations for Venus in the entirety of the lunar zodiac. Qualities of wetness, fecundity, and damp earth found here are extremely conducive to venusian sensibilities. Here she is intensely magnetic, a conductor of electric currents, and is quite capable of harnessing this energy towards her ends. Though it is quite rich here, as it is also a region of great depth, Venus must learn to find her breath underwater for greater lengths of time, so as to imbibe the wisdom that may be found here. This process may remain topical for long periods of time. This station is deceptive as such, and one must not confuse the surface of the ocean for the vastness of its depths. In order for abundance and great potential to be realized, Venus must offer herself on the altar of her Art.

The Presence of the ☉

The Sun's radiance here is like that of the so-called Black Sun or Midnight Sun as it dwells deeply in the underworld illuminating vast reaches below. In this way he may be a great guide in the exploration of hidden matters and occult subjects. Like many placements in this station and the previous one, there is an in-built challenge to them, which requires striving towards less and less conventional directions as conformity is shed for pure spiritual energy. With the emphasis on water here, the fiery Sun is also limited in its capacity to express more fully. Therefore he may feel as though he is doomed forever in this nighttime phase. A guide for the lost, a beacon for the underworld indeed, yet what is he who never rises?

The Presence of ♂

Mars holds a passionate bent towards matters of a hidden nature here. Do not be fooled by his seemingly calm exterior. Like other placements there is a curious relationship between the glimmering surface levels of the matter and that of the obscured depth behind/beyond it. It is the mixing of his heat with the fecund qualities of this station which makes for powerful drives and desires.

Like Venus, there is a strong sexual current here. Mars is something of the boa constrictor in this sign as he squeezes the desired substance from his pursuits only to consume them. Unlike the previous station where his fire is nurtured and instigated further, here Mars moves more slowly, methodical, yet no less powerfully.

The Presence of ♃

Jupiter's natural buoyancy and faith may become waterlogged here as this station is markedly heavy in character. If he is capable of discernment, Jupiter may bring beneficial remnants to the surface while letting sink that which no longer serves. This is akin to the alchemical separation within liquid, wherein the relevant material will float to the surface to be skimmed and removed. He may manifest as a large pocket of air, or the hospitable dimension amidst the great suffocating expanse. Like the Sun, he functions well as guide among the damned, a heretical priest of sorts. The code is abided by yet it is one unfamiliar to the masses and even untenable for most.

The Presence of ♄

Jyotish maintains strong associations between Saturn and this lunar station, as the Vimshottari dasha system has them in correspondence. In terms of weight and downward motion, a strong similarity exists between the two. Saturn, out of all of the classical planets, is closest in disposition to those beings at the bottom of the ocean. Here he marks a place of death and rebirth. As the last visible planet, Saturn was often thought of in this regard. In all matters of great devotion, especially to spiritual or metaphysical pursuits, he excels here. Yet the abyssal nature of this placement feigns the day to day; perhaps the greatest challenge for something of such depth which never sees the light of day.

28.

Water Ways (Veins) / Mouth of the Whale

Precessed Tropical Coordinates:
10° 47' Aries–24° 07' Aries

MANZIL

Al Risa aka *Batn al Hut* 'The Rope' 'The Fish's Belly'
Tropical Zodiac: 17° 8' Pisces–0° Aries
Asterism: Beta Andromeda (Mirach)
Ibn Arabi: و (Waw)
The Hierarchy of the Degrees of Existence, not their manifestation, The One Who Elevates by Degrees
Picatrix: Image of fish with a colored spine. Talisman for fish to congregate. Spirit name is Abliemel. Fashion out of brass and suffumigate with the skin of a sea fish. For increasing merchandise and profit, to destroy wealth, get rid of things, peace between men and women, and to inflict evil on sailors.
Liber Lunæ: Face of Jupiter. For goodness, profit.
Agrippa: Spirit name is Amnixiel. Increase harvests and profit.
Al Buni: غ (Ghayn)

Things set aright. Make talismans and perform good deeds. Spiritual healing, work with precious stones. All done in it shall go well. Traveling, marriage, weather, moving, and mingling with officials. Those born here are blessed and have a righteous character. Pleasant appearance. Blackseed.

IBN AL HATIM: Spirit name is Anush. For gathering fish.

AL ASHRAF: Blackseed.

SOLOMONIC RING (CUNNING MAN): Spirit names are Pergor and Naith. For the purposes of turning iron into gold.

NAKSHATRA

Revati 'THE WEALTHY' 'FISH'

ASTERISM: Zeta Piscium
TEMPERAMENT: Soft, Divine
CASTE: Worker
DIRECTION: East
MOTIVATION: *Moksha*
ANIMAL: Female Elephant
SOUNDS: De, Do, Cha, Che
TREE: *Madhuca Indica* (Mahua)

It is a huge, sheddy evergreen tree found in all the forests of Southern India. They are grown in some plains of Northern India and some regions of Southern India. Oil is extracted from the seeds of its fruits to make soap cakes. In some villages on the outskirts of forest, this oil is used in cooking. It is believed that this oil is used as a mixture in vegetable ghee. Healthy cattle food may also be made from it. The flowers are also used to prepare wine so it is called wine-tree. Wood is used for building material and leaves are used as fodder for domestic animals. The flowers of this tree are also used as medicinal herbs.

VIMSHOTTARI: Mercury

DEITY: Pushan (God of Roads/Paths, Guidance, Nourishment), Revati (Protector of Herds and Animals), Lakshmi, Vishnu

SHAKTI: Power to nourish.

TAITTIRIYA BRAHMANA: "The nourished nourisher needs cows for calves"

BRIHAT SAMHITA: "will be dealers in water-flowers, salt, gems, conch shells, pearls, creatures of water, fragrant flowers and perfumes; they may also be boat-men."

TIBETAN: *Namdru*. He who makes knowledge grow. She who heals. Perfect body. Courageous, even heroic. Scorns other's money. Subtle orator. Rich, has a weakness for women.

XIU

Kui 'LEGS'

AKA: 'FROG' 'HORSE' 'BOAT OF HEAVEN' 'WATER STAR'

UNEVEN TROPICAL ZODIAC: 14° Aries–1° Taurus (4–21 April)

ASTERISM: Beta Andromeda (Mirach), Delta Andromeda, Eta Andromeda

SKY QUADRANT: White Tiger of the West

PLANET: Jupiter

ANIMAL: Wolf

ARTLEY: Suspicious of all except the master. Doing business on this day brings ruin. Burials bring disasters. Starting buildings is the only auspicious activity. Considered a treacherous and rapacious animal. Psychopathic temperament. Seen to be entirely evil. Deity holds the keys to balance. Man with his legs astride. No digging or construction. Said to be the arsenal of the Emperor. Textiles, laundry, and military action.

ELEMENT: Wood

MATANGA SUTRA: Offerings of boiled rice with curds. Those born here are vulgar.

GEOMANCY

TANNERY: Carcer

PGM/GREEK

Key, 'SILENCE.'
DEITY: Hermaia (Hermes) (alternatively, Pan)

PROTO-SINAITIC/HIEROGLYPH

Dagh, Samekh 'FISH'

WORDS

Nourishing, Gathering, A New Microcosm, Swaying of Trees, Connecting Roads, Star Dew, Growth, OMEGA, A Gaping Toothless Mouth, Keys, Gruel, Gathering of Animals, Placental, Wealth, Magnetic Dispersal, A Time Away from Humans, Grass

Consuming Herds, Nectarine, Two of Every Kind of Beast.

One of the names for this station, *Al Risa,* is the star imaged as a rope connecting two fishes moving in separate directions. The Chinese constellation refers to legs set astride, mirroring this movement in two directions. Both seem to emerge from the same body or place yet go on to step away separately from one another. Constant motions of splitting and coming back together illustrated by the constellation speak to how the lunar station functions as well as much of its symbolism.

The solar zodiac holds this portion of the sky as a division between winter and spring in the northern hemisphere. As it corresponds to the sign of Pisces, it is also considered to be a place of transition between life and death. It is from this vast darkness in which the spark of the Pleiades (third station) initiates life's vitality forward. Like many of the nearby stations, there are less visible stars in this region of the sky giving it certain aquatic and oceanic associations. There are strange mysteries of fertility emerging out of death and emptiness. This is a space of the wilderness, yet it is not devoid of life by any means. In this light, many of the Arabic images relate this station to a gathering of animals; specifically fish. The nakshatra has similar associations, as the deity Pushan is thought to be a kind of herdsman and steward of animals. There is also a tenderness with such creatures, both aquatic and terrestrial, as distinctions begin to blur between species amidst the waters.

Even more than the stars of Pisces, this station's primary stellar relationship is to those of Andromeda (briefly mentioned in the previous station and even more relevant here). As her head is found in the preceding station, here lies her body. There are strong connections to the mysteries of Medusa and the Gorgons. Andromeda maintains her magnetism. Primeval currents of the deep waters swell in strangely polarizing ways. Like the Gorgons, there is great power and deep connection to be found here, yet not without trial.

This lunar station is also deeply associated with the biblical story of Jonah and the Whale. The mouth of the fish, sometimes conceived of as the star Fomalhaut or the stars of Pisces, represent an entryway to the otherworld. Lunar stations 26–28 share in the quality of *Barzakh*, or the Islamic understanding of the in-between dimension. This isthmus, or barrier-between, may be conceived as an invisible boundary dividing the fresh waters of Aquarius and the salty ones of Pisces. Perhaps more so than the other two, the 28th station materializes this tendency into actual locations, situated away from the mass of others. The primeval separative act found in the legs astride initiates movement away from the world and into the dimension of the whale. Whether it be a home in the forest or a boat out at sea, this same urge leads to the carving out of a new space all its own.

PLANETARY PLACEMENTS

THE PRESENCE OF THE ☾

The Moon in this station moves further away from the world in increasing preference for the care and company of wild spaces, animals, and alternative lifestyles more broadly. This is often necessary for growth, in the same fashion that one fish splits away from the other into the opposite direction. Yet there remains an ambivalence here, as the movement outwards still necessitates the rope which binds them together As such she may be simultaneously quite caring yet also harsh in character. For it is more than just her life's movements that embody this, but also her persona. The Moon's disposition for gathering together shares many similarities with this station, as they both favor slow and methodical accumulations of necessary resources. Here she is apt at taking stock of life's essential properties. These abilities lead to natural wealth signifiers. The Moon here is connected to the almost limitless abundance of the sea.

The Presence of ☿

Mental processes are bright as Mercury is capable of moving through the darkened realms with a glimmering splendor. They may be a gifted orator as this placement holds a disposition much like a poet in the wilderness. This is not learned or scholarly in the traditional sense, but rather, thrives upon the inspirations of the non- and more-than-human. Here we find a Mercury of wilderness survival and adventure. There is a capacity to transform things unnoticed or banal into treasure and good fortune. They may be the one who starts a business in a niche that nobody else could find. Mercury whispers to animals here, not above them or below them, but equal in status.

The Presence of ♀

This is quite the passionate place for Venus. Other times, she may need much stimulation to feel at home. She must leave the house to find her riches and opportunities. Like Mars, this is an adventurous placement yet not in the ways we might expect. Aesthetics here are made of clashing colors and intensities smashed together. The image of gathering animals is prominent in this station, bringing together disparate elements towards a common end. These expressions do not necessarily fit into the norm. Though there may be an intensity of movement, when she finds that which she appreciates she may become the strongest of caretakers. As this station is deeply related to nourishment, she both protects and feeds those of the wilderness and the outside.

The Presence of the ☉

He often shines the brightest when he has established his own world. By necessity, this world must be away from and outside of the normal arrangement of things. Here we find him exalted as the leader of his own domain, the nature of which may be a small group to an entire nation. The Sun as a radiant individual is quite apparent here, yet he is not exactly selfish. It is the Sun in his life-giving warmth. Indeed capable of shining brightly all his own, he also brings nourishment to those around him. The gravitational orbit is quite strong, which, once more, often creates a microcosm in and around him in this station. Here he is an explorer, a leader, and one seeking glory for his own name, yet also for the sake of principles.

The Presence of ♂

This is a strong placement for adventurous Mars, as he is capable of moving far and wide with power, courage, and much boldness. He is free here in a way he is often not. We must recall the station's image of the legs astride; for like the Sun, it is the vast expanse of the sea that lets him spread out in exploration. If anything, he must be careful to temper his innate connections with the wild dimension of reality. As the xiu holds this station for the wolf, Mars mirrors this animal in beauty and power here. That said, he may also embody some of the more positive martial qualities of protecting those in need or those who are vulnerable. If in a healthier position he may become the strongest of stewards, protecting both his flock as well as the land on which he travels.

The Presence of ♃

A similarly bold placement for Jupiter, he may also be a trailblazer of sorts. The nakshatra emphasizes pathways through the wilderness. Raw wisdom and intense creative urges swell here, where individualistic philosophies of heroism may also be found. Just as likely are the seemingly opposed realities of seclusion through great wealth as well as simple living. As the station represents familial gathering, Jupiter may also feel driven toward children and parenting with this placement.

The Presence of ♄

Though Saturn may be quite at home in spaces we consider wild, he doesn't always possess the boldness and 'on your feet' quality necessary to thrive here. There is a boundless quality to the station that he finds challenging to bring structure to. Though we find endless expanses of land in this sign, it is not that which is cultivated nor should it be. Saturn does his best work here in the renunciation of civilization's tendencies for those of the unseen. In this way, he embraces the position of isolation within the belly of the whale.

1.

Two Horns / Lightning From Heaven

Precessed Tropical Coordinates:
24° 07' Aries–7° 27' Taurus

MANZIL

Al Sharatain AKA *Al-Nath* 'THE TWO SIGNS'
TROPICAL ZODIAC: 0° Aries–12° 51' Aries
ASTERISM: Beta Arietis (Sharatan), Gamma Arietis (Mesarthim)
IBN ARABI: ء (Hamza)
FIRST INTELLECT, AL QALAM (THE PEN), THE DIVINE ESSENCE
PICATRIX: Image of a dark warrior, standing erect, holding a weapon in his hand. Talisman for destruction and depopulation. Craft in an iron ring and suffumigated with liquid storax. Seal in black wax. Spirit name is Geriz. For beginning journeys and the crafting of medicines. For creating discord between husband and wife, for making friends hostile towards each other, and for servants to flee.
LIBER LUNÆ: Face of Mars. For separation.
AGRIPPA: Spirit name is Geniel. For discord, and beginning of journeys.
AL-BUNI: ا (Alif)
Suitable for workings having to do with women. Remain silent, seclude if possible. Do not craft things. If

you must do something, it is suitable for malefic acts. To be born here one will be depraved, argumentative, and restless. Prone to mischief and problems with partnerships. Black pepper and black seed. Place of Jinn King *Al Ahmar*.

IBN AL-HATIM: Spirit name is Haaris. For destruction.

AL ASHRAF: Pepper and black seed.

SOLOMONIC RING (CUNNING MAN): Blood of an eel. Spirit names are Pharap, Giaray, Luneyl, and Bayag. For the purposes of opening up a stream and creating flowing water. To split the land in half.

NAKSHATRA

Ashwini 'THE TWIN HORSES' 'HORSE'S HEAD'

ASTERISM: Beta Arietis (Sharatan), Gamma Arietis (Mesarthim)

TEMPERAMENT: Swift, Divine

CASTE: Merchant

DIRECTION: South

MOTIVATION: *Dharma*

ANIMAL: Male Horse

SOUNDS: Choo, Che, Cho, La

TREE: *Strychnos Nuxvomica* (Strychnine Tree)

Shell-plants such as this tree are used as medicinal herbs in ailment of fever, weakness, and hair loss. In poultice form the leaves of this tree soothe wounds, skin-boils, and abscesses. Nowadays this plant is used as an insecticide to protect crops. It is dangerous in excess amounts. The seeds of this plant can be used only after complete purification.

VIMSHOTTARI: Ketu

DEITY: Ashwini Kumara, The Twin Horse Healers/Doctors

SHAKTI: Power to reach things quickly.
TAITTIRIYA BRAHMANA: "Twin horsemen use twin horses to get soldiers from the city"
BRIHAT SAMHITA: "will keep horses, will be commanders of the army; physicians, servants, dealers in horse, riders, tradesmen or masters of horses."
TIBETAN: *Takar.* Equine. Shining daughter. Fine appearance. Love of finery, jewels, and display. Great charm and elegance. Loved by all. Intelligence and understanding. Prosperity.

XIU

Lou 'BOND/MOUND'
AKA: 'RABBIT' 'TAIL'
UNEVEN TROPICAL ZODIAC: 2°–13° Taurus (22 April–4 May)
ASTERISM: Alpha Arietis (Hamal), Beta Arietis (Sheratan)
SKY QUADRANT: White Tiger of the West
PLANET: Venus
ANIMAL: Dog
ARTLEY: The Dog is both a guardian and a scavenger. When a strange dog follows a person it is an omen of good luck. Fidelity, honesty, and humor. Lifelong friendship. Steady worker. Conservative. Will tolerate considerable hardship and inconvenience rather than make changes. Not particularly adaptable. Defensive of family and friends. Sympathetic. A good listener. Rare displays of a violent temper. Very forgiving. Active and sporty. Astrologically auspicious. Building today is like building to the gates of heaven. Many joys. Deity holds the key to longevity. Dark or hidden god. Good time for communal

events, feasting, gathering, and unveiling of monuments. Good for weddings.
ELEMENT: Metal
MATANGA SUTRA: Offerings of milk gruel. Born here one is skilled in dealing with cattle and horses.

GEOMANCY

TANNERY: Aquisitio

PGM/GREEK

Ox, 'SILENCE'
DEITY: Dioscuri

PROTO-SINAITIC/HIEROGLYPH

Aleph 'Ox'

WORDS

Lightning, Sudden Change, The Carnival Around Every Corner, Friction, Travel, Grindcore, Dangerous Perfection, Splendor, Hacking the Ouroboros, Portions, Alter-Ego, Thundering Hooves, Dead Ringer, Speed, Horns, The Spring, Persuasion, Obliterator of History, Trembling, Twoness, Fitness.

As we see with the Arabic letter ا (Alif), resembling both a horn and a pole-axis, the nature of this station is planar and moving in two directions. It represents the spring equinox and the zodiac sign of Aries, whose stars are aligned to this station. In its relationship to spring, we see the double mystery of *Al Khidr*, or 'The Greening,' found here in the symbolism of the horns. As he is intimately connected with both Moses and *Dhul Qarnayn* (both being of 'The Two Horns') we see an esoteric understanding for the station referred to as 'The Two Signs.' Emerging out of both Pisces and Pegasus, the figure of the two horns rides atop creatures of land (in his form as Saint George) and that of water (in his form of *Al Khidr*) to stir the firmament along the *qutb* or pole, initiating the season of spring in the northern hemisphere.

The nakshatra speaks to twoness and splitting into binaries as the associated deity are the Ashwin Kumara. These twin horse gods were thought to be experts in medicine and healing, though their techniques were not always what we would consider conventional. Known for slicing and separating bodies for the sake of surgical operations, these gods used their scalpel equivalents to effect change and administer medicines. In this way, the present station represents attractive forms obtained through the means of supplements, surgery, craftsmanship, and altogether novel compositions. If the previous station represented the movement away from a common origin yet still bound to it, then here we find the fully materialized other in the form of the twin.

Though *Procession of the Night Theatre* begins with the stars of the Pleiades, it must be mentioned that this lunar station will typically initiate the sequence. It is its association with the stars of Aries that assures this, as the beginning of spring and the nature of the Ram's sign, connote beginnings for both the Western and Vedic astrological paradigms. Similar to the ram, the horse is a primary image for this sign, as well as their various connotations.

Horses represent beauty, grace, power, majesty, and martial prowess. In this way, the station is an initiatrix all its own, as it leads the way in stampede-like fashion.

PLANETARY PLACEMENTS

The Presence of the ☾

The Moon's placement here will be restless, vigorous, and active. Activity often comes in the form of creativity as the nakshatra in particular is related to assemblages capable of attraction worthy of being followed (seen through the beauty of horses and their importance here). She can be incredibly magnetic. This is a station of buzzing activity and experimentation, yet with a keen eye towards the aesthetic dimension. Many of the images around this lunar station deal with cutting and splitting apart. The deities associated with it, the Ashwin Kumar, as already mentioned are doctors skilled in the arts of surgery. This is not cutting for cuttings sake. Surgical tools used towards the ends of beauty give us practices such as cosmetic surgery which enhance bodies through violence. This is one way we might conceive of a soft planet such as the Moon interacting with the sharper forces therein; the molding of flesh. Consequently she may exceed in fitness, exercise, and those endeavors which mold the body to attractive ends. Doctoring being what it is here, she may also take a keen interest in health more broadly, be it supplements, vitamins, and substances which aid in such pursuits. In this sign health is inextricably linked to beauty. 'Health and beauty,' as the two often go hand and hand.

The Presence of ☿

Mercury feels quite at home in the place of splitting things open and apart. As the planet of analysis is already keen to do, this lunar station facilitates actions of breaking things apart and recombining them for optimization. This is achieved in the manner of 'twinning,' not unlike the horse headed twins who hold sway here. That said, oftentimes these re-creations have a Frankenstein-like quality to them. Mercury becomes a kind of mad scientist here as motley parts may be assembled together, stitched, and prodded for the desired effect of their twisted vision. Like with many placements in this station, they strive towards the effect of a collage, bringing disparate elements together. That said, if more impulsive movements can be tempered, there is a possibility of healing through voice and touch here. For this placement also speaks to the hands of the trusted doctor as much as those of the local butcher.

The Presence of ♀

Venus' preoccupation with beauty aligns well with this lunar station. She is naturally inclined towards the arts and skills of beautification. Aesthetically she is drawn towards things which flash, bright and radiant luminosities, and the like. Arabic associations with this station often image bright streaks of lightning and resounding thunder. She achieves her attention and popularity here through these same means. Clashing colors and patterns make up this similarly 'stitched together' motif so common, as beauty emerges from unlikely combinations. Along with artistic qualities Venus holds connections to sexualual energies here. This is a Venus of the theater, of the drag show, and of the runway.

The Presence of the ☉

The Sun here has a natural glow about him. He attracts followers with relative ease, as his warmth combined with good health and vibrancy are bound to draw attention. Whether he is able to lead and guide people past the point of gaining followers will vary. For this placement in particular it is less important, as the primary function becomes the drawing of attention through expression. He may be inclined towards marketing, advertising, and business practices that do this very work.

The Presence of ♂

More than anything else, the presence of Mars will likely play up elements of health and fitness related to this station. Exercise, movement, and physical activity are strong here, especially if these practices have an aesthetic component to them. If supplements and substances are involved it may become keenly defined, or, on the negative side of things, even a little obsessive. Exercise routines and regimens may take on a similar effect. He may be one who wields cutting implements for the sake of artistic vision and taste, such as a chef or a sculptor.

The Presence of ♃

Jupiter may be quite high-minded in his ideals here. Perhaps even more than the Sun, there is a strong leadership quality as well as a teaching or auditory style capable of captivating crowds and moving larger masses of people. This placement may become quite wealth-oriented, as qualities of attraction manifest through money, as opposed to somatic and or physical characteristics. It is a buoyant place for him, allowing for much flare, pomp, and circumstance.

The Presence of ♄

It is the image of the horses which emphasize this station's speed above all else. Consequently it is the quicker planets that tend to thrive the most here. Emphasizing less egoic elements, Saturn may become the responsible doctor, capable of healing that requires deeper processes and commitments. On the other side of this, he may also fall crassly into over-experimentation; losing touch with the humanity of his subjects and those he sees as resources. In regards to practices of beautification, there may be a stronger focus on the non-human, for example through the lens of plant and animal life. To take this one step further, similar to Mercury, a Saturn placement here may become quite scientific in its analysis and capacity to break down varying elements and synthesize where needed.

2.

Kingdom of the Interior / The Relentless Weight of Existence

Processed Tropical Coordinates:
7° 27' Taurus–20° 47' Taurus

MANZIL

Al Batin 'THE LITTLE BELLY OF THE RAM'
  'THE INTERIOR OR THE WOMB'
TROPICAL ZODIAC: 12° 51' Aries–25° 4" Aries
ASTERISM: Delta Arietis (Botein)
IBN ARABI: ه (Ha)
THE UNIVERSAL SOUL, THE PRESERVED TABLET,
  THE ONE WHO CALLS FORTH
PICATRIX: Image of a crowned king. Talisman for the removal of anger. Spirit name is Enedil. White wax and mastic suffumigated with lignum aloes. For digging streams and wells, to find hidden treasures, for planting a great deal of wheat. For the destruction of buildings before they can be completed. To make firm the incarceration of captives.
LIBER LUNÆ: Face of the Sun. For joining together, mutual love and friendship.
AGRIPPA: Spirit name is Enediel. For finding treasure.
AL BUNI: ب (Ba)
Suitable for things pertaining to men. Good for crafting talismans and for works of alchemy. Good for

beginning studies. Spiritual healing, exorcism, and healing. To be born here is to be beloved and guided. Strength of character. Natural born leaders. Men will be enemies for this same quality and women will be envied. Aloeswood, saffron, and mastic.

IBN AL HATIM: Spirit name is Anakil. For meeting Kings.

AL ASHRAF: Aromatic wood, saffron, and mastic.

SOLOMONIC RING (CUNNING MAN): Blood of a hart, buck, or hound. Spirit names are Aman, Urasian, Eazsail, and Azzial. To make dogs in pursuit of a buck or hart (hunting dogs).

NAKSHATRA

Bharani 'THE BEARER' 'YONI'

ASTERISM: 35 Arietis, 39 Arietis, 41 Arietis
TEMPERAMENT: Fierce, Divine
CASTE: Outcast
DIRECTION: West
MOTIVATION: *Artha*
ANIMAL: Male Elephant
SOUNDS: Li, Lu, Ley, Lo
TREE: *Phyllanthus Emblica* (Myrobalan/Indian Gooseberry)

Jam is sometimes made of the unripe fruits. Pickles of these fruits are also made which help give energy, digestive aid, and immune boosts. Their taste is astringent and it is helpful with urinal and indigestion problems. Dry fruits are useful in for bleeding, diarrhea, and constipation. The fruits have an abundance of Vitamin C. If used with iron, it soothes jaundice, indigestion, asthma, and coughing.

VIMSHOTTARI: Venus

DEITY: Yama, God of the Dead
SHAKTI: Power to take things away.
TAITTIRIYA BRAHMANA: "The restraint of the regulator needs to bear down, to arrest"
BRIHAT SAMHITA: "will deal in precious stones, will be flesh eaters, will be wicked men; will delight in acts of killing and torture; will be dealers in pod grains; will be of low descent or weak-minded."
TIBETAN: *Dranye*. The Dancer. Constant, faithful and trustworthy. Happy and prosperous life. Erudition. Good health. Resistance to disease.

XIU

Wei 'STOMACH'
AKA: 'TAIL OF TIME' 'LONG BREATH'
UNEVEN TROPICAL ZODIAC: 14°–28° Taurus (5–19 May)
ASTERISM: 35 Arietis, 39 Arietis, 41 Arietis
SKY QUADRANT: White Tiger of the West
PLANET: Saturn
ANIMAL: Pheasant
ARTLEY: The Pheasant is the imperial emblem of authority. An animal of the Sun and Thunder. Courage. One of the eight diagrams of the I-Ching: Li (Fire). Auspicious. All things done on this day bring advancement and expansion. Considered lucky. Associated with fortifications, prisons, the accumulation of wealth, boundaries, and barriers. Reservoirs and canals. Good for savings and accumulation. The celestial granary.
ELEMENT: Earth
MATANGA SUTRA: Offerings of sesame. Born here the person is murderous.

GEOMANCY

TANNERY: Aquisitio

PGM/GREEK

Vulture, 'a popping sound.'
DEITY: Hades

PROTO-SINAITIC/HIEROGLYPH

Bet, Beth 'HOUSE'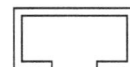

WORDS

Interior/Internal, The Dead, Reincarnation, Cavern of the Skull, Firmness, Ripple on the Water, Knocking on a Door, Karma, Chamber of the Stomach, Esoteric, Bureaucracy, Insulated, Robust, Restraint, Weight, The Secret Child, Of the Cloth, Fertilizer, House of the House, Masquerade, Block, Re-cycle, Judgement.

The stars of nakshatra Bharani consist of the constellation we know as Aries. The shape of the asterism resembles the female sex organ or a downward pointing triangle. This image, often referred to as the Yoni, was for the Vedic culture the great womb of the goddess. Distinct from the birthing process into materiality seen in the seventh station, this is the womb of the otherworld, interiority, as well as the hidden connections and cycles found in this invisible dimension. The image of the downward facing triangle is additionally apt as Bharani means 'to bear down,' not only in the act of birth which is integral to this nakshatra's function but also to the pressure thought to be applied to souls in terms of karmic weight as they are judged.

This nakshatra maintains a strong connection to the Dead and the realm of the ancestors. As the dwelling place of Yama, it is important to note that not only is this the realm of the Dead but of their judgment. It is this vast network of processes which he oversees as karmic cycles, reincarnation, and birth. As he is a deity of judgment there is a strong discerning quality to this station. Decision making based on quality is integral to the functioning of this region. Yama's position in the afterlife is due to his legacy as the first mortal. As the preeminent ancestor along with those found in the 10th lunar station (the psychopomps) they orchestrate the patterns of all mortals through invisible channels.

Though the nakshatra is explicitly related to the dead, both the Arabic and Chinese images for this lunar station connote interiority more broadly. Here we see the Islamic notion of Al Batin (The Esoteric) and the Chinese Wei as stomach; another interior shape found within the body. We see the images of this station pointing towards a darkened-inside. Some cultures may frame this as an underworld. Some cultures may emphasize this as a hellish place. Other cultures may frame this as an otherworld or even a mirror world in reversal to that of the living. With less religious overtones we may call this place the dimension of psyche. Instead of religious precepts, the laws here are psychological. Concepts such as the id and superego, or perhaps that of archetype and collective unconscious explain these mechanisms.

PLANETARY PLACEMENTS

The Presence of the ☾

Just as pressure builds precious stones, so too does the weight of this station bring solidity and strength to the Moon. The ability to exist under weighted states for sustained periods of time may give long-term rewards as well as character qualities such as endurance. It is no surprise then that the Moon here is thought to be resistant to disease. There is a quality of health all around; in particular to that of the body. Similarly, she is likely to have refined senses as discernment is brought to the soul. Strong sensual preferences are common here. As many of the stations' qualities deal with interiority, the Moon has a rich inner life. Beyond a strong sense of imagination, there is a familiarity with hidden processes and dynamics. It is only natural that thinkers such as Sigmund Freud and C. G. Jung, those of a prolific psychological bent, have strong placements here. This inner cavern of the psyche is described as stomach-like (seen through the Chinese imagery), as well as the Arabic *Batin* or esoteric. Inclinations toward so-called hidden and occult sciences are common for this placement.

The Presence of ☿

They may be deceptively intelligent. Logic here takes on intuitive qualities as well as what we call a sense of 'natural law.' Mercury here signifies deeper senses of knowing; that along the lines of interiority discussed thus far. This may manifest in somatic forms, felt senses in a very physical manner, lest we forget that the body is our ancestral inheritance. As this lunar station deals with karmic cycles, like the 10th station, one's Mercurial pursuits may be inspired by traditional byways: learning languages, playing music, writing, and of course running family businesses. As Mercury also signifies the hands and handiwork, we also find them skilled in massage, body, and energy work. Here the hands act as conduits for this same somatic intelligence, allowing intuition to move through the body's channels and roadways.

THE PRESENCE OF ♀

Love and relationships may be challenging with the heavier dimensions of this lunar station. At the same time, its depth and fidelity bode well for matters of endurance in such endeavors. This is a Venus dedicated to her craft, her aesthetic, and those who she loves. Here she appreciates age and that which is long lasting, a more Saturnine-tinged Venus if ever there was one. The strength in judging qualities here bodes well for her, as aesthetic decisions may come quite naturally. She may have strong intimacy with the Dead, but just as much for those internal forms we associate with the unconscious psyche as well as 'skeletons in the closet.' Similar to the Moon there is a strong sensual quality to her, as well as an association with the birthing process more broadly. As the nakshatra specifically connotes birth, or rather, the underlying karmic processes that elicit and frame it, Venus becomes deeply in touch with the invisible aspects of creativity.

THE PRESENCE OF THE ☉

The Sun present here often brings light to the darkness of the interior; that is, unconscious processes, 'the Dead,' and those generally hidden realms of reality. As the Sun is steady in motion and consistent in light, this illumination may take the form of rational principles applied to so-called irrational phenomena. In this way the light amidst the darkness may only observe what is visible within its sphere of clarity, sometimes lacking the nuance of a planet better suited to the darkness. As Yama is born from the Surya (Sun), we see a return of the progenitor to a realm which is fundamentally unlike himself; that of the mortals. Nevertheless like the other luminary of the Moon he is capable of shining light in the most mysterious dimensions, acting as a great explorer of the unconscious.

The Presence of ♂

Laborious efforts are found with this placement as well as long durational actions. Not entirely dissimilar to the Sun, Mars brings fire into the darkness as if a torch. He is a natural explorer of the hidden dimensions. As this station is related to birth and the sensual emerging into manifestation, Mars comes alive through blood and flesh in this station. He may signify trouble or conflict with the Dead, as well as harsher judgements brought on through the afterlife dimension. Unlike Saturn, Mars does not easily fall within the boundaries of the great otherworld bureaucracy and its systematic ways. His desire for freedom may come at odds with traditions and family structures. As this is a station of containment, more often than not he wishes to cut himself out from it as such.

The Presence of ♃

Here Jupiter possesses deep access to the wisdom of the unconscious, yet it is often veiled in a variety of skins and material veneers. Though there are vast spiritual realms related to this lunar station, its weight and 'under the Earth' quality may hinder Jupiter's normally expansive regime. This same materiality may become a gateway for Jupiter's knowledge and educational possibilities. It may feel like an uphill battle,-as the planet's levity does not necessarily coexist with the station's restrictions and containment. If he learns to use discrimination he may become a wise representative of the greater spiritual dimensions; but more often than not we see a disposition towards the laws of human beings in this life. He is a lawmaker of the living here first and foremost.

The Presence of ♄

Saturn's heaviness and position between matter and spirit has him well suited towards this station. He may act as a gateway between tangible and abstract dimensions of reality. Similarly, it is Saturn's restrictive qualities and weight which apply the necessary pressure for forms to emerge into manifestation from the other world. He is capable of withstanding the necessary toil to bring form to the formless. In this way he acts as the final judge; almost resembling the role of Yama himself as arbiter within the darkness. Saturn here is capable of reading beyond the laws of human beings into that of the cosmos at large. Unlike Jupiter, his judgment is less restricted to human laws as well as their mercies. Though he is not cruel as much as he is indeed fair, though not on behalf of what we consider to be familiar.

III
Waning

وَٱلْقَمَرَ قَدَّرْنَٰهُ مَنَازِلَ حَتَّىٰ عَادَ كَٱلْعُرْجُونِ ٱلْقَدِيمِ

> ... AND FOR THE MOON
> WE HAVE GIVEN STATIONS
> SO THAT IT MIGHT RETURN
> TO THE SHAPE OF
> AN AGING PALM FROND ...
>
> HOLY QURAN 36:39

What is the story of stories?

What do they hold in common? Besides character, drama, emotion, accoutrement?

Beyond their furnishings, and all the colorful masks. What is their essence?

It is movement. It is change of any kind. It is a shift from silence, from darkness, from all things which are absolute. It is difference. It is me and it is you.

So the Moon persists in her story. Round and round her starry backdrop. Here and then away again. Here and there, once more. A night, a day. Eyes closed, eyes open. Alive and dead, again and again.

* * *

We return to the archaic movement of consciousness from glimmering points in the vault of heaven to so many stories of animals, humans, kings and queens, weather, warfare, love, death, and society at large. The lunar stations are nothing but dots in the sky. But are they?

Astronomy, now proudly separate from astrology, tells us:

> "Stars are born within the clouds of dust and scattered throughout most galaxies. A familiar example of such as a dust cloud is the Orion Nebula. Turbulence deep within these clouds gives rise to knots with sufficient mass that the gas and dust can begin to collapse under its own gravitational attraction. As the cloud collapses, the material at the center begins to heat up. Known as a protostar, it is this hot core at the heart of the collapsing cloud that will one day become a star."[14]

And, what of the Moon? Who in her interaction with the stars become the lunar stations?

> "Earth's Moon is the brightest and largest object in our night sky. The Moon makes Earth a more livable planet by moderating our home planet's wobble on its axis, leading to a relatively stable climate. It also causes tides, creating a rhythm that has guided humans for thousands of years. The Moon was likely formed after a Mars-sized body collided with Earth several billion years ago."[15]

By the acceptable standards of our modern culture this is the foremost story of our time. No rabbits or intoxication. No shadowy faces gleaming back at us. No word of the divine creator. But of dust particles and numbers. Counting craters and future explorations for precious minerals to power our technologies. In fact, she has already been walked upon. Very literally, physically. Flags hoisted upon

---

14 From science.nasa.gov, "Stars."
15 Ibid., "The Moon."

her fair body. A sight for many millions of amateurs with mass-produced telescopes. Or a graveyard of our hopes for others who might be out there.

They are still stories, no doubt. And we have moved so very far, and seemingly so very quickly as well. So the tales continue. They must for they have no other choice. It is their nature.

But, if our dreams and our nightmares spoke to the stories we told, and the ones the Moon and the stars seemed to tell us back, what would they say? Would they be formulaic? Gravel, particulates, grains of sand upon the endless beach? Do they have heart? Tragedy, comedy? Are they like us or perhaps like the dreaming of a machine? Do they bring us ease, or perhaps fear?

Just as the Moon persists in her story, so too do we. And, it would seem, that our story may very well bring us to a vantage which lacks her very presence in some not so distant night...

Where novel arrangements of dots glitter across new skies, darker and more unfamiliar than the last. Where pixels replace them all together. Where new stars wander, perhaps more quickly and of greater multitudes than our familiar seven.

What of the stations, then?

* * *

To see behind the mirror is to see ourselves.
And the stops we have been making are our own.
The pace we have been moving is our own.
And the others are our own.
We never had them and we never will.

So the story continues, despite them.
whether we appreciate, marvel at their presence,
or not...

Bibliography

*Sources not listed here can be found below in the bibliography section 'The 28 Lunar Stations.'

Andrews, Munya. *The Seven Sisters of the Pleiades: Stories from Around the World. Spinifex Press, 2005.*

Brady, Bernadette. "Images in the Heavens: A Cultural Landscape," pp. 234–58, in D. Gunzburg , ed.,*The Imagined Sky*, Equinox, 2016.

Collins, Andrew and Gregory Little. *Path of Souls: The Native American Death Journey: Cygnus, Orion, the Milky Way, Giant Skeletons in Mounds, & the Smithsonian.* Archetype Books, 2014.

Falk, Harry. "The Early Use of Nakshatras," from *The Interactions of Ancient Astral Science* by David Brown, Hempen Verlag, 2018.

Friedel, David and Linda Schele and Joy Parker. *Maya Cosmos: Three Thousand Years on the Shaman's Path.* William Morrow Paperbacks, 1995.

Furst, Jill Leslie McKeever. *The Natural History of the Soul in Ancient Mexico.* Yale University Press, 1995.

Johnson, Kenneth. *Mansions of the Moon: The Lost Zodiac of the Goddess.* Archive Press & Communications, 2003.

Mursell, Ian. "Mamalhuatzli (Fire Drill)," uploaded August 2nd 2021: https://www.mexicolore.co.uk/aztecs/artefacts/fire-drill

NASA. "Stars" & "The Moon": https://science.nasa.gov/astrophysics/focus-areas/how-do-stars-form-and-evolve/and https://science.nasa.gov/moon/

onesky.arizona.edu, "Jawza' Celestial Complex: A Folkloric Celestial Complex." http://onesky.arizona.edu/arab-star-names/jawza-celestial-complex/

Pellar, Brian R. "On the Origins of the Alphabet," in the *Sino-Platonic Papers,* edited by Victor H Mair, Number 196 (2009).

Segol, Marla. *Word and Image in Medieval Kabbalah*. Palgrave McMillan, 2012.

Skinner, Stephen. *Terrestrial Astrology: Divination by Geomancy*. Routledge & Kegan Paul, 1980.

Stephenson, F. Richard. "Chinese and Korean Star Maps and Catalogs." *History of Cartography*. Ed. J. B. Harley and David Woodward. Vol. II, Part 2, Chap. 13. University of Chicago Press, 1994.

Ulansey, David. *The Origins of the Mithraic Mysteries: Cosmology and Salvation in the Ancient World*. Oxford University Press, 1989.

Varisco, Daniel Martin. "The Origin of the *anwā* in Arab Tradition," *Studia Islamica* Vol. 74 (1991): pp. 5–28.

Yampolsky, Philip. "On the Origin of the Twenty-Eight Lunar Mansions." *Osiris* Vol. 9 (1950): pp. 62–83.

THE 28 LUNAR STATIONS

* Each of the 28 lunar station chapters uses identical texts as information sources. They are listed by section below. The section titled 'Words' utilizes these same sources, as well as the texts listed above in the bibliography. 'Words' also uses astronomical information gathered from the 'Stellarium Mobile Plus' v1.12.0 application, developed by Stellarium Labs S.R.L.

Manzil

Agrippa, Henry Cornelius. *Three Books of Occult Philosophy*. Createspace Independent Publishing Platform, 2014.

Al-Buni, Ahmad. *The Sun of Knowledge (Shams al-Ma'arif): An Arabic Grimoire*, A Selected Translation by Amina Inloes and J.M. Hamade, Revelore Press, 2021.

Allen, Richard Hinckley. *Stars Names: Their Lore and Meaning*, Dover, 1963.

Burckhardt, Titus. *Mystical Astrology According to Ibn' Arabi*. Translated by Bulent Rauf, Fons Vitae, 2001.

Karr, Don. *Liber Lunæ or Book of the Moon*. Golden Hoard Press, 2011.

Lippincott, Kristen and David Pingree. "Ibn al-Hātim on the Talismans of the Lunar Mansions," *Journal of the Warburg and Courtauld Institutes*, Vol. 50 (1987), pp. 57–81.

Skinner, Stephen and David Rankine. *A Cunning Man's Grimoire: The Secret of Secrets*, Llewellyn, 2018.

Varisco, Daniel Martin. "The Magical Significance of the Lunar Stations in the 13th Century Yemeni Kitāb Al-Tabsira fī Ilm Al-Nujūm of Al-Malik Al-Ashraf," in *Quaderni di Studi Arabi*, Vol. 13, Divination magie pouvoirs au Yémen (1995): pp. 19–40.

Warnock, Christopher and John Michael Greer. *The Illustrated Picatrix,* Renaissance Astrology (Lulu.com), 2015.

Warnock, Christopher. *The Mansions of the Moon: A Lunar Zodiac for Astrology and Magic*, Renaissance Astrology, 2019.

Nakshatra

Cornu, Philippe. *Tibetan Astrology*, translated by Hamish Gregor. Shambhala, 1997.

DiCara, Vic. *Nakshatra: The Authentic Heart of Vedic Astrology*. Independently Published, 2019.

Frawley, Dr. David. "Shaktis of the Nakshatras," published November 10th 2022. https://www.vedanet.com/shaktis-of-the-nakshatras/

Mihira, Varaha. *Brihat Samhita.* Translated by N. Chidambaram Iyer, Dev Publishers and Distributors, 2022.

Shah, Dr. Rutesh R. and Dr. R. S. Patel. "Study of Various Plant Species Useful in Each Nakshatra for Human Society." *International Journal of Scientific and Research Publications*, Volume 4, Issue 1, (January 2014).

Sutton, Komilla. *The Nakshatras: The Stars Beyond the Zodiac*, Wessex Astrologer, 2014.

Xiu

Artley, Malvin N. "The 28 Animals of the Lunar Mansions." Online.

 * Artley cites *Chinese Animal Symbolisms* by Ong Hean-Tatt and *Ming Shu: The Art and Practice of Chinese Astrology* by Derek Walters as his two primary textual sources.

Artley, Malvin N. "The Twenty Eight Xiu (Lunar Mansions): A Compilation." Online. *Artley cites *The Complete Guide to Chinese Astrology* by Derek Walters and Richard Hinckley Allen's *Star Names: Their Lore and Meaning* as his two primary textual sources.

Duoduo, Xu. "Lunar Mansion Names in South-West China: An Etymological Reconstruction of Ancestral Astronomical Designations in Moso, Pumi, and Yi Cultures Compared with Chinese and Tibetan Contexts." *Onoma* Vol. 51 (2016): pp. 113–43.

Giebel, Rolf W (trans), "The Mātanga Sutra" (Taishō, Vol. 1, № 1300), *Esoteric Texts*, Bukkyō Dendō Kyōkai America, 2015.

Geomancy

Block, Sam. "On Geomantic Figures, Zodiac Signs, and Lunar Mansions," blog posted April 3rd 2015. https://digitalambler.com/2015/04/03/on-geomantic-figures-zodiac-signs-and-lunar-mansions

* The original source is said to be from Paris Bibliothèque Nationale MS Lat. 7354, reproduced in Paul Tannery's chapter on geomancy 'Le Rabolion' in his *Mémoires Scientifiques* (Vol. 4).

Savage-Smith, Emilie and Marion B. Smith. "Islamic Geomancy and a Thirteenth Century Divinatory Device: Another Look," pp. 211–76, in *Magic and Divination in Early Islam*. Edited by Emilie Savage-Smith, Routledge, 2004.

PGM/Greek

Betz, Hans Dieter (ed), *The Greek Magical Papyri in Translation: Including the Demotic Spells: Texts (Volume 1)*. University of Chicago Press, 2nd edition, 1996.

* The lunar station correspondences emerge from the 'Prayer to Mene,' listed in PGM VII 756–94. These are translated as the "28 shapes of the world," and accompanied by a series of 14 sounds.

Luna, Jade Sol and Michael Santangelo. *27 Stars: Discovering Your True Self with Asterian Astrology*, Jade Sol Luna, 2014.

Proto-Sinaitic/Hieroglyph

Goble, Edwin. "The Origin of the Alphabet from Egyptian Hieroglyphs and the Lunar Zodiac." https://independent.academia.edu/EdwinGoble

* Though the names used in our text match the letter correspondences proposed by Goble, we have chosen to use single characters from the standardized set of Egyptian hieroglyphs for all 28, which he has not done. "The Origin of the Alphabet" proposes a variety of options for each lunar station in terms of possible letter correspondences.

Procession of the Night Theatre WAS
TYPESET BY JOSEPH UCCELLO USING
ANETO, ANETO SKYLINE *(TypeTogether)*, DTL FELL
TOT, DTL VANDENKEERE DOT *(Dutch Type Library)*,
GRAEBENBACH *(Camelot)*, 29LT OKASO *(29Letters)*,
AND NOTO SANS EGYPTIAN
HIEROGLYPHS.

www.ingramcontent.com/pod-product-compliance
Lightning Source LLC
Chambersburg PA
CBHW070126080526
44586CB00015B/1572